BECOMING HUMAN AGAIN

BECOMING HUMAN

AGAIN

AN ORAL HISTORY OF THE RWANDA
GENOCIDE AGAINST THE TUTSI

Donald E. Miller

with Lorna Touryan Miller and Arpi Misha Miller

 UNIVERSITY OF CALIFORNIA PRESS

University of California Press
Oakland, California

Library of Congress Cataloging-in-Publication Data

Names: Miller, Donald E. (Donald Earl), 1946- author. |
    Miller, Lorna Touryan, contributor. | Miller, Arpi Misha,
    1976- contributor.
Title: Becoming human again : an oral history of the Rwanda
    genocide against the Tutsi / Donald E. Miller, with Lorna
    Touryan Miller and Arpi Misha Miller.
Description: Oakland, California : University of California
    Press, [2020] | Includes bibliographical references and
    index.
Identifiers: LCCN 2019026629 (print) | LCCN 2019026630
    (ebook) | ISBN 9780520343771 (cloth) | ISBN 9780520343788
    (paperback) | ISBN 9780520975156 (ebook)
Subjects: LCSH: Genocide survivors—Rwanda—Psychological
    aspects. | Tutsi (African people)—Crimes against—
    Rwanda—Psychological aspects. | Widows—Rwanda—
    History—20th century. | Children and genocide—
    Rwanda—History—20th century. | Rwanda—History—
    Civil War, 1994.
Classification: LCC DT450.435 .M56 2020 (print) |
    LCC DT450.435 (ebook) | DDC 967.57104/31—dc23
LC record available at https://lccn.loc.gov/2019026629
LC ebook record available at https://lccn.loc.gov/2019026630

Manufactured in the United States of America

29 28 27 26 25 24 23 22 21 20
10 9 8 7 6 5 4 3 2 1

To the survivors who shared their stories

CONTENTS

PREFACE

Like most things in life, this book has not progressed in a linear straight line. What began as an opportunity to speak at a conference in Rwanda about the Armenian genocide, the first genocide of the twentieth century, evolved into a love affair with a group of orphans in Rwanda. We had no intention of launching a new research project. Writing a book on the Armenian genocide had been challenging enough. However, sometimes things seem almost preordained to happen.

We had spent a number of summers in the commercial salmon fishing industry in Alaska, and after one of these seasons the owner of the company sent us a substantial check to be used for charitable purposes. Hence, when the orphans we met in Rwanda expressed an interest in doing an interview project with their members, all of whom were heading households of surviving brothers and sisters, the money was sitting in the bank, ready to fund their project. And a few years later, when an association of widows wanted to replicate the orphan project, it only took a single phone call to a foundation to secure funding for their project. At this point, there was no turning back. We had visited Rwanda a number of times, and the material emerging from these two projects was incredibly rich and compelling. We were hooked.

Making a strategic decision, Don decided to contact the John Templeton Foundation to see whether they might fund a new interview project, focusing on the issue of forgiveness, since this was a program area for the foundation. This time we would do the interviews ourselves; we decided to videotape them rather than simply record the interviews on audiotape, as had occurred in the previous two projects. Very rapidly we realized that survivors were not inter-ested in talking about issues of forgiveness and reconciliation unless they could tell their story of what happened during the genocide. We also discovered that the hundred days of the genocide was only one element of their concerns. They wanted to describe the massacres and discrimination that Tutsis faced prior to 1994. And it was clear that the struggle for survival after the killing ended was also important. Consequently, our interview guide kept evolving as we did more and more interviews.

The richness and uniqueness of this book is that it is not just about the genocide, nor is it narrowly focused on forgiveness, which ended up getting only one chapter. We became convinced that it was important to tell a holistic story, locating forgiveness within the context of the killing, rape, and poverty that survivors experienced. This meant that it was also important to examine the themes of trauma and healing as well as the role of religion and the justice system. To ignore any of these elements would provide a simplistic account, since they interact together in the lives of survivors.

It is important to state up front that we have an anxiety about the way the book is structured. The accounts of the genocide in the first five chapters are excruciatingly painful and disturbing. Nevertheless, they are important to read because otherwise the more analytical chapters in the second half of the book are without context. But this is also the strength of the book: The fact that topics like healing, forgiveness, and justice are framed by the experience of survivors during the genocide.

While this book is focused specifically on the genocide against Tutsis, it is paradigmatic of other genocides and acts of mass violence, not only in the role of propaganda but also in the fact that the pain of genocide does not end with the killing—it is ongoing, sometimes for generations and certainly for years as survivors struggle to heal from the trauma they experienced. Therefore, it is our hope that the thematic chapters of the book contribute to the academic literature on healing, religion, and justice from a grassroots perspective of the experience of common people. While we have cited some of the relevant source material on these topics, the book, fundamentally, draws its examples and insights directly from the survivors. The book is based on survivor testimony, grounded in their everyday experience, not what politicians, generals, and the international community were saying and doing.

In conclusion, it is important to say a few words about authorship. Lorna and Don conceived of this project together, visiting Rwanda many times over a fifteen-year period. Together we did all of the interviews at Solace Ministries. In 2006, our daughter, Arpi, joined us in Rwanda and experienced survivors and the country firsthand. After finishing her PhD in sociology at UCLA, she then became actively involved in reading and editing multiple drafts of the manuscript, bringing theoretical clarity to many of the chapters, and drafting some crucial takeaways. In this regard, it is a family effort. Lorna and Don spent hours coding each of the 260 interviews. Don wrote drafts of each chapter, which the three of us then critiqued, struggling for ways to order the material and illustrate the argument of each chapter by citing from our rich database of interviews. A colleague at USC, Professor Beth Meyerowitz, and one of her graduate students, Lauren Ng, worked with us about halfway through the project administering a survey on trauma and resilience to two of the populations that were interviewed for the book. Their analysis focuses on the issue of trauma and is presented in the second appendix.

The book has been gestating for a number of years. The core element is the interviews. The laborious work was coding every interview, line by line, after the interviews were translated from the local language of Kinyarwanda. It is the coding that made it possible to write a thematically ordered book. The insights for the book, however, are based on much more than interviews. Lorna and Don returned to Rwanda multiple times over a fifteen-year period, traveling around the country, sitting informally with survivors, visiting their homes, eating with survivors, going to memorial sites, attending the tenth and twentieth commemorations of the genocide, including accompanying conferences. In the acknowledgments, we mention the numerous people who have assisted us with the project, many of them becoming close friends, both orphans who are now grown and raising families and adult survivors who have inspired us at every point in our journey. While we chronical in this book the process of survivors regaining their humanity after the genocide, it is also true that after every trip to Rwanda, we felt more truly human. The superficial elements of life had been stripped away. The rudimentary fact of living interdependent lives searching for our common humanity had become primary.

ACKNOWLEDGMENTS

Our greatest debt is to the several hundred survivors who were interviewed for this project. We honor their courage in describing their experiences as well as welcoming us into their homes on many occasions. It is to the survivors of the genocide that we dedicate this book. You have helped us to think more deeply about what it means to be truly human. Our lives are forever transformed as a result of these conversations.

We have extremely fond memories of our first visit to Rwanda, when we met François Ngarambe, president of IBUKA, and Bonaventure Niyibizi, vice president, at the conference organized by IBUKA, "Life after Death," in 2001. François was very helpful in working with us on the interview guide for the members of AOCM. And Bonaventure was the very first person we interviewed in some depth about his experiences during the genocide. Without their welcoming embrace of us, we might not have continued to venture more deeply into the complex history of the genocide.

It was the early interaction with the officers and members of AOCM that really captured our hearts, especially Naphtal Ahishakiye, the president. We also want to thank the team that did the interviewing: Alfred Habinez, Modeste Gashayija, Jean Pierre Kalimba, Agathe Mukasine, Delphine Mpinganzima, and the skilled translator of the one hundred interviews, Sylvie Rutayisire Isimbi. Jean Munyaneza was the project director for the AOCM interviews. In addition to the memories of traveling around the country with the AOCM team, we also have great memories of team meetings and various dinners, including one that celebrated Don's birthday.

Fairly early in the project we invited photographer Jerry Berndt to join us in Rwanda from his home in France. After several trips to Rwanda, he produced an amazing exhibit of photographs, *Orphans of the Rwanda Genocide*, that was accompanied by a photo essay designed by Margi Denton. We were delighted when the African American Museum in Los Angeles agreed to host the exhibit, which was followed by an exhibition at LA's Catholic Cathedral, Our Lady of the Angeles. We estimate that more than twenty thousand people viewed the exhibit, including the president of USC, Stephen Sample. The Survivors Fund (SURF) in the United Kingdom played a crucial role by enabling us to use signage they had prepared for an exhibit.

This book would never have been possible without generous funding from Bob and Beverly Bingham, friends of ours from the fishing industry in Alaska, and Howard and Roberta Ahmanson, who funded prior research in the Republic of Armenia. The John Templeton Foundation then gave a big boost to the project that enabled us to do one hundred video interviews at Solace Ministries. We also want to acknowledge donors who support the education of orphans, including Mary Lou Dauray.

We were delighted when AVEGA expressed interest in doing interviews with their members. Jean Munyaneza once again served as the project director. The leadership of AVEGA embraced the project and gave us permission to quote from the interviews. Early in our research, AVEGA also hosted us as we visited a number of their programs, including our first visit to an AIDS clinic for survivors. Since the interviews were done in Kinyarwanda and then translated into French, we needed an English translation. Lorna's sister, Helen Touryan Reynolds, graciously translated all of the interviews from French to English so that we could code them.

We have enjoyed good relationships with the staff at the Kigali Genocide Memorial Center, including being part of a symposium on genocide denial that was organized by Peter Balakian and Deborah Lipstadt. The Kigali Center is engaged in a very fruitful collaboration with the USC Shoah Foundation at my [Don] home institution, the University of Southern California. One of our memorable experiences was taking some of the visiting Kigali staff sailing in Santa Monica Bay when they visited California.

Solace Ministries and its staff deserve special thanks. The director, Jean Gakwandi, was one of the first individuals we met after arriving in Rwanda. On subsequent trips, he took us to visit numerous orphans, widows, memorial sites, and Solace projects—ranging from farms to housing projects and their medical clinic. We also enjoyed leisure time traveling with Jean and his wife Vivian to Ruhengeri as well as dinners in their home. All three of his daughters, Jessie, Florence, and Muyco, helped at different points in the project. His staff also drove us to numerous home visits. And we enjoyed wonderful meals at Solace that were prepared by Jean-Marie, a very talented chef.

Two individuals associated with Solace Ministries require special mention. The first is Agnes Mukankusi, who was our project manager at Solace. Not only did she arrange interviews and do screening interviews with every one of the hundred survivors, but she also translated during our interviews and then laboriously transcribed and translated the interviews so that we could code them. In addition, she accompanied us to the home visits and maintained contact with survivors after the interviews. We came to thoroughly enjoy her Pentecostal spirituality as well as interacting with her husband, a former professional footballer (soccer player), and her adorable kids. The second individual is Mama Lambert. She is truly a saint, a mother to hundreds of orphans, and a steady shoulder to cry on for many widows. For some people, words do not describe their depth or character.

Beth Meyerowitz's contribution is spelled out in the second appendix, but it is important to acknowledge her help in introducing us to the complex literature on trauma. She has also been a steadfast friend throughout the project and we have enjoyed traveling with her in Egypt, Iraq, Lebanon, and Armenia. Anahid Yahjian assisted us greatly at the end of the project in organizing mountains of video interviews and photographs. Daniela Hinsch served as our video editor in putting together a number of clips for presentations and, in addition, subtitled a number of interview clips that reside on the website of the Pomegranate Foundation, hosted by Carla Garapedeian. We also want to acknowledge that it was Yael Danieli who originally invited us to be part of the conference in 2001 at the Mille Collines Hotel. And, finally, the Center for Religion and Civic Culture at USC has been a supportive institution at every stage in the process.

PART I

The Genocide

CHAPTER I

Encountering the Genocide

In a recording studio at Solace Ministries, Mama Lambert described in detail how her husband and five of her children had been killed during the genocide against Tutsis in 1994. She escaped the slaughter of more than 800,000 Tutsis by Hutu extremists by hiding in the bushes for three months with her one-year-old son.[1] To the interview she brought a picture of her murdered husband, the letters written from prison of the young man who confessed to killing her two daughters, and the little shirt that her son had worn while she carried him on her back. At the end of the interview she volunteered to take us [Don Miller and Lorna Miller] to the actual location where the deaths of her family occurred. She wanted us to see the foundation stones of her destroyed house, the beautiful hillside where their cows had grazed, and the memorial where she had buried her family members and other loved ones.

At the top of the hill we climbed out of a four-wheel-drive vehicle and made our way down the side of the hill. Stopping at a clump of bushes, Mama Lambert said, "this was the entrance to our garden," and pointing, she said, "there was where our house stood." Describing their property, she continued: "We had a very big land that was fertile. We cultivated and grew all kinds of crops except rice." As Don set his video camera on a tripod, Mama Lambert looked across to the green valley and the hills in the distance, populated with houses and small farming plots. When she turned to face the camera, tears were streaming down her cheeks.

On a not too distant hill, in April 1994 they had the first warning sign of an impending disaster. Houses were being burned. Suddenly their Hutu neighbors with whom they had enjoyed good relations became hostile. Her husband, who was the headmaster of a school, was loaded onto a truck at the roadblock up the hill from their house, and along with other leaders in the community he was taken down the hill to a lake where he was killed and his body along with hundreds of others was discarded. Mama Lambert has been able to exhume the bodies of her children and give them proper burial, but her husband's bones are mired somewhere in the sediment of this lake. Many times, she has wondered if the lake could be drained so that she and other survivors could uncover the skeletal remains of their loved ones and bury them properly.

Amid the tangled brush, we then made our way to the actual site of her house. The foundation was completely overgrown. In addition to slaughtering Tutsis with machetes and clubs, the "killers," as survivors refer to them, looted the houses of their victims, stealing kitchen items as well as door frames, windows, and metal roofing sheets, and then lit the houses on fire to make certain that no one would return so that they could assume ownership of the land. Later Mama Lambert said that she wanted to rebuild this house, not to live in it herself, but so that the neighbors would say, "This was Placid's home." For her, it is important that her husband's name not be erased.

And then several surprising, unscripted encounters occurred. As we walked a short distance to a neighboring house, we saw a young woman and her child. Mama Lambert greeted her and then told us that they had been godparents to this girl's elder sister. "Whenever we had parties, we would share together." She said that her children had taught these kids how to read, and her husband had generously supplied milk and even paid the school fees of Hutu children in the area. After greeting her, Mama Lambert turned to this young woman and said, "Could your family have not hidden at least one of my children?" In response, the woman said, "Please forgive us. . . . It hurts me that I have no neighbor, that my child has no one to play with." She was a girl at the time of the genocide and protested that she didn't have any control over what was happening. Reflecting on the events of the genocide, she said, "We did not benefit anything by killing you."

We then looked up the hillside and saw an older woman walking down the path from the road. Mama Lambert embraced this woman—a Tutsi who was married to a Hutu—and turning to us, said, "This woman's son killed my two daughters." In 1998 this young man wrote a letter to Mama Lambert from prison in which he explained what he had done. In the letter, "He narrated how he killed my children. Some were stoned in the chest and others had their heads cut off. When I read this I was so confused, and I actually got angry with the leaders of the prison for having allowed him to send me this kind of letter. I knew that my children were killed, but I did not know all those horrible details."

We then made our way back up to the road where our vehicle was located. Mama Lambert pointed to a house that had been owned by a Hutu who now is hiding in France, or at least this is her assumption since he escaped Rwanda with French troops. It was in this house that her daughters were raped, along with many other girls. After the *gacaca* courts,[2] where many killers confessed to their crimes, survivors found twenty-six bodies that had been thrown into a pit latrine behind this house. Everyone was naked, including her two daughters and the body of her mother-in-law. In this latrine, they found the decapitated head of one of her daughters. Across from this house Mama Lambert had built a memorial with the names of those who were buried there. She went down the list, one by one, recalling the names of each person, including her two daughters, other relatives, and a neighbor who is buried there along with her five children.

Collecting ourselves after these rather dramatic encounters, we crossed the road and made our way up another hill. Mama Lambert waved her arms in all directions saying this entire area was populated with Tutsis; now only an occasional house was in sight. She said that what hurts her is that Hutus now live in nice houses, but houses of Tutsis are destroyed. In her view, perpetrators of the genocide look at the lack of Tutsi homes and say, "What we did was a success." The fact that she has forgiven the killer of her daughters does not alter the bitterness that she feels about the genocide.

Near the top of the hill we entered a small banana plantation. There was an indentation in the earth, which in 1994 was the pit where the bodies of Tutsis were being thrown as they were slaughtered. Miraculously, a young woman survived the killing and gave witness to what happened. The woman who survived said that she saw her own mother's head being cut, falling on the stomach of one of Mama Lambert's sons. It is also in this pit that Mama Lambert found the remains of her other son, who wanted to be a doctor.

At a nearby memorial, where 109 bodies were exhumed from this pit, flowers had been put on the gravesite. One bouquet said, "We cannot forget you." Another one read, "You left when we still needed you." Mama Lambert said that they had hurriedly buried these bodies after they were discovered so that they would not be dug up and eaten by dogs. From the banana plantation, we trudged up to the top of the hill. Mama Lambert pointed across the valley to a hillside some distance away. It was there that she and her one-year-old son hid for three months. At this site and throughout the day, Mama Lambert wiped away her silent tears.

•

SURVIVING

Mama Lambert's personal odyssey of the genocide began on April 24, 1994, when her husband was killed, although she did not witness his death nor that of her children. These details were revealed in the *gacaca* court and in the confession that was sent to her from prison by the individual who had killed her daughters. Her own memory of the following three months is absolutely vivid, however. She survived with her one-year-old son, Lambert, whose name she took after the genocide—the "mother of Lambert" or Mama Lambert.

During the three months from April through June, she experienced several different moments when she could have been killed. On one occasion, with Lambert on her back, she remembers being chased through a banana plantation by the killers. A Twa[3] woman saw her running and motioned for her to crouch behind some pottery that she was making. "I hid behind the pots and they did not see me. The Twa woman told them that neither Hutus nor Tutsis are allowed to step near unfinished pots. That's how I survived." This woman then made porridge for Lambert and this kept him from going hungry for the moment, but they were sent away since it was dangerous for anyone to harbor a Tutsi.

After leaving the Twa woman she narrowly escaped death again. Killers were placing Tutsis into three different lines—men in one line, women in another, and children in a third line. One by one they were cutting them with machetes and throwing them into a pit. She recalls people calling on God for help. "Some were praying, Catholics were reciting the rosary, and children who had been cut and were still alive in the pit were saying, 'Please forgive me, I will not do it again.' Others were saying, 'I did not urinate in bed.' And still others were pleading that they will never be a Tutsi. And others were asking God, 'Please receive my soul.'" In remembering such things, Mama Lambert said, "My heart becomes unstable."

When her time came to be cut and thrown in the pit, she asked the lady in front of her whether she or her daughter was going next. "I told her that I was scared seeing our children being cut down, and she answered me, 'All I know is that we are entering heaven. Just be silent.'" Then, just as she was putting Lambert down from her back, a boy appeared who had once been her student. He said to the leaders, "Look at my teacher, just hand her to me. I will kill her the way I want." This boy then started kicking Mama Lambert, leading her away from the rest of the group. This was his strategy for saving her.

When they were at a sufficient distance, Mama Lambert remembers the boy saying to her that you are not going to die. That she had treated him well and encouraged him to study. She remembers him saying, "If you die, you will die from another place, but I cannot stand seeing you killed." He told her to stay in the bushes and not enter any houses, because the next day they were going to search to see if anyone was hiding Tutsis.

During the period of hiding, Mama Lambert began to question God's intentions, saying, "You protected me in '59, '63, '73, why don't you protect me in this war of '94?" She told God that if she survived, she would serve as a witness to what happened to the Tutsis. Meanwhile, her son Lambert was very near death. He groaned for a while and then grew silent, so she put him on her back and continued hiding. Some fleeing mothers would put their babies near the home of a Hutu, hoping that a sympathetic woman would take the child. Mama Lambert refused to do this, but in the month of May she thought that her son was nearly dead from lack of nutrition and water. She said that Lambert developed a very thick yellow fluid in his mouth, which she tried to extract without success. He was literally dying in her arms and she began to wonder, "If he dies, where am I going to bury him, and what will I do?" In fact, she began to regret that she and Lambert were not killed at the pit where people were being slaughtered.

During this time, they were surviving on wild fruits that would cause sores in their mouths. Because it was rainy season, they would wet their mouths by licking wet leaves. She even remembers putting damp soil in her mouth, trying to suck out the moisture. And other times, when it was raining hard, she would cup her hands to catch falling drops. At one point, in anger at God, she threw a Bible that she was carrying into a bushy area. And when she looked to see where it landed, she said, "I saw wild fruits which were ripe." She immediately picked them and squeezed the juice into the mouth of little Lambert, which revived him from a coma-like state. Momentarily, they both regained strength.

But life was miserable in this location. Caterpillars kept falling on them, and Lambert would make a sign to her so that she would brush them off him.

He also would sometimes alert her to danger that he sensed. And somewhat miraculously, he never cried. Perhaps he lacked the strength.

Finally, she grew tired of the rain and caterpillars and thought of going to the house of a Hutu man to whom her husband had given a cow. They had also paid the school fees of his son who lived with them, and she thought he might take pity on her. But instead, when they arrived the man got his *panga*— a machete—and was going to cut her. Heroically, the boy whom they had supported protested, saying that the rest of the family has been killed, let us save just one. So, he took the two of them inside the house and told Mama Lambert to climb up into the ceiling area, saying, "They will have to kill me before they kill you."

That night the father brought some men to the house, and one of them said that he could smell a Tutsi and started stabbing his spear into the ceiling, searching for someone who was hiding. The spear pierced Mama Lambert in her rib cage but did not fatally wound her. And in the process of poking around in the ceiling their eyes met, and Mama Lambert held out a 5,000 franc note for him to see, and he stealthily tucked it in his pocket in a way that the others could not observe—which in turn saved her life, since he didn't want to share the money with the other men who were present. (Ironically, in the *gacaca* court he acknowledged this event and wanted to refund her the money, but she refused, saying that he had actually saved her life.)

After leaving this house, with Lambert once again on her back, she had another narrow escape with a group of killers, but she spotted a grinding stone that she started to turn and, pretending to be a Hutu, told them she was going to make them beer. Eventually, however, she grew so discouraged that she sought out a leader of the Hutu militia and asked him to shoot her, but the man refused, saying that the Tutsi rebel forces were nearby and that she could testify to them that he had protected her. At this point, she said that she had become nearly insane and had given up all hope of survival. Shortly thereafter the Rwandan Patriotic Army[4] took control of the area and she was safe, with many of the killers fleeing to Zaire[5] and other neighboring countries.

Somewhat miraculously, in addition to Lambert, two of her children survived the genocide, although five were killed, along with her husband, mother, and father, and other relatives. One son was hidden by an Italian Catholic priest who found him under a pile of dead bodies and then hid him under a bed. After the genocide, this boy was returned to Mama Lambert, although the priest was very interested in taking the child with him to Italy. A daughter was saved by a Hutu servant who fled to Zaire. When they were reunited after the genocide, the daughter, who was quite young, did not recognize her mother but did recognize the older brother whom the priest had hidden.

Mama Lambert said that her oldest surviving son is very quiet. "He was taken out of the dead bodies and saw his sister raped and later killed. When anybody begins talking about the genocide, he avoids the conversation. He refused to participate in *gacaca*. He puts his effort into studying and has completed his degree at the National University in Butare." The younger daughter avoided seeing many of the traumatic things witnessed by her brother since she was taken to Zaire by a Hutu servant. Heroically, Mama Lambert has also adopted four surviving children of relatives.

Mama Lambert's story is just one of several hundred interviews that compose the data for this book on the genocide and its aftermath. But her story is a defining one that touches on key themes throughout the book—how the genocide was experienced, what precursors were in place, and, perhaps even more importantly, how survivors deal with the ongoing trauma of the atrocities they experienced. We will revisit her story in later chapters on healing and forgiveness, since she deals with survivors on a daily basis at Solace Ministries, where we did a number of interviews and ethnographic observations for this book.

THE FOCUS OF THIS BOOK

Many good books have been written about the history of the genocide against Tutsis, including books that draw on oral history testimony.[6] Some of these books focus on the colonial legacy of this small country that placed it under German and then Belgian governance, both of whom favored the Tutsis in part because of their physiological resemblance to western Europeans.[7] Other books examine the failure of the West to intervene in the slaughter of the Tutsi population, including the cowardly role of the United Nations and the American government.[8] Several books examine the role of religious leaders in the genocide.[9] And a number of books focus on the attitudes of the perpetrators, the role of the *gacaca* courts, and the International Tribunal to try the masterminds of the genocide.[10] Recently, there are several books that deal with the political context after the genocide, challenging the narrative offered by the RPF and the president of Rwanda, Paul Kagame.[11] Then there are those books that address the task of preventing genocide in the future, referencing the mistakes that occurred in Rwanda.[12] And, of course, there are books that deal more generally with genocide.[13]

In this book, we have taken a very holistic approach rather than focusing on a specific issue or topic. The stories and analysis presented here draw on 260 interviews and fifteen years of experience with Tutsi survivors. We spent months coding every paragraph of our interviews, identifying patterns and themes in survivors' descriptions of the one hundred days of genocide, their lives before April 1994, and, importantly, their experience of trying to rebuild their lives following the killing.[14] We have followed many of these survivors from 2001 onward, through the various phases of their postgenocide experience. Additionally, for two of our sample groups there are also quantitative data that assess their trauma.[15]

These data have led us to several important big-picture conclusions and many subpoints found throughout the chapters and reviewed in the conclusion. First and foremost, we assert that it is impossible to really understand genocide without studying the aftermath of the killing. Yes, the hundred days of killing in Rwanda were horrific—beyond the grasp of people outside Rwanda as well as those who experienced the killing themselves. But to understand the immensity of genocide one must follow survivors through the process of rebuilding their lives. It is there that one sees not only the psychological damage of genocide but also how far-reaching the destruction is—from the microcosm of the social reconstruction of identity, to the ways cultural capital is passed from one generation to the next, to the rebuilding of key institutions in society.

Second, the data teach us important lessons about the context of healing. Survivors' well-being—their ability to cope with trauma and reengage the world in a productive relationship with the present as well as a hopeful connection with the future—is filtered through many things such as their health and physical well-being, their level of poverty and material conditions, the political climate, and their social context and religious worldview. In this sense, the first steps in healing the traumatic wounds of an individual and a society are addressing issues of poverty, health, and political stability.

Third, the data also raise many questions about the healing process itself. For example, what is the role of social life and community in healing individual psychological trauma? Can religion play a negative role during the genocide and a positive role in the healing process? Is forgiveness for the killer, or is it for the victim, and are there different types of forgiveness? What about trials, tribunals, and the daily performance of normalcy—can they be experienced as destructive for a victim while still being positive for the larger society? Finally, what are the meaning-making processes that survivors grapple with? And have models of healing communities emerged in Rwanda that are effective and might be adapted to other genocides or forms of individual and collective trauma?

This book is based on oral history testimonies with common people, who many times lacked knowledge of policy formation at a national or international level. Although chapter 2 gives some historical background on why the genocide occurred, most of the book focuses on the grassroots experiences of everyday people. What precursors to genocide did interviewees note? How was the killing experienced? How did they survive? What key struggles followed the killing, and what does the healing process entail, both individually and politically?

It is our hope that some of the insights gained here might be relevant beyond Rwanda and even beyond genocide. The aftermath of the killing takes us outside a formal definition of genocide[16] to an understanding of ongoing trauma and the postgenocide reconstruction process. As an extreme form of trauma—about as extreme as it gets—does the study of genocide and the rebuilding process reveal insights into social dynamics and human well-being that are otherwise hard to see in the banality of daily life?

THE JOURNEY FROM ARMENIA TO RWANDA

This book is not our first encounter with the topic of genocide. During the first ten years of our married life, we were focused on the first genocide of the twentieth century, which claimed the lives of approximately 1.5 million Armenians in Turkey. Lorna's parents were both survivors of this genocide. Out of nine family members, her father and a sister survived, and half of her mother's family were killed. Over a ten-year period, we interviewed one hundred elderly Armenian survivors and published a book, *Survivors: An Oral History of the Armenian Genocide.*[17]

In 2001, we received a surprise invitation to speak at an international conference in Kigali, Rwanda, on genocides of the twentieth century. This was seven years after a genocide that had claimed the lives of at least 500,000 and likely as many as one million Tutsis. Rwandans were trying to understand and contextualize their own genocide, and so they had invited scholars and survivors of the Holocaust, and the Cambodian, Bosnian, and other genocides to speak about their experience. We felt honored to represent the Armenians and decided that Lorna would talk about her father's experience and Don would give a historical overview.

The meeting was held at the Hôtel des Mille Collines, made famous by the influential movie *Hotel Rwanda*, which only later did we realize was heavily criticized by many survivors who disagreed with its happy Hollywood ending and the heroic portrayal of the manager, Paul Rusesabagina. The conference was appropriately titled "Life after Death," and the keynote speaker was Rwanda's president, Paul Kagame, who was the leader of the rebel army that ended the genocide after one hundred days of slaughter by leaders of the Hutu Power movement.

As soon as Lorna gave her presentation, a small group of young Rwandan survivors gathered around her. They had formed an association of orphan heads of households (AOCM, L'Association des Orphelins Chefs de Ménages). They were fascinated by Lorna's story of her father's survival and the fact that he had gone on to have seven more children—the same number as had been in his nuclear family prior to the genocide. This encounter started a journey that led us back to Rwanda more than fifteen times in the subsequent decade and gave birth to three different oral history projects, and a total of 260 interviews, which form the basis for this book.

The officers of AOCM, who were attending the conference, wanted to tell us their stories. Although they had missed a few years of school after the genocide, many of them were in their early to mid-twenties and were university students, but of a special sort. They were also parenting their surviving siblings, and, in some instances, they had adopted orphan children who had no other parental figure in their life. They were balancing attending school, sometimes at night, and working hard to provide shelter and food for their younger siblings.

It was with some trepidation that late one afternoon, just as it was getting dark, Claudine invited us to her home. We hired a taxi that drove us about fifteen minutes from the Hôtel des Mille Collines, down a dirt road, until finally the driver had to stop because of washed-out areas in the road caused by pouring rain. At the time, we didn't realize that Rwanda is probably the safest country in all of Africa. Nevertheless, as the small living room grew dim and Claudine brought out an oil lamp, all we could think about as she recounted her family's experience of the genocide was how are we going to get back to our hotel.

Later in the week, the conference organizers took us in vans to some of the memorial sites that populate this small landlocked country. Claudine sat next to Lorna on our trip to the Murambi Memorial, where hundreds of bodies have been laid on low wooden tables in classrooms of a former school, École Technique Officielle. More than fifty thousand people were killed in this area in a period of three days, from April 19 to 22, 1994. Although a preservative of lime has been sprinkled on the bones, there was still the discernible smell of death as we moved from one classroom to another. Infants were laid next to adults; some still had fragments of clothing on them; others had beaded necklaces holding crosses—reminders that this genocide was one where Christians killed members of their same faith.

Evidence of the means of death was apparent from machete blows to the back of the neck that had severed the spinal column. Other skeletons revealed fractured skulls where their victims had been clubbed. And in several cases, we saw where the Achilles tendon had been cut so that victims could not run from their killers. After going through a dozen rooms or more, we came to one that had nothing but clothing. Tutsis were often stripped of their garments before being killed so that they would not be stained with blood and could be given by the "killers" to their family members.

We were both deeply shaken. It is one thing to read or hear about a genocide; it is quite another to meet it face-to-face. Lorna in particular was grateful that Claudine kept a tight grip on her arm as we made this gruesome tour of man's inhumanity to man. However, once we got back into our van, Claudine's pent-up emotions unleashed as she started to cry. Far from entwining her arm in Lorna's to give Lorna support, Claudine was grabbing onto Lorna for emotional support herself. This was the first time Claudine had been to Murambi. Like many survivors, her emotions related to the genocide were far from resolved.

The other memory that stands out from our first week in Rwanda was a visit to an AIDS medical clinic that was run by AVEGA,[18] an organization of surviving widows. We were joined by a psychiatrist from Bosnia and a young Rwandan Canadian who served as our translator. After some informal introductions, the director of the clinic asked if we would like to interview one of their clients. A tall, slender young woman entered the room; she fit the stereotype of a Tutsi. She told us that her child and husband had been killed, but for unknown reasons her baby had been spared. She was locked in a room and kept as a sex slave where every night men would rape her.

Finally, they decided to kill everyone in the village, and so a pit was dug for disposing of the bodies. By the time they got to her, she said they were tired from the hard work of killing, and so they pushed her into the pit and threw a grenade on top of the bodies. She survived because she was clutching her baby to her chest, who took the brunt of the shrapnel and was killed, but the mother's arm was severed. That night someone came in the darkness and asked if anyone was still alive. She called out and this person threw the end of a rope down into the pit and she was able to climb out. Within days her severed arm was filled with maggots, and eventually she found someone to amputate it. During our interview, she motioned at the stump of her arm saying that she needed another operation because the bone was starting to poke through her skin. Although she was taking antiretroviral drugs for her AIDS, like many victims of rape in Rwanda, we don't know if she is still alive.

A second woman also volunteered to be interviewed. She had been raped but did not know that she was infected with HIV when she later remarried a survivor whose wife had been killed. Subsequently, her husband died from AIDS, being unintentionally infected by her. She was currently taking care of thirteen children, only two being her own. The others she had adopted, which is true for many of the widows who survived the genocide. During the interview she started to cry, saying that it was okay for her to die, but who would take care of her children?

THREE INTERVIEW PROJECTS

We arrived home after that first conference and assumed that this was the end of our encounter with the Rwanda genocide. Perhaps we could write a check to a charity. However, we kept in email contact with the leadership of AOCM, the officers of the association of orphan heads of household. Clearly a bond had been created. Lorna could see in these young adults her own father who, at the same age, was surely struggling to find dignity and meaning as he ventured into adulthood after losing his parents and six of his siblings. Over dinner we kept talking, just as we had when Lorna was doing the Armenian survivor interviews. At last we came up with an idea—what if we offered to assist AOCM with funding an oral history project with their own membership of several thousand orphans, all of whom were raising younger siblings?

The next morning, Don fired off an email to Naphtal, the president of the organization. We received an almost immediate affirmative response. They would like to do the same sort of interviewing that we had done for the research on our Armenian genocide book, namely, interview one hundred of their members. So, we asked them to write a proposal and prepare a budget. Within weeks we had a full-fledged proposal that outlined the goals of the project, indicating that they would hire their own members to do the interviews, those who were social science undergraduates, and they had also secured a first-class translator, someone who had been studying in India when the genocide occurred and was now working for the local radio station. They also included funds to rent an office, hire a coordinator, and offer a small gift to each interviewee. (See appendix I for the methodology of this study and the other two projects.)

A few months later we were in Singapore on another research project and bought a number of tape recorders and other equipment necessary for the project. We flew into the Kigali airport a few days later and spent a week working with the newly appointed research team on developing an interview guide, which was approved by IBUKA,[19] the umbrella organization of the various survivor groups in Rwanda. We had the team members practice interviewing one another, which proved to be interesting since several of the female interviewers spoke so softly that their voices were not discernible on the tape. We were now firmly enmeshed in a new genocide project, and very quickly we had a number of orphans who were addressing us as "mother" and "father." In emails they would begin, "Dear Parents . . . "

Eight months later we had several thousand pages of interview transcripts, translated into perfect English. After reading through these heart-wrenching interviews, we decided to involve Jerry Berndt, a photographer who had worked with us on a project in 1993 after the Republic of Armenia became independent from the former Soviet Union.[20] After several trips to Rwanda with Jerry, we worked together on a photo exhibit of orphans that was seen by over twenty thousand people in Los Angeles.

With the AOCM project completed, AVEGA, an association of widows, asked if we could find funding for them to do an interview project similar to what AOCM had done, but with questions adapted for their membership of women. This project led to another sixty interviews, translated into both French and English. The coordinator for the AOCM project agreed to work with them in designing the study.

Our largest undertaking, however, was one hundred interviews that we conducted ourselves with survivors associated with Solace Ministries, a nongovernmental organization that was started in 1995 by Jean Gakwandi, who survived the genocide with his family.[21] All of these interviews were videotaped and, like the other projects, translated and transcribed so that they could be coded by theme and topic.

Although we draw heavily in this book on the interviews with members of AOCM for references to the experience of child survivors, and use the detailed interviews with AVEGA members in descriptions of the experience of widows, it is in the context of Solace Ministries that we spent the most time wrestling with questions about reconciliation, forgiveness, and the power of a community to facilitate the healing process of survivors. At two different points, we also worked with Professor Beth Meyerowitz, a psychologist at the University of Southern California, who developed quantitative measures of trauma and resilience, which are reported in appendix II. But our primary data for this book is qualitative—the interviews with survivors, time spent in their homes, visiting memorial sites, and observing survivors at weekly meetings and commemorations over a fifteen-year period.

VICARIOUS TRAUMA

When we began the interviews at Solace Ministries we were scheduled to do five interviews the first day. By evening we were completely exhausted and emotionally spent. The next day we told our dutiful project manager that we could only do three interviews a day. Even then we went to bed with nightmares of machetes and sadistic acts of violence. By the time the weekend arrived, we were ready for a break. And at the end of our three weeks' stay we flew to Italy for a two-week vacation to collect our thoughts and regain our moral bearings. When we returned to Rwanda six months later for another round of interviews, we decided to interview in the morning and spend the afternoon visiting the homes of survivors. This was very helpful because it enabled us to experience the humanity of our subjects, not simply the terror of their past. In subsequent trips to interview survivors we followed the same pattern: interviewing in the morning and doing home visits in the afternoon.

Nevertheless, when one is on a schedule—we were committed to do one hundred interviews with survivors—it was not possible to invest oneself emotionally in each survivor's story. In many ways, this came later when we were coding transcripts of interviews, one by one. Therefore, it is with some regret that we admit that we began to experience a degree of emotional blunting at points in the project, the same thing that we observed in some of the survivors we interviewed. It is a coping mechanism to shut down one's emotional response, including empathy toward another person's problems. Our personal good fortune was that we could return home, play with grandchildren, and invest ourselves in other activities. Survivors did not have this same luxury.

If we felt any discomfort about the structure of our interviews at Solace it is that we had limited time for each interview, which was not the case for our Armenian survivor interviews, where no more than one was scheduled each day, and we often lingered for coffee and sometimes returned for a follow-up visit. Because of our schedule, Tutsi survivors did not have time to tell us their full story, which could have taken many hours since survivors could often give a detailed moment-by-moment, day-by-day account of what they experienced in the hundred days of the genocide as well as how they put their lives back together after the genocide. Fortunately, our project manager had heard their stories in detail in a preinterview when survivors agreed to be part of our project; she had taken good notes and she continued to stay in touch with them long after we left.

CONTEXT MATTERS

Were this study based on interviews alone, our story would be quite different. Altogether, we have spent more than fifteen years not only interviewing widows and orphans but also visiting their homes and attending group meetings on economic development and housing projects. Also, we have traveled with our participants, observing their daily encounters with both fellow survivors and Hutus whose family members were responsible for the deaths of their loved ones; we have met with government officials, visited museums, observed commemorations and *gacaca* trials; we have visited schools, attended weddings, and been present to meet the children of survivors just minutes and days after they were born. In short, we have seen a much larger context than is afforded in a single interview, which in turn allows us to appreciate the degree to which context really matters.

Our Solace interviews were done in three different settings: a sound studio that had excellent acoustics but got uncomfortably hot without the cooling system being on, which added considerable background hum to our recording; our apartment, which was directly across the street from Solace Ministries;

and a guest room that was within the Solace compound. Perhaps the most "foreign" location was our apartment, which was nicely furnished and was certainly not typical of survivors' homes.

Some of our most joyful experiences were visiting survivors in their homes. They were surprised and delighted that we would visit them. The tenor of the exchange was completely different from the formal interviews we had done with them. We were on their territory, not ours. We were their guests; they were not our interview subjects. The vicarious trauma that we often felt during an interview, including a sense of helplessness in assisting survivor after survivor, was completely gone. We chitchatted; we were blessed; we were prayed for; and we were introduced to surviving children, siblings, and neighborhood friends. Survivors who had cried during our interview and seemed terribly traumatized were typically filled with smiles and relaxed during our visits to their homes. Several examples illustrate the contrast.

As one survivor entered the studio at Solace for the interview, we were shocked when the first thing she did before sitting down was to pull up her blouse and show us her internal organs that were barely held together by loose folds of skin. During the genocide, she had been severely cut by a machete and had miraculously survived. Someone had stitched her skin back together but clearly the stomach wall that holds in her internal organs was very damaged. At the end of the interview we were pessimistic about her prospects, both emotionally and physically. However, when we visited her home, which was neat and clean, she immediately took control, welcoming us and being the perfect host. When we stood to leave, she asked to pray for us, blessing our children, and our grandchildren. We walked away from this visit questioning the impulse to classify people based on external appearances.

Another memorable experience was with a woman who, prior to the genocide, had nine siblings and seven of her own children. All but two of her extended family were killed and only two of her own children survived. During our interview, she remembered witnessing the killers forcing her brother to dig his own grave, plus two others. He was then buried with his head exposed so that the birds would come and peck out his eyes. She also witnessed killers sadistically cutting off the limbs of Tutsis, one at a time, until they died. How can one recover your humanity after experiencing such events?

When we visited her home, it was larger than most, although the tin roof was punctuated by holes. When asked what they do when it rains, she said they simply move to locations in the house where the rain is not streaming through. After a very pleasant conversation she disappeared into a bedroom and reappeared with a beautiful basket that had taken her two months to make. She wanted us to have it, and in this gift-giving culture one must accept presents that are offered. There was no expectation of reciprocity. The gift was a pure expression of her humanity, offering us a gift in appreciation for having listened to her story. This basket sits in a prominent place in our living room at home as a reminder to be as generous and hospitable to others as this survivor was to us.

While many other examples of home visits could be given, there is one that resides indelibly in our minds. This survivor had been raped multiple times by many different men. She escaped eventually to a church with her baby and a number of other people. Once they were locked inside, grenades were thrown into the church. She remembers huddling on the floor with body parts of others falling on her from the explosions. After the genocide, she said she used to drink herself to sleep after having sex as a way of supporting her two surviving children. Her sister had gone mad and left her with two more children to raise. So, they were a family of four, plus an aging asthmatic mother who was in bed when we went to visit.

Going to her home, we drove up a very steep dirt road that was so rutted that only a four-wheel-drive vehicle could negotiate the climb. We were welcomed into a narrow hallway and offered a seat on a bench. Our host and her children sat opposite us a few feet away on makeshift stools. After some informal conversation, our host asked if we would step into one of the two bedrooms to see her mother. There on a narrow bed, covered with a blanket, was a shriveled old woman, and snuggled behind her was a small child sleeping. The room was dark and dank. Our project manager, a devout Pentecostal, prayed for the grandmother. And then our host said it was Rwandan tradition to offer guests a gift, such as soda. But they didn't have any to give. Instead, she asked one of her daughters, maybe eight or ten years of age, to sing a song. And taking a cloth this young girl came to us, one by one, wiping away the dust from our feet as she sang, "You have walked a distance to visit us; we now clean your shoes."

In Western society, which is so materialistic, pragmatic, and utilitarian, such gifts—whether a basket or a song—are reminders that dignity and humanity are expressed in many forms. Had we limited our research to formal interviews on our own turf, we would have never experienced the multiple dimensions of our survivors' humanity. After every one of our trips to Rwanda we returned home feeling more human ourselves, having glimpsed, if briefly, not just the way categories such as race and ethnicity can divide us but also some of the more fundamental aspects of what unites us as human beings into one interconnected family.

We have tried to reciprocate in our own way by helping orphans with college tuition and leveraging the resources of others to help in several construction projects at Solace Ministries. We also made certain that each survivor received a gift within a few days after their interview. But the primary responsibility we feel is to communicate the experience of survivors via the written word, which is a complex task given the massive data from which we are drawing.

AUTHENTICITY AND VALIDITY OF INTERVIEWS

It is legitimate to ask whether the descriptions of the genocide offered by survivors are an accurate reflection of what actually occurred, or, stated more bluntly, did survivors fabricate their accounts for some political motive. These are complex issues, and we do not approach them lightly, especially given our experience in writing a book on the Armenian genocide that the Turkish government denies.[22] In the case of Rwanda, very few people question whether a genocide occurred.[23] The visual documentation is simply overwhelming since evidence of the genocide was screened on television and there were multiple independent observers of what happened in the course of one hundred days. However, one can still ask whether the content of our interviews is trustworthy. In responding to this question, it is important to note that no memory is a mirror image of what occurred. Every memory is contextualized and therefore interpreted in response to a question that is being asked or a story that is being told. Furthermore, as we will argue in the chapter on healing, one way of coming to grips with traumatic events is to develop a narrative about what happened and the meaning of past events in light of present possibilities.

In some of our interviews, it was obvious that survivors had not digested their experiences during the genocide. They would jump from one event to another with very little linkage between events. They clearly had not developed a script of any sort and, in some instances, they showed very little emotion as they described the most horrific events. More typically, however, survivors gave detailed and coherent accounts of the genocide, oftentimes day-by-day litanies of what they saw and experienced personally. Somewhat surprising was the lack of hostility or anger in these descriptions; rather, the dominant emotions were pain and sadness. And it was very rare for the description of their experience to be enveloped in political rhetoric beyond references to "the war" as the context—by which they meant the civil war between the government and the Rwandan Patriotic Front (see chapter 2).

While survivors sometimes generalized about rape or killing based on what others had told them, in the chapters that follow we have been careful to cite examples of things that survivors experienced themselves or personally witnessed. In coding interviews, we looked for patterns across all 260 interviews, and while there were geographical variations related to the killing, there was also substantial resonance in the descriptions that matched observations by other scholarly studies that we read. The main difference within our three different interview cohorts is that orphans, which obviously were younger during the genocide, tended to give less complex and detailed descriptions, especially of their postgenocide experiences and emotions.

We have no way of evaluating whether our sample of interviewees is typical of all survivors, and, in some ways, it probably is not. It is highly likely that AVEGA selected women to be interviewed who were articulate; likewise, AOCM undoubtedly interviewed orphans who were more senior and were willing to be interviewed. In the case of the interviews done at Solace Ministries, survivors came to Solace seeking comfort because of the traumatic events they had experienced.

Consequently, we are not writing from a random sample of survivors. But we have no reason to think that these survivors were exaggerating or not telling the truth. And this is where subjectivity comes in play. In the one hundred interviews that we personally did at Solace, not once did we feel that survivors were manufacturing stories. There was something transparent and heartfelt in their accounts of the genocide as well as their response to questions about forgiveness, reconciliation, and so on.

At this point, however, it is important to make a technical distinction. We cannot assert that "such and such" literally occurred in any particular circumstance. Rather, we are dealing with *perceptions* of what occurred. For example, Hutus fleeing from advancing RPF troops would undoubtedly have a different narrative of events. Furthermore, it would be naive for us to say that survivor perceptions are not colored by multiple factors—experiences prior to the genocide (e.g., by parents and grandparents who were killed or faced discrimination); conversation among fellow survivors from their same village or region; or even political discourse that they heard on the news. On the other hand, descriptions of particular events, especially the killings of family members, have a strong ring of authenticity to them.

One other distinction is important. Part of the healing process is developing a narrative about what one experienced during the genocide, potentially enveloping these experiences within the context of a purposeful life trajectory. This is especially true of orphans who have married and have children—many of whom are struggling with what to tell their children about the absence of grandparents and relatives. Sometimes rape victims have discovered a new sense of dignity and self-worth in spite of what they experienced. Hence, the "envelope" in which survivors encase genocide experiences may be imbued with new meaning, but this does not imply that the "contents" within the envelope have been falsified. The rapes still occurred and the circumstances surrounding them remain the same. Likewise, the death of a child or a spouse occurred, and the details of the killing remain the same. But life also moves on, at least for some survivors, and the events of the genocide may not have the same traumatizing effects that they once did. Nevertheless, particular experiences are seared into their memory, and these are the events described in the chapters on orphans and widows.

ROADMAP TO THE BOOK

In the next chapter, we draw on a number of studies of the genocide to provide historical background as to why the genocide occurred and the political context that led to mass killing of the Tutsi population during the civil war. From that point forward, the book takes the readers on a journey that draws directly on our interviews. The next two chapters are full of horror; horror as the victims themselves experienced it. However, pushing through these chapters is important because it allows the reader to come out on the other side with a real sense of the arduous ordeal of survival. Specifically, chapter 3 focuses on the experience of orphans, drawing primarily, but not exclusively, on the interviews with orphan members of AOCM. Chapter 4 examines the one hundred days of the genocide from the perspective of women survivors and uses the AVEGA interviews as well as interviews with widows at Solace Ministries. In chapter 5, the tone moves from horror to deep sadness and desperation as the survivors begin to find one another and put little pieces of their lives back together. Here we hope to impart a realistic sense of the difficulties confronted in the aftermath of the genocide. This chapter tells the story of how survivors tried to reestablish their lives, seeking shelter, jobs, and physical sustenance.

In the second half of the book, glimpses of hope begin to return, just as they did for the survivors. This second half is less descriptive and more analytical, with chapter 6 tackling the problem of trauma, its symptoms, and the loneliness, including suicidal thoughts, as survivors faced the reality of living without their loved ones and the social fabric that had sustained them prior to the genocide. Chapter 7 deals with the healing process and describes in some detail how this occurs within the context of Solace Ministries, a model healing community. Chapter 8 analyzes the thorny issue of forgiveness. Chapter 9 deals with the political processes associated with justice, reconciliation, and commemoration in Rwanda. In the concluding chapter, we offer some updates on survivors as they enter their third postgenocide decade. We also offer a review of the themes we have presented as well as some summary theoretical conclusions for further study.

One might legitimately ask what is distinctive about this book since every theme mentioned above has been discussed in various books or articles on the genocide. Without claiming too much originality, the uniqueness of this book is that it tackles all of these issues in a holistic way, drawing on the same set of interviews. A limitation of this book is that we did not interview Hutu survivors of the civil war in Rwanda.[24] As several recent books have indicated, they would undoubtedly reveal a different view of events that span the period from 1990 to 1994.[25] Furthermore, this book does not engage political debates about the current governance of Rwanda.[26]

In the next chapter we sketch the broad outlines of some of the political events that led to the genocide. Initially, we struggled with making sense out of how such mass killing could occur, but after reading extensively in the literature on the genocide, it is clear there were a number of "tipping" points in the political process that explain how the genocide unfolded, involving large numbers of peasant Hutus who prior to 1990 often enjoyed positive relations with their Tutsi neighbors. Understanding the causes of a genocide is quite different from thinking that it was inevitable or that it is morally justified.

CHAPTER 2

How Did It Happen?

On April 6, 1994, Rwandan president Juvénal Habyarimana was flying in his private Mystère Falcon 50 jet, piloted by a French crew, with the president of Burundi, Cyprien Ntaryamira, and other advisors.[1] They were returning from a meeting in Dar-es-Salaam, with the president of Tanzania, the vice president of Kenya, and the president of Uganda, where they had discussed the political situation in Burundi, various other regional issues, and the peace treaty between the Rwandan government and the Rwandan Patriotic Front (RPF)— the refugee organization based in Uganda that was dedicated to the return of Tutsis to their homeland. Just as they were about to land at the Kigali Airport, two surface-to-air missiles[2] shot down the plane from close range and the fuselage landed in the garden of the presidential palace, where the two presidents were pronounced dead.

Because of the conflict between the RPF Tutsi refugees and the Rwandan government, the implication was immediately drawn by much of the population that the RPF had assassinated the president. To this day, there is debate about who shot down the plane.[3] One argument is that the missiles could not have been fired from the Tutsi stronghold in Kigali and were more likely shot from the Kanombe military camp—the highly fortified location of Rwanda's French-trained elite unit known as the Presidential Guard, which was directly under the pathway of the plane. According to this explanation, extremists within the Hutu Power movement assassinated their own president knowing that the public would then immediately jump to the conclusion that it was an attack by Tutsis, mobilizing the majority population of Hutus to carry out the genocidal plans of extremists within the government. This would enable the radical element of Hutus to reject the peace accords that had been signed by their president and to implement the "final solution," which was the extermination of the Tutsi population in Rwanda.[4] The alternative explanation is that the RPF, and specifically Paul Kagame, did not want a political solution to the civil war but instead believed that a military solution was the best alternative.

Regardless of who shot down the president's plane, a swift and extreme mobilization of local Hutus against Tutsis is precisely what followed.[5] The plane was shot down at 8:30 P.M. and by 9:15 P.M. there were roadblocks set up in Kigali and houses were being searched, which is further evidence that extremist elements within the president's own party had planned the assassination.[6] However, this was not the perception of the Hutu peasant population. The death of Habyarimana became the catalyst for justifying the elimination of the Tutsi population, fueled by fears that the Tutsis living in Rwanda would align with the RPF Tutsi refugees from Uganda. Influential Tutsis and moderate Hutus who might resist the plans of the interim government that came to power after the president's assassination were targeted for immediate death. Included in the initial "hit list" for assassination were the prime minister, the president of the Constitutional Court, various priests and civil rights activists, the negotiator of the Arusha agreements, journalists, and influential Tutsis, including businessmen, even if they had no connection to the RPF.[7] It is estimated that 10,000 to 30,000 politically moderate Hutus were killed along with 800,000 or more Tutsis.[8] Gérard Prunier states, "They started killing during the night [of April 6] and they managed to dispose of most of the 'primary targets'—the politicians, journalists, and civil rights activists—within less than thirty-six hours."[9]

By April 7, just one day after the president's assassination, the genocide was in full swing. The radio station RTLM,[10] funded by the extremist CDR[11] opposition party, was not only spewing poisonous rhetoric about the Tutsi "cockroaches" that were responsible for the assassination but also issuing detailed instructions regarding the mobilization, including lists of specific people who were to be killed. Many Tutsis who had lived in Rwanda for generations were identified as being aligned with the foreign rebel forces under General Kagame's command and were labeled as spies and collaborators of the RPF, even if they had no actual connection. Over the next three months, all Tutsis were targeted for death, including women and children.

No distinction was made between local Tutsis living in Rwanda and the "rebel" forces of the RPF.[12]

Many Tutsis had a fatalistic attitude right from the onset of the violence; it was not a matter of whether they would be killed, but when. Nevertheless, Tutsi families tried to flee the inevitable, hiding in bushes, congregating at churches where they had found safety during previous massacres, and running to the homes of Hutu friends, assuming they would hide them. For the next one hundred days, slaughter occurred at a rate that had never happened in human history with such deadly efficiency. Eighty percent of the killing occurred in the first six weeks, and it is estimated that the daily killing rate was at least five times that of the Nazi death camps.[13]

In this chapter, we address the question of how the local Hutu population could be mobilized so quickly to participate in the mass extermination of their Tutsi neighbors, and we also focus on what happened during the first few days of the genocide. As is the case in all genocides, mass killing doesn't occur because of a single madman or even a few co-conspirators who are the architects of a genocide. There is always a political, social, and often an economic context in which genocides occur.

As we examine the historical context of the genocide, it is important to not get lost in the details. The big framework is this: Prior to the early 1960s, Tutsis were the ruling class even though they were the minority. In 1961, the Tutsi monarchy was abolished and the Hutu majority came to power. There were subsequent massacres of Tutsis that resulted in tens of thousands fleeing to neighboring countries, with Uganda being a prime destination. In Uganda, Tutsi refugees united together to form the Rwandan Patriotic Front, which in the 1990s demanded their rights as Rwandan citizens. This led to a civil war, and it was in this context that the genocide occurred.

HISTORICAL CONTEXT

The earliest inhabitants of Rwanda were the Twa, now only about 1 percent of the population.[14] The Hutu and the Tutsi were to migrate later, and there is considerable dispute about the origins of both groups.[15] What is known is that the population coalesced into various clans and that the Tutsi Nyiginya clan became politically dominant by the mid-eighteenth century.[16] At the time of the genocide, Tutsis were approximately 15 percent of the population in

Rwanda, Hutus were 84 percent, and Twa were 1 percent, although there is debate about these specific numbers.

In 1885 at the Berlin Conference, Rwanda was assigned to Germany for oversight.[17] After World War I, under the League of Nations mandate, Belgium was given Rwanda to administer.[18] Both countries noted the European features of the Tutsi population, deemed them to be the superior "ethnicity," and chose to rule through the monarchy of the Tutsi kings, even though Tutsis were the minority population. This decision set up obvious conflicts between the Hutu majority and the Tutsi minority, with the former being pushed to the bottom of the political, economic, and social hierarchy despite their large numbers. This is not to say that all Tutsis were wealthy, but they were favored by the monarchy that was governing the population and setting social policies, such as access to education.[19]

In 1933 these distinctions were solidified when Belgian administrators organized a census, classifying every Rwandan by whether they were Hutu, Tutsi, or Twa, thus institutionalizing these ethnic classifications within the state and society.[20] Preserved in various photographs of the period are Rwandans being measured by the length of their nose, their height, and the shape of their eyes. In actuality, despite various stereotypical features of the population, the distinctions between Hutus and Tutsis were quite fluid, since there was a history of intermarriage. Furthermore, the categories referred to occupation as well as ethnic background, since Hutu were traditionally farmers tilling the soil and Tutsi were herders raising cattle. But these distinctions were put in black and white when everyone was issued an identity card unambiguously labeling them as Hutu, Tutsi, or Twa. Stereotypically, Tutsis were perceived to be tall, thin, and with angular features, whereas Hutus were viewed as shorter, squatter, and with broad noses.

By the early 1930s, the Catholic Church was the major institution in society, and the European clergy in Rwanda strongly favored the Tutsi monarchy. The Tutsi king was a Christian and in 1946 consecrated the country to "Christ the King."[21] The church was the primary educational institution and gave priority to Tutsis. This had a ripple effect in other institutions as well, so that by 1959, forty-three chiefs out of forty-five were Tutsi and 549 subchiefs out of 559 were Tutsi. And at the college in Butare, 279 of the pupils were Tutsi and only 143 were Hutu.[22] Education clearly resulted in economic opportunities, and even at the time of the genocide Tutsi were overrepresented in many professions and employment in international NGOs, even though in the thirty prior years the Hutu government had imposed quotas for students and occupations that more nearly resembled the 15/85 percent ratio of Tutsis to Hutus.

HUTUS COME TO POWER

In 1957, supported by foreign Catholic clergy who recognized the injustice of the political system that favored Tutsis, Hutus published a manifesto in which they demanded their rights.[23] The church's affirmation of reform is somewhat ironic given its earlier support of the Tutsi monarch. Two years later in 1959, the Tutsi king died under somewhat suspicious circumstances, and in the same year Hutus attacked elements of the Tutsi population, burning their homes and driving many into exile. The rationale for much of this violence was summarized in the Bahutu Manifesto, drafted by nine Hutu intellectuals in 1957. By 1964, it is estimated that at least 336,000 Tutsis had fled Rwanda in response to killings and discriminatory practices.[24]

In 1961, national elections abolished the monarchy, and the Hutu majority elected Grégoire Kayibanda. This change in the political context resulted in further violence against the Tutsis, and thousands more fled to Zaire (Democratic Republic of the Congo), Burundi, Uganda, and Tanzania—which are the countries surrounding Rwanda on its various borders. Between 1959 and 1973, as many as 700,000 Tutsis had left Rwanda because of political persecution.[25] In our interviews, frequent mention is made of massacres of Tutsis in 1959, 1963, and 1973. These memories were etched indelibly in the minds of Tutsis when the killings began in April 1994.

As one might predict, the Tutsis who had occupied power for many decades did not go quietly. On November 14, 1963, a group of "monarchists" who identified with the old regime and had fled to Uganda organized themselves into a fledgling military force and invaded Rwanda from Burundi.[26] This operation was poorly planned, with the rebel forces lacking equipment, and about a dozen miles from Kigali, they were decimated by Rwandan soldiers who were commanded by Belgian officers. Between December 1963 and January 1964, 10,000 Tutsis were killed in Rwanda.[27] In many ways, this set the pattern that was to follow in the 1990s when Hutus identified the local Tutsi population living in Rwanda with invading rebel, exile forces, leading to their slaughter by the tens of thousands. The perception by many Hutus was that if they didn't kill Tutsis now, they would once again live in servitude.

In the years to follow, the Hamitic myth, this pattern of labeling Tutsis as "other," flourished: Tutsis were not real Rwandans; they were imports from Ethiopia, which explained their different features.[28] Even though for generations they had shared the same language, religion, and culture, Tutsis were now increasingly viewed as not being "true" Rwandans. The extension of this argument was that Tutsi rebel forces should be repelled with force and that their "cockroach" relatives living in Rwanda should be removed. Tutsis were "aliens," and only Hutus were truly Rwandans.

Under President Habyarimana, who came to power in 1973 following a bloodless coup, Tutsis were scarcely represented in government. In fact, Tutsis were barred from being officers in the army, and Hutu soldiers were not permitted to marry Tutsi women. A quota was put in place that capped the number of Tutsi children who could advance to higher education.[29] Between October 1972 and February 1973, vigilante committees went from schools to the university to civil service and businesses to enforce the quota system.[30] It was a reversal of what Hutus had experienced under the monarchy of Tutsi kings.

In 1972, an event occurred in neighboring Burundi that further solidified antagonism toward Tutsis. Burundi had become politically independent a decade earlier in 1962, about the same time as the independence struggle in Rwanda against Belgium, except with the difference that the Tutsi minority ruled over the majority Hutu in Burundi. In 1972 there were massacres of tens of thousands of Hutus in Burundi by the Tutsi-led army, which led to massive migrations of the Hutu population into Rwanda and other neighboring countries, and this, in turn, led to further oppression of Tutsis in Rwanda. These massacres stirred the imagination of the Hutus' leadership in Rwanda of what might happen if they were not vigilant.[31]

THE EMERGENCE OF THE RPF

Meanwhile, Tutsi refugees in Uganda had been organizing themselves. By 1990 they had developed newspapers and magazines that romanticized the home country. A number of Tutsis had become educated and some had even entered professions, leaving their cow herding traditions behind. Gérard Prunier says that a pattern occurred that resembled Eastern European Jews who went to Western Europe and the United States in the early twentieth century.[32] Landless and without a home, Tutsi refugees focused on education for their children, since they could no longer depend on herding cattle for a living. In 1979, Tutsi refugees created a welfare foundation[33] to assist victims of political repression after Idi Amin was toppled. In 1980, they changed the name to RANU: Rwandese Alliance for National Unity. And in 1987 the name of the organization was changed to the RPF (Rwandese Patriotic Front), focused on return of exiles to Rwanda.[34]

Among the Tutsi refugees in Uganda, one particularly bright young man, Paul Kagame, became the deputy head of military intelligence and participated in the coup that put President Museveni into power in 1986. He and Fred Rwigyema, another Tutsi refugee, had joined the resistance in Uganda led by Yoweri Museveni against Milton Obote who was elected Uganda's president in December 1980, along with three to four thousand other Tutsis, many second-generation refugees. In Museveni's National Resistance Army (NRA), Tutsi refugees received excellent training and had ample access to weapons.

Nevertheless, many Tutsis living in Uganda became disillusioned when a law was passed that they could not own land as foreigners. And in November 1989, Rwigyema was removed from his position as commander in chief and minister of defense, which further led to Tutsis questioning their long-term status in Uganda. This and other events prompted a desertion from the Ugandan army; the refugees instead joined the Rwandan Patriotic Front (RPF) and brought their weapons with them.[35]

On October 1, 1990, a well-disciplined army of Tutsi volunteers from Uganda invaded Rwanda, seeking to put teeth behind their political demand for representation and democracy in Rwanda, which included abolishing identity cards and ending the ethnic divide. However, the invasion met with disastrous results. Troops from neighboring countries joined with President Habyarimana's forces and routed the rebel army of the RPF, aided by four hundred paratroopers from Belgium and spotter planes from France.[36] General Rwigyema was killed on the second day of the rebel attack, which was a serious blow, since he was a charismatic and loved leader.[37]

On October 5, the Rwandan government faked another attack during the night by setting off explosives that the population assumed were from the invading Tutsi rebels. The shooting began shortly after midnight and went until 7:00 A.M. This was all for show, although the press reported (falsely) that there was heavy fighting. In response, the French sent more troops and also ammunition, thinking that the RPF was about to attack Kigali. While this invasion inflamed the local population of Hutus and resulted in new arrests of Tutsis, it did not completely dampen the spirits of the Tutsi refugees living in Uganda, even though between October 11 and 13, 1990, five hundred homes of Tutsis in Rwanda were burned and nearly 350 Tutsis were killed.[38]

Paul Kagame had been training in the United States when this invasion occurred, and on his return he took command of the Rwandan Patriotic Army (RPA), the military arm of the RPF. In Fred Rwigyema's absence, he reorganized the army, recruiting additional volunteers, including Tutsis from Burundi, Zaire, and Tanzania, although almost all of the RPA officers were from Uganda. Under his leadership, the numbers increased, from 5,000 men in 1991 to 12,000 by the end of 1992, to 20–25,000 by April 1994. Meanwhile, funds were being collected for arms from refugee Tutsis all over the world, from Kampala to Brussels, Paris, Canada, and the United States. And it is quite likely that Museveni looked the other way when the RPF took ammunition from his stockpile in Uganda.[39]

On January 23, 1991, a group of Tutsi rebels attacked a prison in Ruhengeri, in the northern part of Rwanda.[40] They liberated a thousand prisoners, including some Tutsis, took military equipment, and held the city for one day until they withdrew. This attack restored some of the confidence of the rebel forces and also alarmed and weakened the Rwandan government. In response to this attack and internal dissension, President Habyarimana was forced to approve a multiparty political system. In March 1992, the CDR (Coalition for the Defense of the Republic) was born, which was a radical Hutu party to the right of the MRND (National Republican Movement for Development, Habyarimana's party), and the MDR (Democratic Republican Movement) also gained strength. The magazine *Kangura*, connected with the CDR, was spewing racist rhetoric. And the radio station RTLMC became a mouthpiece of the opposition to President Habyarimana.[41]

CIVIL WAR, PEACE ACCORDS, AND THE UNITED NATIONS

What unfolded in the next few years was a civil war between Tutsi refugees living in Uganda who were demanding their rights and the Hutu-led government based in Kigali. In response to this conflict, negotiations began in nearby Arusha, Tanzania, to iron out a peace agreement between the RPF and the Rwandan government. Hardliners within Rwanda felt that President Habyarimana was being too soft in his negotiations, and after the Arusha Accords were signed on August 4, 1993, there were demonstrations against the peace agreements by the CDR, beginning in October 1993.[42] Because the government of President Habyarimana had actually been quite civil toward the country's Tutsi minority, compared to the opposition factions that developed, rhetoric started emerging from the RTLMC and *Kangura* about "brush clearing," which was a euphemism for getting rid of the local Tutsi population. Small-scale massacres, echoing those of 1963 and 1973, became more frequent, often in response to actual or perceived rebel threats.

What forced the peace agreement was the strength of the RPF. On February 8, 1993, the RPA invaded, and this time they got within 23 kilometers of Kigali before being turned back. Even though they did not succeed, the attack strengthened their position at the bargaining table with the Rwandan government as details were being hammered out in the Arusha Accords.[43] The accords called for a classic power sharing agreement, but one that favored the Tutsis compared to their percentage of the population. Paul Kagame's military advances and the growing sophistication of the RPA were having an impact, and it left President Habyarimana looking very weak in the view of the opposition parties, and especially the CDR, the hardliners opposed to the president. Gérard Prunier says about the fallout from the RPF's February attacks: "Even the most resolute and honest opponents of the regime began to feel that they had been naïve and that, through their actions, they were running the risk of exchanging a Hutu military dictatorship for a Tutsi one."[44]

In response to this peace agreement, which ended three years of civil war, there were divisions within President Habyarimana's government[45] with hardliners thinking he was too soft in acquiescing to the RPF's demands. This was the fertile soil in which the Hutu Power movement grew, including increasingly vitriolic propaganda inflaming the local population against their Tutsi neighbors. But there were other factors. The economy was in bad shape due to collapsing coffee prices. The government had dramatically increased spending on armaments, including ramping-up the number of troops, which resulted in increased taxes for the peasant class. It is in situations of social and political discontent such as this that racist ideologies oftentimes brew. But there were other important triggering mechanisms that contributed to the genocide.

On October 21, 1993, President Melchior Ndadaye, the first popularly elected Hutu in the history of Burundi, was assassinated by Burundi Tutsi military forces.[46] In response, there were anti-Tutsi pogroms as well as anti-Hutu killings in Burundi, resulting in as many as 50,000 deaths. Upwards of 300,000 Hutus fled Burundi, mostly to Rwanda, and the assassination of

Ndadaye had a substantial effect on the psyche of politicians in Rwanda. According to Gérard Prunier, "It was the murder of President Ndadaye which convinced the CDR and their allies that time had come for action."[47] The airways of RTLMC were filled with hysterical rhetoric: Kill the Tutsis or be killed by them. This was a very dangerous turn because it justified preemptive action against the minority population.

Because of the oppression of Tutsis after Rwanda's independence, turmoil in Burundi after the assassination of their Hutu president, and various invasions by the RPA and counter massacres of Tutsis, there were hundreds of thousands of people, both Hutu and Tutsi, who had fled their homes, creating a huge refugee problem in the region. By February 1993, there were 600,000 on the move. Rwanda was in a full-blown civil war, and this attracted the attention of international governments and aid agencies, and also led to the decision to deploy UN troops in Rwanda.

On October 5, 1993, the UN Assistance Mission for Rwanda (UNAMIR) was created under Resolution 872.[48] It was a relatively small force, led by General Romeo Dallaire from Canada, that had a weak mandate and limited funding. In November 1993, the first six hundred UNAMIR troops arrived, eventually building to 2,519 by April 6, 1994.[49] In the months prior to the genocide, General Dallaire predicted the possibility of mass killing and cabled his superiors at the United Nations informing them that a genocide was imminent, but to no avail.[50] On October 3, 1993, eighteen Americans had been killed in Somalia and another eighty-four wounded. Government officials in the United States did not want to hear the word "genocide," which would have put them under legal obligation to respond. Knowing this, the interim government that formed after President Habyarimana's death was very strategic in killing ten Belgian peacekeepers, which prompted the Belgians to immediately withdraw their troops that were part of UNAMIR. Within days, France sent in planes to evacuate French nationals who were living in Rwanda. Meanwhile, the US government turned a deaf ear to the crisis that was unfolding. It was not until 1998 that President Clinton acknowledged the failure of the United States to intervene in the genocide.[51]

SUMMING UP: MAKING SENSE OF THE GENOCIDE

Simplistic theories regarding the genocide need to be dismissed. It did not occur because of ancient tribal hostilities or because these sorts of things happen in Africa. Also, the genocide was not simply a result of payback for the years that Tutsis dominated political leadership under the monarchy. Nor was any other single factor the cause of the genocide, such as the high rates of population density in Rwanda, the dehumanizing role of propaganda, or the passive response by Western governments, although all of these factors played a role. Rather, there were multiple factors and a variety of tipping points in the political process that coalesced in the attempt to annihilate the Tutsi population. In the next few paragraphs—and at the risk of some repetition of the history to this point—the goal is to explain why and how the genocide was able to take place.

First, any attempt to understand or explain the genocide must acknowledge that it occurred during a civil war. Had there been no war, then it is unlikely that the genocide would have happened. People do not kill each other to the point of extermination simply for the joy of killing or the loot that can be secured. In the case of Rwanda, there was fear that the rebel Tutsi might retake the government and once again subjugate the Hutu majority. This fear was exacerbated by events in neighboring Burundi and by the success of the RPF in its various incursions into Rwanda. Furthermore, these fears were being concretized by the favorable negotiations of power sharing with Tutsis that was agreed to by the president in the Arusha Accords. Acknowledging the context of the civil war does not blame the RPF for the genocide, nor does it exculpate the political leaders that planned the genocide, such as Theoneste Bagosora. Instead, it acknowledges that genocides often occur within the context of war.

In unraveling the root causes of the genocide, it is important to acknowledge that the German and then Belgian governments fostered antipathy between Tutsis and Hutus by favoring the former over the latter. This discrimination led to the perception that one race was superior to the other, and, in more practical ways, it resulted in the minority population receiving favoritism in education as well as government positions. By current standards of human rights, these colonial policies were unjust, and it is not surprising that even foreign clergy began to acknowledge this fact in the political climate of the late 1950s and early 1960s.

When Hutus asserted their rights, there were discriminatory killings of Tutsis. More importantly, it was these killings in the early 1960s that led to large numbers of Tutsis fleeing to neighboring countries—and this is what eventually set the stage for the civil war. In Uganda, Tutsi refugees developed a political consciousness, gained military training by joining the resistance of

Museveni against President Obote, and created the RPF, which sought to undo the injustice of being forced out of their homeland.

Meanwhile, back in Rwanda, there was political jockeying. The first Hutu president, Grégoire Kayibanda, who was from the southern part of the country, was overthrown by Juvénal Habyarimana, whose constituency was primarily from the northwest of Rwanda. These geographical tensions would continue to express themselves politically, including after Habyarimana was killed and an interim government was installed. During Habyarimana's reign the balance of power between Tutsis and Hutus was completely reversed. Gérard Prunier states: "Throughout the Habyarimana years there would not be a single Tutsi *bourgmestre* or *prefet*, there was only one Tutsi officer in the whole army, there were two Tutsi members of parliament out of seventy and there was only one Tutsi minister out of a cabinet of between twenty-five and thirty members."[52] Discrimination was further reinforced in the schools where Tutsis advancement was capped at 9 percent; members of the army were prohibited from marrying Tutsi women; and, of course, this information was being communicated to the Tutsi diaspora, which inflamed them against the ruling government in Rwanda.

Consequently, it is not surprising—in fact, it might be expected—that a movement such as the RPF would surface. What gave this rebel movement its impetus, however, is that Tutsis were being excluded from integrating into Ugandan society. And what gave the rebel group its power is that a substantial cohort of Tutsis had been trained in the resistance army in Uganda and therefore had access to weapons from their training.[53] Equally important is the fact that a smart, capable leader, Paul Kagame, had emerged from its ranks. Without his leadership and intelligence, it is doubtful that there would have been a successful civil war.

MOBILIZING THE KILLING MACHINE

Although the RPF failed miserably in their first invasion of Rwanda in 1990, it was the tactical strategies and efficiency of the rebel forces that created the context for the following to occur in Rwanda: (1) the creation of two Hutu militia groups—the Interahamwe and Impuzamugambi—which were made up of young thugs who were extremely efficient killers; (2) the poisonous rhetoric that equated Tutsis with cockroaches and snakes and justified "brush clearing" to eliminate this venomous presence in the country; (3) political divisions in response to the Arusha negotiations that created hardline racist extremists, some of which began planning a genocide as early as 1992; and (4) an atmosphere of fear and anxiety that enabled Hutu peasants to do things against their Tutsi neighbors that never would have been imaginable in a different political context.

Because of the strength of the RPF, the Rwandan government began to build the Rwanda Defense Force (FAR) troop numbers. In October 1990, there were 5,200 FAR; by mid-1991 there were 15,000; by 1991 there were 30,000; and by mid-1992 there were 50,000.[54] As much as $100 million was spent between 1990 and 1994 purchasing large quantities of armaments from abroad.[55] Machetes and other "farm" implements were imported from China, which became the killing instruments for the Interahamwe,[56] the youth militia created by President Habyarimana's party (the MRND), and the Impuzamugambi ("those with the same goal"), created by the CDR. Without the creation of these two militia groups, the killing would never have been as effective and fast in 1994. Gérard Prunier says, somewhat cynically regarding these militia groups: "For these people the genocide was the best thing that could ever happen to them. They had the blessings of a form of authority to take revenge on socially powerful people as long as they were on the wrong side of the political fence. They could steal, they could kill with minimum justification, they could rape and they could get drunk for free."[57]

This takes us to the question of how 800,000 people or more could have been killed in one hundred days, especially when the army was involved in fighting the RPF. The answer relates to the participation of the peasant class, but first, it is important to note that the organizers of the genocide realized that they had to eliminate the moderate Hutu within their own ranks, which they did within the first few days by going down the "death lists" that they had prepared in advance. The next step was to enlist the rank and file, and they did this through the established hierarchy of the political structure, which began with the national government, and then cycled down through the prefectures, communes, sectors, and cells. At every level there was a political structure and leadership, and people were used to following orders from the leaders above them.[58]

WHY DID NEIGHBORS KILL?

Scott Straus interviewed over two hundred prisoners who were accused of participating in the genocide, and he found them to be rather ordinary people, with no prior history of killing, not particularly ideological, and not trained in military tactics. On the other hand, they were frightened by the civil war and feared invading RPF forces that might threaten their homes, livelihoods, and families. And they were angry at the death of their president, which they blamed on the RPF.

Furthermore, the peasant class was used to following orders, especially related to *umuganda*, which is known as "community work"—something every able-bodied person did on a regular basis and is still practiced in Rwanda today. It varied from repairing roads to various tasks that contributed to the civic welfare of the community. Hence, when the order came to kill neighboring Tutsis, it was oftentimes not done with any enthusiasm but out of duty, even if the work was distasteful. Prunier states, "Killings were umuganda, collective work, chopping up men was 'brush clearing' and slaughtering women and children was 'pulling out the roots of bad weeds.'"[59]

Straus argues that ordinary peasants feared punishment if they did not follow orders. Furthermore, if other neighbors were participating, even in limited ways (e.g., manning roadblocks) there was peer pressure to also participate. And once the killing began, it gained momentum. Straus states: "Once a point was reached when those promoting violence consolidated control and once men started killing, they themselves became increasingly violent and demanded conformity from their peers. Men traveled through their communities telling other men, in effect, 'Since we have killed, so must you.' And 'Since killing has started in neighboring regions, it must start here too.'"[60]

Scott Straus says that there are a number of comparative and theoretical possibilities for the genocide, with self-protection being a primary factor: "Many ordinary Rwandans participated in genocide because they feared for their safety in war and because they calculated that committing violence would be less costly than openly disobeying."[61] In his view, fear played a substantial role in motivating ordinary people to kill innocent neighbors. Straus states, "Once the hardliners authorized and ordered the population to fight Tutsis and once coalitions of actors at the local level emerged to heed that call, genocidal killing became the order of the day. Those who participated in turn pressured others to kill. Conformity ruled; open disobedience was punished."[62]

According to Straus, it is difficult to explain the genocide simply in terms of ethnic hatred between Tutsis and Hutus.[63] Nor does he agree with the material deprivation thesis that this was class warfare. He says, "Men participated in the killing because other men encouraged, intimidated, and coerced them to do so in the name of authority and 'the law.'"[64] While one might justifiably be skeptical of the perceptions of prisoners, he says that many of his interview subjects said that they killed because, if they didn't, they would be punished by the authorities ordering the extermination of the Tutsis or else they feared they would be killed by advancing RPF troops. He cites the famous Milgram experiment that indicated in experimental settings that ordinary people can do horrific things when following the orders of authority figures.[65] Killing does not require one to be a rabid ideologue or sadist. Rather, people were following orders.[66] They saw other people killing. They were fearful of not following government mandates. And there were material spoils associated with killing people and taking their household goods and property.[67]

In addition to political authority, the other institution with authority was the church.[68] It was oftentimes complicit, with many clergy and religious figures supporting the Hutu government while the genocide was being enacted.[69] The complacency or outright collusion of the church altered the traditionally accepted religious mandate against killing. According to Linda Melvern, "So overt was the Catholic support for Hutu nationalism that, when the 1994 genocide happened, the archbishop of Kigali, Vincent Nsengiyomva, was on the central committee of the ruling party, and closely linked to the inner circle of Hutu Power which organized the genocide."[70] Timothy Longman, who studied the role of the churches in depth, states: "As the primary voices of moral authority in Rwanda, the churches not only failed to speak out forcefully against the increasing exclusion of Tutsi and the growing violence against Hutu activists and Tutsi in the years leading up to the genocide but also lent strong support to the regime that was encouraging the exclusion and violence."[71] Hence, the priestly class made the genocide morally acceptable, contributing to the climate where genocide was possible, and on occasion actually giving leadership to policies that resulted in the genocide. In Longman's view, "The Christian message received in Rwanda was not one of 'love and fellowship,' but one of obedience, division, and power."[72] The only religious people who resisted participation in the genocide were adherents of Islam, which constituted about 1.2 percent of the population. They refused to divide themselves by ethnicity.[73]

CASUALTIES OF THE WAR

The RPF is to be credited with stopping the genocide. After April 8, they started making their way toward the capital, aware of the mass slaughter of

Tutsis that was occurring. As they took various areas, many Hutu residents fled, often in a very organized manner, led by the Hutu leaders of their region. By August 1994, there were two million displaced people. From Kigali alone, there were three hundred thousand people on the run, including dispirited Interahamwe, civil servants who had commandeered cars, ordinary peasants, exhausted FAR troops, middle-class businessmen with overloaded cars, and abandoned children, says Prunier.[74] Officials of the defeated government ordered people to flee, and in Butare, they would be shot if they did not.[75]

On July 19, 1994, the new government was sworn into office, with Paul Kagame as the vice president, and shortly thereafter diaspora Tutsis started flooding back into the country, some four hundred thousand by November. Meanwhile, the condition of Hutus in the refugee camps was deplorable. A cholera epidemic swept the camps in places such as Goma, across the Rwanda border in Zaire. In response, multiple aid agencies came to their rescue, focusing on Hutu refugees from Rwanda more than on the Tutsis who had survived inside Rwanda. The country was completely decimated. Two million of seven million Rwandese were living outside the country; the economy was shattered—the fleeing Hutu government officials had taken with them all the cash in the Central Bank; the court system was completely nonfunctional; and many surviving Tutsis were homeless, traumatized, and unemployed.[76] One hundred fourteen thousand children were without parents.[77]

Because of reported abuses by the RPF, the United Nations High Commissioner for Refugees (UNHCR) sent a three-person team to investigate, headed by Robert Gersony. From August 1 to September 5, this team traveled the country and conducted a number of interviews. Although the report was never formally made public, there may have been around thirty thousand revenge killings between July and September 1994.[78] Prunier acknowledges that reprisal killings occurred and says that this was, in part, because recent Tutsi recruits had witnessed violence against their own families. He says that the highly disciplined RPF army necessarily had to bring on new recruits as the civil war expanded, and these individuals were not as disciplined as the rebel troops from Uganda.[79] This does not dismiss the killings that undoubtedly occurred by RPF soldiers, but the proportion is on a completely different scale from the eight hundred thousand or more Tutsis who were killed.[80] Furthermore, the idea of a double genocide has no legitimacy since the RPF-related killings were not an attempt to eliminate an entire population or category of people, which is the definition of genocide.[81]

CONCLUSION

In the next two chapters, we take the reader directly to the experiences of survivors during the genocide—first orphans and then widows. At no point did we interview prisoners or Hutus, which is a limitation of our study. However, our goal throughout the rest of the book is not to decide who is right or wrong, nor do we venture into the contested debate regarding the current political situation in Rwanda. From here on in the book, we are focused exclusively on the testimony of Tutsi survivors. When appropriate, we footnote relevant literature on the topic being discussed. However, fundamentally, this is an oral history of the genocide, its immediate aftermath as survivors attempted to put their lives back together, and the experiences of trauma, healing, and justice as perceived by the survivors themselves.

CHAPTER 3

Orphan Memories

Francine, in her early teens in 1994, said that on the night Habyarimana's plane crashed she was visiting her grandmother when her aunt came to them saying that they must flee because otherwise they would be killed.[1] She said that because her grandmother had many cows, their home was immediately attacked, and Francine and other relatives spent the night in a sorghum field. That night several of her uncles were killed and other relatives were killed the next morning. Francine and her mother were hiding in the woods when the killers[2] brought dogs to search specifically for them, based on a list of Tutsis that they had not yet found. Francine said that she eluded the killers, but they took her mother, raped her, then cut off her fingers one by one and left her there to die. Meanwhile, Francine said that she could not make any noise, or they would have found her, so she witnessed her mother bleeding and screaming until around noon when they came back and hit her on the head with a club and she fell silent.

Francine ran around in the woods all that night, not knowing where she was going, and the next day encountered a group of Interahamwe. "They took me to a place with other people. There were so many people there, many Interahamwe. But one took me to the woods and raped me. I felt that I was going to be killed the same way that they had killed my mother, for they had started off by raping her. After raping me, he called three other men who also raped me. I was still a virgin. I felt . . . I was very hurt and this has affected me very much."

After raping her, she said they tied her hands and legs together and took her to a nearby river and threw her in the water. "I was drowning in the river and I prayed to God and told him that if he saved me I would serve him for I didn't want to die." Nearly unconscious, she washed up on the bank of a river where a Hutu man and woman cultivating their land found her. They helped her vomit out the water she had swallowed and took her into their home.

Francine's account illustrates a number of themes common to the experience of orphan survivors. First, news spread very quickly about the crash of the president's plane. Most Rwandans had small radios, and blame for the crash was immediately attributed to the RPF. As we saw in the last chapter, beginning in 1990, the RPA had made strategic attacks from their base in Uganda. Hence, it was quite plausible to Tutsis and Hutus alike that the RPF had successfully shot down the president's plane. Few local residents would have theorized the possibility that it was Hutu extremists who had killed President Habyarimana in an effort to seize power.

Based on past massacres of Tutsis since 1959, it is quite understandable why their first impulse would be to hide from potential attackers. In our interviews, most survivors said that they fled to the forests or spent the night sleeping away from their home in bushes or sorghum fields, especially beginning April 7. Later they would hide in swamps and other locations, because it was difficult to evade attackers. In terms of size, Rwanda was the most populated country in all of Africa. Nearly every arable plot of land was being cultivated, so it was not that easy to hide. Roadblocks were set up on streets, making transiting from one area to another difficult without being detected. And, furthermore, the attackers used dogs to flush out Tutsis from their hiding places in fields, forests, and brush areas.

Several other important facts are mentioned by Francine in her account. Francine's grandmother had many cows, which singled her out as being wealthy. Looting homes and stealing cattle were extremely common. In fact, an incentive for killing Tutsis was that one could benefit personally by taking their property, including land. Also, killing the cows of Tutsis and feasting on them was part of the collective celebration that for many Hutus took place nightly. It was not only the men who were enjoying the carnival-type atmosphere as they ate and drank at night before going to "work" the next morning. Their wives were also the beneficiaries of cookware and other household items. While many houses with straw roofs were burned after being looted, those with metal roofs were viewed as having special value, and the benefits of looting were measured in some cases by the number of metal roofing sheets that one was able to accumulate.

Francine also notes that their attackers had a list of Tutsis that they had not yet found. Amid the fervor of killing, which sometimes was quite chaotic when mass slaughters were occurring, such as in churches, there was actually a very methodical process of creating lists of Tutsis in every community and then systematically identifying who had been killed and who was remaining on the list to be killed. It was very common for the killers to come looking for even a single individual on their list. Until this person had been killed, they had not done their job. Tutsis lived intermingled with Hutus, and residents typically knew the ethnicity of their neighbors.

As Tutsis fled from one area to another, and therefore were not personally known to attackers, identity cards were used to determine one's ethnicity. Although Tutsis had certain stereotypical features, including long fingers—the reason Francine's mother's fingers were hacked off after she was raped—it was not always that easy to distinguish Hutus from Tutsis. Therefore, identity cards were extremely important in identifying Tutsis, prompting some individuals to destroy or hide their cards. Finally, Interahamwe who did not know the local population were extremely careful not to kill Hutus; this is why some Tutsis escaped, especially children, if their ethnic identity could not be determined.

Also, notable in Francine's account is the fact that she witnessed the rape and killing of her mother. What was especially difficult was that she could not show any emotion during this time or else she would have been discovered. Hence, like many survivors, she suffered silently, feeling completely helpless to assist her mother. And as we will see later in the chapter on trauma, it is the image of others being killed, and especially family members, that continued to haunt survivors, resulting in flashbacks, insomnia, hysterical outbursts, and other symptoms of PTSD. During the interviews, it was descriptions of the deaths of parents and children that frequently brought tears to survivors' eyes.

But survivors also experienced direct violence, such as the multiple rapes that Francine said have affected her so much in later life. It was very common for Tutsi women to be gang raped or else taken as sexual slaves to be shared day after day until the attackers grew tired of them and finished their business by killing them. Teenage virgins were targeted as well as women, sometimes of any age. There was a sadistic element to rape, as women had sticks and other objects shoved in their genitals. And in one instance in our interviews, it appears that males were sometimes raped by their attackers as well.

Several other observations in Francine's testimony warrant mention. First, she was thrown into a nearby river to drown. The point of this act was not that this was the easiest way to kill her. Rather, decomposing bodies smell, attract flies, and are a public health problem. Consequently, various means were used to dispose of bodies. Throwing them into rivers was one common means, and at the height of the genocide there were literal logjams of bodies in some rivers as well as decomposing bodies that ended up in Lake Victoria. The more common means, however, was putting bodies in the pit latrines that dotted the landscape; many of these were quite deep and therefore allowed for a number of corpses to be piled on top of each other. The other option was to throw bodies in pits or holes in the ground and cover them with dirt. In the cities, dump trucks picked up bodies to dispose of them in mass graves.

Finally, there were sympathetic Hutus who did not participate in the mass killings and either attempted to hide Tutsis—usually for a brief period since such acts potentially resulted in death or fines—or else tried to feed or bind up the wounds of survivors before they went on their way. After the genocide, over one hundred thousand individuals were put in prison, accused of violence against the Tutsi population. Most of these were men, but some women were also charged with crimes. It is incorrect to generalize that all Hutus were guilty of the crime of genocide.

CHURCHES AS KILLING SITES

Churches are supposed to be places for praise, hope, and renewal. But because half the deaths during the genocide occurred in church buildings and their surrounding courtyards, some churches in Rwanda have been turned into memorials—or, alternatively, there are memorials located on church grounds. At the Catholic Church in Ntarama and the immediate vicinity, approximately five thousand people were killed. It is a relatively small church with several side buildings, including a room where the children met for Sunday school. As one enters the church, visitors to this memorial encounter shelves where hundreds of skulls are neatly placed, one next to the other. They are of different sizes and include those of children.

The first time we visited this church, there was debris between the pews, remnants of what people had brought with them when they fled to the church for safety, including clothing, food containers and plates, and other household items. Clearly people thought they might need to stay there for several days. On the altar at the front of the church, someone had placed a skull, and rosary beads were hanging on a wooden cross that was propped up against the altar.

There was a gaping hole in one of the side walls. As we stood in this church in silence, we tried to imagine what had occurred during the slaughter.

Six years later we returned to Ntarama with Yves, a staff member of Solace Ministries who is in charge of several development projects for survivors, including farming, beehives, and dairy cows. He was twelve years old at the time of the genocide when his family fled to the church in Ntarama to escape the killers. As we entered the church with Yves, we were surprised at the change. The debris between the pews had been cleaned up. Clothes that had been scattered in the church were now hanging on lines. Other debris had been neatly organized in a building adjoining the church. The Rwandan government had built a metal roof over the church to protect it from the elements. Because it was the period of commemoration, the church was draped with purple cloth. A guide prohibited taking pictures in the church. Somehow the church had been sanitized. But Yves's account of his experience was not.

He took us directly to the pew where he had lain with bodies on top of him. The killers thought he was dead because of the blood running over him. He thinks he lay there from 10:00 A.M. to 3:00 P.M. while individuals were killed one by one. When he finally tried to get up, his arm and side were numb from the weight of bodies on top of him. Standing in the middle of the church he recalled that a number of Tutsi men tried to prevent the killers from entering the church, but they finally gave up and fled, including his own father. His mother and several sisters were hiding in an adjacent building, so he was alone in the church. He remembers that the killers threw a grenade into the church before entering, which may account for the hole in the wall that is still there. The church was packed with people so that there was scarcely any place to sit. He was one of the only individuals to survive the mass slaughter that ensued.

As we approached the altar, Yves spotted an identity card. He held it up and said, "I knew this boy." Then as we walked out of the church, we entered a small room where the belongings of people who had gathered in the church were stored. On the shelf was a notebook with calculus functions that someone had written. It was next to a soiled dictionary. From there we went to a separate building in the church compound. On the floor was a burned mattress. After the slaughter in the church, Yves's father returned to see if any of his family had survived. He found Yves in the church, a daughter who had been killed, and the mother who had been severely cut but was still alive. Sometime later, the killers came back to the church and set the building on fire where the sister had been killed, which was the reason for the charred mattress. They also found the burned remains of their sister in this building.

A wall separated this room from the Sunday school classroom next door. There were little pews where the children would sit for their lessons. Yves walked to the front of the classroom and pointed to a bloodstained wall. This is where children's heads had been bashed against the bricks. They must have been fairly small children who were held by the feet and slammed against the wall to break their skulls. We stood in horror as Yves demonstrated what must have happened, and, to our surprise, he did not shed a tear or express any emotion. The only indication of trauma was a slight stutter as he explained what had occurred.

We piled back into our van and the driver took us down the road to a flat tree-covered area. Somewhere under these trees, Yves and his father had buried his sister and mother after they died. Although Yves had dug around in various areas, he could not locate their bones. He simply could not remember the exact spot where they had buried them, and his father later died during the genocide and therefore could not assist him with the search. This obviously troubled Yves and perhaps played a role in his own inability to process the loss of his family.

Later he said, "I can't forgive the killers." In fact, even if they apologized he wasn't sure if he could forgive them. His conviction was manifest one afternoon in our apartment as we witnessed a heated exchange between the cook at Solace Ministries—also a survivor—and Yves. The cook during his spare time preached in some of the local prisons where genocide perpetrators were serving time for their sentences. He insisted that some of the prisoners had repented of their crimes and that Christian survivors must forgive, but Yves was not convinced.

After leaving the site where his mother and sister were buried, we thought our tour with Yves was over, but he insisted on taking us to the swamp where he lived for forty-five days, along with hundreds of other Tutsis. During the day they would hide in the murky water, filled with snakes, mosquitoes, and other wildlife. At night, they would walk back up to a cluster of abandoned houses where they would sleep, since the killers only "worked" during the daytime. As we stood on a hill overlooking this huge swamp, Yves kept repeating over and over how he, as a twelve-year-old boy, kept looking up through the reeds and brush at the sky. This was obviously a vivid memory of his time in the swamp.

Eventually, the RPA entered the area and they were safe. The soldiers took him and other survivors to a camp in nearby Nyamata. He had malaria from being bitten by mosquitoes in the swamp and recalls sleeping for nearly a month while he recovered. He stayed with the RPA soldiers for four months. After he was well, he went looking for his house, but it had been destroyed.

His father had married twice and there were fifteen children between the two wives. He eventually found one stepsister and one stepbrother, but none of the other children survived. Later he moved to Kigali and lived with a cousin who treated him as if he were her son. He completed secondary school and was fortunate to have a sponsor through Solace Ministries, which enabled him to graduate from Kigali Independent University. Currently he is working on a master's degree.

ORPHAN TESTIMONIES

As indicated in chapter 1, in 2002, eight years after the genocide, we collaborated with the leadership of an association of orphans (AOCM) who were parenting their surviving siblings, and sometimes nieces, nephews, and/or other children with no surviving relatives.[3] One hundred interviews were done by a research team of orphans in their twenties and early thirties who were members of AOCM and were majoring in the social sciences at various universities in Rwanda.[4] We worked with the leadership of AOCM in developing the interview guide, but they were responsible for doing the interviews, transcribing them into Kinyarwanda, and then having the interviews translated into English. This chapter also draws on interviews with orphans that we did at Solace Ministries. In both sets of interviews, at the time of the genocide in 1994 these orphans were typically teenagers. Hence, in reading these accounts, it is important to view them from the perspective of young adults who were reflecting back on experiences that happened in childhood or their teenage years.[5]

The interviews with orphans cited in the rest of this chapter are remarkable in terms of the unfiltered and fresh character of the interviewees' memories. In the case of the AOCM interviews, orphans were talking to fellow survivors who understood their experience. The youth answering questions trusted their fellow child-survivors with intimate details of what they had experienced, their present difficulty supporting themselves and their children, their struggle to get an education, and the quest for meaning in a context in which the support system and guidance of parents and grandparents no longer existed.

Names of killers, details of the deaths of parents and siblings, and places they traveled to escape the killing are explicit in the interviews, although we have intentionally avoided citing some details in order to protect our subjects' anonymity and also to avoid legal issues or recriminations by genocide perpetrators mentioned in the interviews. Furthermore, it is important to protect the confidentiality of orphans who were raped. In time, survivors may write their memoirs and be public about their experiences, but in the meantime, they have entrusted us with their memories—to share with the world, but confidentially.

PRECURSORS TO GENOCIDE

Prior to independence in the 1960s, Tutsis were overrepresented in the schools as a percentage of the population. For example, it is estimated that nearly 90 percent of the students at the National University in Butare were Tutsi.[6] This was due to the favoritism of the colonial powers that ruled Rwanda. However, beginning in the 1960s a quota system was imposed on advancement of students from one schooling level to another, regardless of individual merit on tests. By the 1980s, Tutsis were no more than 15 percent at the National University.[7] Many Tutsi children felt that their effort no longer counted in school, and they began to feel like second-class citizens because of overt discrimination by their Hutu teachers.

Orphans remember that their teachers would single them out by asking all Tutsis in the class to stand. Some of the younger children did not know their identity and would return home to inquire from their parents whether they were Hutu or Tutsi. But teachers often knew the ethnicity of their students and would get angry at Tutsi students who did not identify themselves. In addition, orphan survivors said that their teachers often aligned their subject content with the views of the government: "They used to teach us history about how Tutsis had ruled over the Hutus for a long time. They were actually sowing division among people," said one orphan. Teachers also reinforced the Hamidic ancestral interpretation that Tutsis were foreigners, from Ethiopia, and that is why they were tall, had long fingers and long noses.

Singling out Tutsi children in class often resulted in shunning by fellow students. "From my first-grade class in primary school, teachers used to tell us to stand up to see which ethnic group we belonged to. I was always alone or sometimes we were two but not more. They used to laugh at us and I was very sad because of that." Another interviewee said, "During break you could notice that your closest friend is staying some distance from you." This sentiment was echoed by many other orphans who were interviewed, such as in this case: "Since that day our classmates changed their attitudes towards us. We stopped playing together and from that day there was a big distance between us." Sometimes nastier and more violent things were done. "They used to spit in our faces. When we would accuse them to the director, he did nothing. They used to beat us on the way back home or order us to bring them money. We had to do it. When we reported this to our teacher he did nothing."

Numerous orphan survivors said that they were doing very well in class until they took the entrance exam for secondary school and then they scored poorly. Other Tutsi students said that they were not called on by teachers in class or were told that their answers were wrong. This discouraged many bright Tutsi students, as articulated in this comment: "When I was in primary school, people used to stone us while going to school or pierce us with thorns. Another thing, our schoolmasters used to tell us to stand up. We were one or two in the whole class. Because of that, many of us, including me, decided to stop our studies. We thought that even if we would study we would not get a job in this country."

Negative views of Tutsis were also being reinforced in the households of Hutus. When one of the interviewees asked her classmate why she wasn't playing with her anymore, she was told that her parents told her that she was the "enemy." Another young survivor said that her classmates told her that "I was a Tutsi and I was not supposed to go with them so that I would not hear their secrets and tell them to my parents who were 'inyenzi' [cockroach] and could kill them." Tutsis were also labeled "snakes" or serpents, and the myth was being spread that the RPA soldiers had "tails." Especially after the October 1990 invasion by the RPA (Rwandan Patriotic Army), Tutsi students were identified with the Inkotanyi, the rebel Tutsi force from Uganda.

HOSTILE ENVIRONMENT FOR TUTSIS

Orphans recalled that RTLM[8] was broadcasting hate messages about Tutsis on a regular basis. Songs were played on the radio that inspired prejudice. Various commentators called on "sleeping Hutus" to "wake up" and fight the enemy. One interviewee recalled hearing President Habyarimana say in a broadcast that "when a forest has grown up, it has to be thinned out," meta-phorically referring to the need to eliminate some of the Tutsi population.

Once the genocide began, the broadcasts became more explicit. An orphan survivor said that he heard announcers stating exact locations of where the RPA (Rwandan Patriotic Army) had advanced. "In the evenings, we could hear on the radio that the RPA had reached such and such place; therefore, they could ask the killers to 'work' hard with courage to accomplish their 'task' before the RPA reached their location." The RTLM was owned by members of the Akazu, an extremist network that supported President Habyarimana. There was also Radio Rwanda, the government station that was more liberal and included commentary by various political parties in Rwanda, including even the RPF. The RPF also owned a station, Radio Muhabura, but it did not cover all of Rwanda. If one was caught listening to this station it was evidence of sedition.

While there was a multiparty system in place prior to the genocide, one orphan survivor stated: "I remember that just prior to instituting multiple parties, MRND[9] people came in the rural area to distribute MRND cards among people so that they would not register in other parties. If one did not take their card, he was considered an RPA accomplice and was in danger." Another orphan survivor equated the message of the MRND and CDR:[10] "Where I was living there were political parties such as MRND and CDR, which used to say they would kill Tutsis since they were 'inyenzi,' like animals—with tails and long nails—that they should kill them because they were not Rwandans but should go back to their original place that is Ethiopia."

Many orphan survivors viewed the CDR in particular with considerable alarm. Members of the CDR were the most vocal party in the local community stating that Tutsis were an internal threat to the country, and that they were spies for the RPF and were potential traitors. There was also harassment of students that was inspired by the CDR. "In our classroom, I used to sit near a girl whose parents were members of CDR. That classmate of mine used to poke me with her pen in my back, and they used to tear up our books and notes." He said that he didn't really understand why she was doing this. Also, he and other orphan survivors experienced harassment at roadblocks. "At the time of school holidays, we used to cross a roadblock. On that roadblock, we had to show our identity cards and whenever they would find 'Tutsi' in your identity card we had to sit down near the roadblock in water."

Orphan survivors said that members of these different political parties held secret meetings to which they were not invited. In retrospect, they assumed that it was at these meetings that plans were being laid for the extermination of the Tutsi population in Rwanda. Young Hutu men were receiving military training, and they would sometimes disappear for periods of time from the local community and then reappear with uniforms and various armaments, including rifles and grenades. Also, students who identified with the CDR started to wear scarfs and clothing that clearly identified their political orientation. The instruments for genocide were also being distributed among the local Hutu population prior to the genocide. "In the districts, they used to distribute machetes and hoes among Hutus under the pretext that these were the only people who tilled the land. We couldn't imagine what was the purpose of all that."

During each of the RPA invasions in the early 1990s, there would be repercussions for the local Tutsi population. Many orphan survivors recall their parents being taken to prison for questioning, where they were often beaten. Apparently, women were not immune. One survivor said that her mother was accused of being an accomplice of the RPA, teaching students seditious things, and she was put in jail for six months in 1990. Another orphan said that local Tutsi who were regarded as leaders within their community were often imprisoned after each invasion, while less important Tutsis were ignored. The homes of Tutsi were also searched on a regular basis to ensure that weapons were not hidden on the premises.

There were also localized massacres after each invasion with the homes of Tutsis being burned. Consequently, orphan survivors recall sleeping outdoors at night, fearing attack by local Hutu residents. There were also frequent acts of intimidation, such as stoning the roofs of houses at night or breaking windows of Tutsi homes. And schoolmates would sometimes tell their Tutsi friends that they were going to be killed, based on what their parents were saying at home and what was being discussed more generally among Hutus, fueled by incendiary radio broadcasts from RTLM and a publication called *Kangura* (*Wake Up*), which was frequently mentioned by survivors as being filled with hateful rhetoric.

If a young Tutsi male was no longer present in the community, it was assumed that he had joined the RPF rebel army. This had immediate consequences for his family, typically resulting in imprisonment of the father and sometimes the death of family members. This created a dilemma within some families. As the local Tutsi population experienced greater repression, they were potentially more inclined to side with the rebel army. At the same time, any overt expression of sympathy with the opposition led to further repression at the local level.

One orphan survivor said that he was very sick in 1990 when the civil war started. Because he was absent from his village, going from hospital to hospital for treatment, he was suspected of having joined the RPA and was taken directly from the hospital to prison in 1993. "We were beaten in a bad way. Our arms were tied from the back and then our feet were beaten. Until this day I have problems with my feet. . . . While others were having their breakfast, we were being beaten, harassed and called 'inyenzi,' the betrayers of the country."

Cows figured prominently in the discussion of some orphan survivors as they recalled that every problem in the country was being blamed on the Tutsis. A survivor said that his father attempted to buy a more peaceful environment for Tutsis by giving cows to the local Hutu authorities. Another survivor said that his father gave cows to an official for something as simple as trying to get the certificate of educational accomplishments so that his son could advance to the university. Other orphan survivors said that their fathers gave cows in acts of friendship to neighbors, especially prior to the civil war. But as tensions grew stronger, some Tutsi began selling their cattle fearing that otherwise they would be stolen and eaten by Hutus, especially as security for the Tutsi population became more precarious. And for those who still were raising cattle, there were attempts by Tutsis to safeguard them, even as they were fleeing personal attack and the burning of their homes.

For many younger orphan survivors, they said that they didn't really understand what was happening politically. One survivor simply recalls feeling ashamed that he was a Tutsi. During the various RPA invasions, there were exaggerated reports of rebel forces slaughtering Hutus as they attempted to advance toward the capital. References to "divisionism" were frequently made in the interviews. Orphan survivors experienced discrimination at school as a result of the poisonous rhetoric that was being promulgated on the radio. Tutsis were identified as "other" in a variety of ways, and there was continual insinuation that their loyalty was to their "brothers" in the RPF in Uganda. One orphan survivor said, "It was like we were not citizens of this country." Nevertheless, until the genocide was actually launched on April 7, Tutsis were still trying to make appeals to local officials for protection and fair play. It was only after the president's plane was shot down that many Tutsis said that they were doomed.

APRIL 6, 1994

Orphan survivors learned of the crash of the president's plane from parents, radio broadcasts, and friends. The response of some parents to their children was, "We will die." Other parents told their children that they needed to hide in the bushes for a few days or else flee to the local church, but they assumed that the incident would blow over. For example, one survivor said, "We were asleep. Then our father told us that it was over with us. We asked him why and he told us that Habyarimana was dead. We didn't understand the relation between Habyarimana dying and it being over with us. We thought that if anything would happen it would be just the way it had been, meaning that we would flee to the church and then come back home. But things didn't turn out that way; instead, the situation became worse." An orphan survivor who had fled with his family to a Presbyterian church said, "We thought it would be about eating cows and burning houses. Then that would be all, as my father told me was the case in 1963."

Another orphan recalled, "We went on top of a mountain, our whole family. From there we saw houses being burned, people being cut into pieces. We heard that so and so—especially rich people—were being killed. We thought it would last at most three days and then we would go back home, because we were used to such incidents."

The timeline of killing Tutsis varied from place to place. But based on orphan accounts, the pattern tended to be the same. People were ordered to stay in their homes or return home if they were at school or work. Looting and killing followed, and simultaneously Tutsis started fleeing for their lives. Roadblocks were set up almost immediately, which impeded flight by Tutsis who were asked for their identification cards at roadblocks. They were either killed on the spot or sometimes the possessions they were carrying were taken; other times they were able to bribe their way through the roadblock with money. There was perhaps some reticence in the first few days to simply kill people wholesale, without regard to gender, age, or class. Morally, it was easier for local residents to start looting homes, steal cattle, harvest crops of Tutsis, and so forth, rather than kill Tutsis en masse.

An orphan survivor recalled, "When the genocide started we left our house. Our neighbors immediately started stealing. I remember my father telling my brother and me to go back and bring his radio since he had forgotten it. When we reached our house, the neighbors told us to leave. We obeyed. They were guarding it and waiting for evening in order to steal the things inside. When it was night, we saw them stealing, pouring petrol on it, and putting it on fire."

Accounts of houses being looted and then destroyed abound in our interviews. In addition to cookware, bedding, and food, neighbors were very keen on removing the doors, windows, and metal roofing from the houses of Tutsis. Many orphan survivors then saw their house being burned, because they were hiding nearby in sorghum fields, banana groves, or sometimes even in trees.

In some regions, people were killed within the first twenty-four hours. And in other areas it was a week or more. For example, one orphan survivor said, "President Habyarimana died on the sixth. On the seventh people started to do meetings and take Tutsis' cows. On the eighth they were told that they had to first kill the owners of those cows and then eat them." Another orphan survivor said, "There were political parties like MRND and CDR, and many in our area were PL people. Therefore, they started killing us immediately."[11] Child survivors were often very detailed in their memories of the first day of the genocide. For example, a survivor said that he heard about the president's death on the radio. When his parents returned home later that night he told his father, who didn't believe him, but his father immediately became very fearful the next morning and left the house to find a safe hiding place. Later that morning the Interahamwe came to look for his father, but family members told them that he had gone looking for medicine. "They didn't believe us and surrounded our house with every kind of weapon to hinder us from escaping. Around 12 noon, they threw a grenade on us. My youngest brother and mother were wounded but not killed, so they took her [his mother] and cut her with machetes. After that we ran and fled toward a nuns' convent, but we heard that papa also was killed the same day, that is April 7, 1994."

The military and Interahamwe militia mobilized very quickly after the president's plane was shot down. For example, an orphan survivor said that by 6:00 P.M. the next day they were seeing people with machetes saying that they were there to revenge the death of the "father" of the nation. "The soldiers asked local people to show them where Tutsis lived because they wanted to revenge their 'parent.' . . . We really wanted to flee but we couldn't because there were roadblocks all around." That same evening his parents were killed by soldiers as local Hutu residents watched. In contrast, another orphan survivor said that the killing didn't begin in her area until April 13. In fact, people were fleeing to escape the slaughter. But on the thirteenth, they were attacked, and everyone fled. Other survivors said that even though the killing had not yet happened in their area, they started to see bodies floating in the river near their house, which were coming from upstream.

In addition to hiding in the fields, banana groves, swamps, and forests, families sometimes fled together to locations that they thought would be safe. For example, one orphan survivor said that they went to a place where the UNAMIR soldiers were stationed, but he said, "After three days those UN soldiers left us in the hands of FAR [the government troops]. We tried to tell them to take us with them, but in vain." About fifty people then tried to reach a location where there were RPA soldiers, but many died on the way.

Indicative of the close relationship between Hutus and Tutsis prior to the genocide, a more common strategy was to flee immediately to the home of a trusted Hutu neighbor. Initially, they took in some Tutsi families. But typically, within a few days, they realized their own lives were at stake if they were hiding "cockroaches." An alternative strategy was to flee to a local church, but, as we will see, that simply concentrated Tutsis in a way that enabled them to be killed more easily. Other strategies involved trying to alter one's identity card or simply throwing it away in the hopes that one could pass as a Hutu. "My uncle called me inside the house and asked me for my identity card so that we could erase the 'Tutsi' word marked in it, but we failed. Then I threw it in the toilet and decided to use my face to show that I was not a Tutsi." This orphan survivor was hiding in the ceiling of his uncle's house when he saw the Interahamwe enter the home and kill his uncle.

A strategy for survival by some parents was for the father to go one way and children and the mother to go different directions, with mothers carrying infant children and toddlers. An orphan survivor recalled: "It was the night of April 7 and we didn't sleep well because our mother told us that something would happen." The parents were killed the next morning and from where they were hiding the children saw the killers taking away their cows. Returning to their home, she saw the following: "My father was cut inside the house, while our mother was killed behind the house."

The important thing to note is that early in the genocide, many children either became separated from their parents or their parents were killed. Thus, many children were left to survive on their own during the hundred days of the genocide. Consequently, children as young as six and seven years of age were oftentimes traveling long distances by themselves or in small packs. Sometimes they mingled with other Tutsis who were fleeing. They often sought out relatives, including those who were married to Hutus, only to be rejected, or they discovered that they were already dead.

PARENTS' LAST WORDS

One of the more poignant elements of our interviews with orphans are the final words that parents spoke to their children before they were killed or separated. Sometimes their comments had a heavy dose of fatalism. Referencing earlier massacres, such as in 1973, parents, and fathers in particular, simply said that they didn't have a chance. Everyone would be killed. Nevertheless, they instructed children to flee. From our interviews, it appears that many fathers departed from their families, perhaps assuming that they would be killed first and that their children and spouse would have a better chance of survival if they were not with them. In some testimonies, it is also clear that the men were singled out to be killed and then days, and even weeks later, the women and children were killed, although this was certainly not always the case—especially when mass extermination seemed to be the intention of the killers.

Some parents, especially right before they were about to be killed, told their children that they would meet them in heaven. Rwandans are a very religious people, and at times of tragedy, in particular, it is not surprising that they referred to life after death or, in some cases, that they would survive if it was God's will. "I recall my father telling me, if we didn't meet on earth we would meet in heaven, and he asked me to have faith in God." Other times, religious values were mixed with practical advice. "When I met my mother, she told us that we are all going to die and that we had to commit our lives to God. She told us that our only sin was being Tutsi. She said that if any of us survives, he must live in peace with everybody so that he might live a little longer." Another orphan remembers his father's instructions "to look after my siblings and God would bless me."

When children were being sent off to fend on their own, parents said things that could be viewed as truisms, but at the time they gave hope to children. They were told "to have courage," "to be strong," "to not be afraid," and "to love each other," should they survive. Another survivor recalls a more fatalistic set of instructions: "My mother told us to go together and die together, but father was telling us not to do so, but instead he was directing us to his friends."

Orphans recalled that sometimes parents also gave very practical advice, telling them to seek out a particular family where they might stay, or a place where they might hide. An orphan survivor also recalled his mother's last instructions, which were to "put on your pullover" since it was raining. And a father who had sold all their goats and cows prior to the genocide showed his children where he had buried money, telling the children that they should dig at this location if they survive. Other times, parents were simply pragmatic in what they said. An orphan survivor remembered her mother's last words as follows: "She told me to go because I was able to run and that she would die with the small child who was unable to walk."

An orphan remembered her mother's last words: "She told me that she could be killed at any time, but her prayer was that she would not be thrown into a latrine." Other advice was more inspirational, such as this survivor's memory of his father's statement, which he considers to be his "inheritance": "He told me this, 'My son, I have seen many wars, in 1959, 1963 and 1973. . . . Our family members are already killed, but whoever survives must remain what he is, a Tutsi, and love others who survive with him.'"

METHODS OF KILLING

Multiple methods of killing were witnessed by orphan survivors, including some that were quite efficient. For example, several survivors said that Tutsis were formed into lines in front of a large pit, where they were then hit in the head with a spiked club, and then were pushed into the pit, which was later covered with dirt. Apparently, many Tutsis believed that their time had come, so they neither tried to offer resistance nor run away from the slaughter, although this was certainly not always the case—as will be shown later in this chapter.

Several orphan survivors described another event in which hundreds of Tutsis were hiding in a cave carved out from past rainstorms, hoping to escape their attackers. Rather than kill them individually, their assassins instead built a large fire on one side of the perimeter of the cave and directed the smoke into the cavern where almost everyone died from smoke inhalation. Another orphan survivor said that an entire hillside was set on fire as a way of flushing out Tutsis who were hiding in the brush.

According to orphans, grenades were another common method of killing more than one person at a time. They were thrown into locations where groups of Tutsis had gathered, such as churches. Sometimes grenades were also thrown through the windows of homes. And other times grenades were tossed onto a pile of bodies in a latrine or pit when the killers did not know if everyone they had hit with clubs or cut with machetes had died.

While mass killings such as these were common, identifying individual Tutsis to be killed also frequently occurred. There seemed to be a perverse pleasure taken in cutting people with machetes. Several orphan survivors recalled watching killers sharpen their machetes before beginning the task of killing. Another orphan said that the person who attempted to kill him actually wiped the blood from his machete on this individual's clothes after a blow to his neck. Sometimes this "cutting" was sadistically done, slicing off both arms and legs and then leaving the individual helpless, without limbs. A more common practice was to force someone to kneel and then sever their spinal cord with a blow to the neck.

In our interviews, there is also reference to spears that were used to pierce people in the chest or vital organs. Swords and machetes were sometimes used to cut unborn children from their mother's stomach before killing the woman. An orphan recalled Hutu women involved in sadistic acts: "Three ladies [they are named in the interview] were killing her, seriously, and then they pushed a piece of stick into her sexual organ." Other methods of killing were much cruder, such as taking an infant by the legs and smashing the head against a wall. And we also have instances of "stoning" as a way of killing Tutsis, especially once they were captive in a pit or latrine. Even Hutu children participated in this primitive means of killing people. Because of the torturous ways in which people were killed, Tutsis sometimes begged Hutus to shoot them, if they had a gun. Guns were also sometimes used to kill people who were attempting to run away or had been flushed out of the bush.

If someone was wearing clothing of any value, they were frequently stripped naked and then killed, which avoided getting blood on the cloth. For example, an orphan recalled being caught by killers as they were trying to flee to a hospital. "They told us to separate. Girls on their side, men, children and old people on their side. We did it. So, they asked children of killers to kill our children, men to kill men, girls and women to kill other women. They started to kill, but before that they took off our clothes and everything we had." An orphan survivor recalls seeing his father's coat being worn by someone after he was killed.

Sometimes clothing collection was done systematically, as revealed midway in this orphan's description of killing: "They started shooting on us, throwing grenades on us. Some people died on the spot; others got their legs cut; still others got their arms cut. We were lying there among the corpses. The Interahamwe divided themselves into two groups: one group was collecting items and the other group was killing. By evening, we were able to get out of that place and went to a nearby bush. Two days later, the Interahamwe brought dogs to look for us. They caught us and brought us back to the district office. People were still killing; others were burying."

When people are being killed in such numbers, it becomes a massive problem to deal with the odor of rotting bodies, which is the reason that dumping victims into pits, latrines, or rivers was an efficient way of disposing of corpses. However, sometimes this was not possible. For example, one child who was fleeing the carnage recalls entering a church for refuge, only to discover that there were hundreds of decomposing bodies in the church from a previous massacre, and she left because she could not stand the smell. Another survivor recalled stepping on a rotting corpse. "Even after the genocide I used to get that smell."

Survivors also said that Hutus who might have temporarily hidden Tutsis sometimes rejected them because their wounds smelled so terrible. For example, a female orphan said: "Around 6:00 P.M. we saw our grandfather's neighbor coming and immediately they beat him with a wooden weapon called 'ntampongano,' which means 'no pity for our enemies,' which had nails in it. They said that they had to bury him nearby, but one of them told them not to bury him near his house because he could smell bad. Then they threw him near my feet [where she was hiding], but they didn't see me. I ran and found an animal hole [in which to hide]."

One gets the impression from the interviews that exterminating the entire population of Tutsis was such a big job that sometimes the killers did not want to take the time to finish off their victims. Illustrative of the physical work of killing is this statement by an orphan: "Others were brought near the place where I was, and killers said that they needed to rest first and then kill those people. So, they did a small feast, then they killed them. They buried them, but not deeply. After their departure, dogs came and ate those people who were buried. I witnessed all that."

Deception was used in some areas to get survivors to come out of hiding. Several orphan survivors said that local officials broadcast news that there was a peace settlement between the RPF and the Rwandan government. Then when people left their hiding spots, the Interahamwe started killing them in large groups, throwing grenades at those who gathered.

There are also insights in the orphan interviews about the overarching tactics used in killing. Initially, the killers worked from lists of influential Tutsis. The local population could easily identify where these individuals lived, and the local police or militia came to their homes and either killed them on the spot or took them away for questioning and killing. Orphan survivors also said that they saw busloads of Interahamwe entering their community. These were trained killers and very efficient in their task. Whereas the local population might have difficulty killing a neighbor, these individuals went about the task without apparent conscience. In fact, they threatened to kill local Hutus who resisted killing Tutsis they knew.

SADISTIC ACTS

Killing people efficiently and without mercy is one thing. Torturing them and killing them sadistically implies another level of human depravity. For example, an orphan survivor said that his father was killed and shortly thereafter they caught his brother who had been hiding. The killers then ordered him to take off all of his clothes and lay in his father's blood. He complied and then they decided to kill him with a sword, but his mother gave the killers money and he was spared.

In our interviews, we have two instances of killers pulling out the tongues of children. "My mother had a child with her. When they wanted to kill that child, my mother let go of him. The killers pulled that child's tongue out. But the child didn't die immediately. He was not able to speak, not even to eat. That night we went to sleep in a school. Early in the morning the killers came and killed my mother. That morning they killed almost everybody except a few youngsters who were able to escape through their legs."

In another instance, an orphan survivor said her cousin was beaten with a club. When he fell down, he was hit on the head with a machete, but did not die. A friendly Hutu brought the cousin to where they were hiding, instructing him to stay under a bed while they left to hide elsewhere during the day. However, because of his injuries, he could not leave the house and he defecated in the same room where he was hiding under the bed. "When the killers entered that house, they saw it [the feces] and knew that someone was there. They took him and pulled out his tongue. In the evening when we came back, we found him dead with his tongue out. We dug a small pit and buried him nearby."

It is very clear from our interviews that sadistic acts had a traumatizing effect on orphan survivors. We have already referenced babies being cut out of the stomachs of their pregnant mothers, but it is appropriate to quote directly from one of our interviews: "There was a beautiful lady who was pregnant. The killers killed her, opened her belly, and pierced the fetus with a spear so that the fetus was taken out on a spear." Another orphan witnessed his father's head being cut off and then carried around on a stick for everyone in the village to see. Another orphan saw a woman's eye that was pulled out.

And sometimes children were forced to do sadistic things by the killers, which they cannot forget. For example, Tutsi boys were forced to kill other children in order to prove that they were Hutus and not Tutsis. In another case, at a roadblock an orphan recalled that a boy was forced to kill his own brother. And with a sense of painful regret, an orphan recalled the following: "There is one child who was brought to me and I was asked to kill him as a sign that I was a Hutu. I told them, I am not able to do this. So they gave me a cup full of pepper mixed with water and asked me to pour it in his eyes. I did it and then they told me that I was one of them."

EXPERIENCES OF FAMILY MEMBERS BEING KILLED

Our interviews with orphans reveal the intimate connections between children and parents. For example, an orphan survivor recalls hiding in the forest with her mother when they were surrounded by Interahamwe. The mother started running while her daughter hid next to a fallen tree. She witnessed the following from her vantage point: "They took mummy and cut her on the heel and beat her with those traditional wooden weapons. She died there. Late in the evening I went to see her. I lay near her and called to see if she was still alive, but she was dead." Another survivor said that their father was beaten with clubs and machetes and left for dead. The children discovered him in a pitiful condition. His request was that they would shave him, seeking dignity as he lay dying. But before they could do this, "The one who had cut and beaten papa came and finished him off."

Repeatedly orphan survivors gave accounts of the trauma of observing their own parents being slaughtered. For example: "We continued on our way but in about 100 meters we met another roadblock. They called my father and told him that they would kill him if he were a Tutsi. And directly they started beating him with wooden weapons. They took out his scarf and money.

Another person came and took off his coat. I was witnessing all that, but behind me I heard someone telling me to save my life because that was my father's end. So I climbed the mountain and when I reached the top I saw killers beating my father still. As I was afraid and very much tired, I just slept there." Another orphan survivor explained that killers surrounded them: "My mother was carrying our last-born baby. They took her and beat her with machetes. She was cut into pieces. I was able to escape with others and went in the big forest. We sat there and said that if they want, they could come and kill us because we were too tired, and we didn't have another safe place to hide. At nightfall, we went back to that place [where the mother was attacked]. We found her and the child dead."

An orphan also recalled the last hours with her mother. They were fleeing as a family but had split up to enhance the possibility of survival. She said that she was hiding in a banana plantation while her mother was in a forested area nearby, with a baby wrapped in a cloth around her back. It started raining at around 6:00 P.M. Finally, the rain quit in the morning, but they were soaking wet. After this miserable evening, they decided they would simply give themselves up to be killed and so went to a hill and took off their outer clothes to dry them. It was still misty, and the sun had not come out. From this vantage point on the hill they could see houses being burned. And then around 3:00 P.M., a crowd of people came toward them. Several young men approached her mother and said they were going to kill her, but she pleaded to let her first pray. One person then hit her on her knees and another hit her on the head as she was bending over. There was a long pause in this orphan's testimony as she started crying, saying, "I saw all that with my own eyes . . . I eventually spent a night there with many dead bodies which were left there on that hill." In the morning, she came out of hiding because whistles had been blown announcing a meeting at the commune building. "So that's when I got a chance to get out. I went close to my mother's dead body. . . . I found this child [who had been wrapped on her mother's back]." The baby was still breathing. She untied the blood-saturated cloth that was glued to her mother's body since the child had been there all night. Weeping, she said, "I put him on my back." She then covered her mother's body with the bloodstained cloth that had been holding the infant. Quite miraculously, this baby survived and at the time of the interview was in primary six school in the town of Butare.

Witnessing the deaths of family members was clearly traumatizing. One child survivor said that they were very hungry, and his brother decided to go in search of food. "I urged him to stay with me, but he refused. So, he left but immediately encountered a group of killers who knew him [he gives the name of one individual]. They cut him with machetes; he was cut into pieces. Because I witnessed all that, I wanted to shout aloud and to come out of hiding, but I stayed there, laying down and crying."

CHILD/ORPHAN SUICIDE

Many orphan survivors contemplated suicide at some point during the geno-cide. After losing father and mother, and in some cases all of their family members, they felt there was little reason to continue living. Furthermore, many of them assumed that it was just a matter of time until they were killed, so why should they continue to struggle by hiding, enduring thirst and hunger—both of which were cited as pervasive issues by survivors—as well as dealing with medical problems, including fractures, amputations, and other wounds.

Sometimes specific incidents also provoked the desire to take one's life. For example, an orphan said that she witnessed a man who had been killed by burying him up to his neck in the ground. "In fear of being killed like that, I thought I was of no use in this world." Another orphan referenced seeing people's arms and legs being cut off and left to die and said that she wanted to die before this could happen to her. One survivor said that after his entire family was killed, "It was useless for me to stay alive." This sentiment was echoed in the statement of a fellow orphan survivor: "I said to myself that it is better to take my life than be tortured for nothing [and then die]." And, finally, an orphan said that he was ready to take his life, "but a voice encour-aged me to be bold enough to not commit suicide."

These instances of suicidal attempts and thoughts are balanced by the affirmation of life by orphans. For example, we have already cited examples of child survivors burying their deceased parents and relatives, which were attempts to provide a modicum of dignity in the face of moral chaos. Children also frequently risked their lives in order to care for a younger brother or sister, even carrying the child on their back, as they escaped killers. And on a daily basis, especially after parents had been killed, orphans, who were some-times quite young, roused themselves from sleep to continue fighting for survival, day after day.

A CHILD'S PERSPECTIVE OF RAPE

The subject of rape was not discussed nearly as much by orphans—compared to our interviews with widows—but it nevertheless was mentioned frequently.[12] Women's bodies seemingly had no sanctity. One orphan survivor said, "Before killing they used to check people to the extent of uncovering them and inserting fingers in the vagina saying perhaps they had hidden some money inside." Another orphan said that Hutus escaping to Tanzania took with them Tutsi "wives" that they had abducted. She said that the men used to exchange their "wives" with each other. Taking beautiful girls as sex slaves also appeared to be common. Sometimes they were gang raped and then killed, being raped by as many as twelve people according to one account.

Another child survivor said that a member of the Interahamwe took a young girl as a sex slave. They would kill all day, she said, and then his friends would come back to the house where this girl was held, and they raped her all night. Other times, killers would happen upon a Tutsi girl and simply rape her on the spot, such as in this account. "I witnessed the rape of my cousin. We were together in the sorghum plantations. When we heard killers coming we ran. They were young men. When they saw her, they ran after her and she fell down. They took and raped her. I was around in the bushes and heard my cousin crying. They did what they wanted and left her in a bad condition. I approached her, and she asked me to bring water from the rain, and I then helped her to go in the bushes again. I witnessed that."

Another orphan survivor said that after an attack the men were taking home any girl they wanted, "according to his taste." She said a man with a spear and "impiri" (wooden club with nails in it) took her to a classroom and raped her, saying that he was afraid to take her home for fear that she might poison him, since he and his group had killed her mother and father. She went back to the group of Tutsis that remained, but "in the night one boy who was our neighbor came and raped me too." The next day another person attempted to rape her, but she laid down and told him to kill her since her life was not worth living.

In only a few instances did protesting rape seem to have any effect, but these cases should be mentioned. "When we reached Rwamagana, a group of people came and took girls for rape. But I refused saying that I am still young. They accepted." Another survivor said, "They tried raping her [referring to another girl] but some of our neighbors shouted and those Interahamwe left her." We also have an instance of a potential rape victim being brought into the home of an Interahamwe. "Around twenty-five killers came with their dogs and found me. One of them told me how they had killed my mother and my young sister. I kept quiet and he took me to his house. I thought that he could rape me any time. His wife received me—she had been my schoolmistress in the third year of primary school—and put me under the bed to hide me. They used to say how they had killed people, my family members included. . . . They also said how they had killed my maternal aunt. But I saw that, also. One day the men wanted to rape me, and I refused. So, they told me to go out."

FLEEING AND HIDING

Those who survived moved from one location to another, hiding in bushes, forests, swamps, sorghum fields, and banana groves. Sometimes children were traveling many miles in a day, often alone or in small packs. They would join groups of Tutsis who were fleeing violence in their area, only to discover that the killing had spread to the location that they thought was safe. Children would run to a neighbor or relative who was married to a Hutu, thinking that they would surely take them in, only to be rejected.

A child survivor recalls separating from her mother at a roadblock where they were stripping off the cloth that her mother used to carry her baby. "So, I left her there and continued walking with the rest of the people who were fleeing. You would see somebody taking another direction and you would think he or she might be of help if you followed them. So I followed a woman who went up the hill because many people had been killed in the valleys." When they entered a coffee garden they were discovered. "They started stoning us from the home that was near that garden." The two of them began running, but the killers surrounded the woman. "I remember she was pleading with them to forgive her." But they instead killed her on the spot. "I thought they might have seen me, so there was a bush nearby and I thought maybe I can hide in it. So I laid there with my head down." The killers called out to her since they had apparently seen the two of them together, but she decided not to surrender. "They threw a very big stone and it fell close to my head. I was not very far from where they were at that time. I just think that God wanted to protect me. Later as it was getting dark, I saw a tree that was cut down and decided to go and hide under it. . . . I went and sat there, and I spent two days there."

An orphan graphically described their uncertain existence during the genocide. "We kept on hiding in and out of the bushes. Sometimes I would sleep in sorghum plantations. There was a time I spent three days, very worn out, and ants would fill up my ears and I still experience difficulty hearing when a person talks to me from behind. People used to tell me to put water in my ears, which was scarce at that time." Instead, she said that she put urine in her ears to try to drive the ants out.

Some of the child survivors said that they would hide during the day and move only at night when there was less risk of being caught. For example, a survivor said that they would travel when it was raining, because it was less likely that they would encounter Interahamwe. The rain also provided opportunity to get water. "We spent almost two weeks in the sorghum living on water that settled on plant leaves."

In the process of fleeing the killers, orphans survived in a variety of ways. For example, an orphan said, "There was a lady who hid me in her garments," meaning that the child was small enough to hid under her dress. In some locations, girls were not being killed—at least initially. "I got very scared when the Interahamwe said that all boys have to be killed first; so I would dress like a girl most of the time to hide my identity." Nevertheless, this boy said, "I would think and worry a lot and get scared" when the killing was occurring.

Sometimes surviving relatives assisted children. "Along with another child, my grandfather dug a small pit, put us inside and covered it, letting his cows roam around [in the area] in order to hide us." While children were sometimes able to stick together, often they were fending on their own, such as this orphan survivor who said, "While hiding, it was not advisable to hide with many people in one place, because the killers could find you. So, we used to hide in a scattered way. You could then meet in the evening or after several days."

INTERVENTION BY HUTUS

Sometimes there was outright intervention by altruistic Hutus. For example, a survivor was traveling with his brother and several others when he was accused of being an accomplice of the RPA at a roadblock. "So, they made me sit, waiting to kill me. . . . One man [gives his name], a born-again Christian, came and said that I was a Hutu. The killers said if anyone else would come and tell them I was a Hutu, they would release me. A man called [gives his name] came and said I was a Hutu. They let me go." This small band of Tutsi boys continued down the road after this ordeal. "We encountered another roadblock. We told them we were going to buy items at the market for our father, which was a lie since he had been killed a few days previously. They asked us where he was. We told them he had preceded us. They asked us where the containers were in which we would put the items to be bought. We told them he is the one carrying them. They asked us for our identity card. I showed my student card. One man [at the roadblock] said his son was studying at the same Red Cross school that I was. So, they let us go."

Frequently orphans fled to the homes of Hutus thinking they would be protected, and instead they were rejected. "During the night, we decided to go to our neighbors and spend the night there." Not only did they turn them away, but "they immediately sent people to kill us." This orphan said that they ran away only to be stopped at a roadblock. "They told us to sit down and that they would kill us the next day. They were cooking meat from the cows of those killed. But late in the night they slept except for one of them. He took us to his home and asked his wife to prepare food for us. However, she refused saying that she can't cook for serpents."

But on occasion, Hutus were instrumental in saving Tutsis children. For example, one child survivor said, "I had a friend who was a son of Interahamwe. I chose to go with him everywhere he went. But we met people and when they wanted to kill me, he asked them to leave me alone." Another survivor said that the students of his father, who was a teacher, spared their lives, even though he had to tell them where the family cows were located so that they could steal them.

One woman hid an orphan in her latrine, which was away from the house where Hutus were slaughtering cows that they had stolen from Tutsis. Another woman hid an orphan in her chicken house. Although the Interahamwe came to check if anyone was hiding there, they didn't check very thoroughly since the husband was a well-known Interahamwe. "The next morning that lady told me to do some work and to reply to whoever would ask me that she was my auntie, because I was not known in that area. Immediately after starting my job, the Interahamwe came. I was afraid. I ran inside the house. They asked the house owners if they had hidden somebody. The lady said I was her niece. They slapped her, but the husband confirmed it. They agreed because he was a 'great' Interahamwe."

INTERVENTION BY THE RPA

In addition to the ways already described, some orphans survived by being rescued by advancing RPA soldiers. They were often given food and clothing. Many times, they were resettled in homes, including those of Hutus who had fled the RPA advance—since their own homes had been destroyed. They were also taken to hospitals for medical treatment. And children who were sole survivors, without anyone to care for them, were sometimes placed in orphanages. In general, accounts of intervention by the RPA are cloaked in language of care and compassion, which is somewhat surprising given the fact that the RPA was also involved in a military operation. Soldiers took great care to try to find survivors, including many who were hiding in the bush from potential attacks by the Interahamwe.

Exploding shells exchanged between the government army and the RPA were the first indication to survivors that the RPA was nearby. When the RPA reached their actual hiding place, many times child survivors could not readily identify which side the soldiers were on. For example, this child noted her confusion. "I reached the river and I heard people shouting, so I went back near a bush to hide. I spent almost two days there. But I was hearing bullets bursting just near me. One day I saw soldiers. It was around 9:00 A.M. When I saw them, I fled toward the bush. They came after me and surrounded the bush, then found me. They asked me why I ran away from them. I said nothing. Then I asked them to let me pray before they killed me." They asked her if she knew who they were, and she replied that they were Habyarimana's soldiers. At this point they identified themselves as RPA, and immediately offered her help. "I was not able to walk. They carried me until we reached a river where they gave me soap so that I would wash myself. They took off my clothes and gave me women's clothing. One of them got out his T-shirt and gave it to me." They then arranged for a vehicle to pick her up and she stayed with the RPA for almost three weeks before she was settled in a home.

An orphan said that they attempted to fight with the killers, but then the Presidential Guard came with rifles and started to shoot them. They escaped to a house, only to discover the owner and his children lying dead in the home. "We laid near them and spent two days there. Then we heard someone passing nearby saying that the RPA has come. At nightfall, we tried to wake up though it was very difficult. We met soldiers, but we didn't know if they were RPA or RAF [Rwandan government soldiers]. They told us not to worry and that they would not kill us. They took us to Rwamagana hospital and we were treated there."

Another survivor said that her mother died on July 2, which was when the war was winding down, and her sister took her to Kigali for medical treatment. On July 4, she was sitting on the street with her siblings; everyone had left the area, and she felt very alone. "A soldier of the RPA came and met us there and asked me where my parents were? I couldn't contain myself. I started weeping. Then he asked me what he could do for me. I told him that the only thing you can do for me is to take me home." This was impossible, so he took them to Saint Andre church where there were other orphans the same age.

This story was repeated in various ways in many of the interviews with children. Survivors were rounded up by the RPA. They were often put on buses or otherwise transported to safe locations, including refugee camps. Many of the surviving children were extremely hungry and malnourished by this point. They were given food and if injured their wounds were treated, including one orphan who said she had been infected from being raped. "Since I was suffering a lot, my sex had swollen; it was as if I was suffering from syphilis." She was given antibiotics, and once she got better she started assisting nurses who were caring for the injured.

ORPHAN REFLECTIONS ON SURVIVAL

Numerous orphans credited their survival to God. Peppered throughout the interviews are statements such as these: "It's only God who helped me." "It is God who saved me." "God allowed us to survive." "God alone delivered me." "It is God who protected me." "It was only by God's grace that I was not killed." The children did not address the profoundly theological question of why they survived and others perished. By all counts they should have been killed, but they were not. In gratitude they credited God for their safety.

Survivors also acknowledged the role that Hutus sometimes played in hiding them for a day or two. However, in the one hundred interviews with AOCM members, there were very few references to heroic acts by Hutus. Instead, it appears that many Hutus, even those who had been neighbors and friends of the family, quickly capitulated to the threat of being killed if they were harboring Tutsis. When intervention did occur, it was often fleeting and not sustained. And what was inexplicable to survivors was the fact that many people who previously were good citizens, and even family friends, were turned into killers almost immediately after Habyarimana's plane was shot down.

In the interviews with orphans, there was almost a complete absence of political analysis. The context for the genocide was typically framed as "the war," but survivors did not give sophisticated answers about why there was a civil war or why the Tutsis were being exterminated. Perhaps the interview questions did not invite analysis, but it is also quite possible that these were "kids" who were caught in a civil war. They could accurately describe what occurred, and how, but not "why" it was happening, which may have implications for their ability to deal with their trauma—something that will be addressed in a later chapter.

Outsiders may wonder why there was not greater resistance by Tutsis. Did they simply go like sheep to the slaughter? In some instances, this may have been true. As previously mentioned, there was a spirit of fatalism when they heard about the crash of the president's plane. On the other hand, people did flee their homes. Fathers were sometimes strategic in telling children to separate from them, thinking that this would increase their likelihood of survival. Also, child survivors often demonstrated remarkable tenacity in escaping assaults. And in a few instances, there were active acts of resistance.

At several locations, orphans said that men tried to fight back, often courageously, until reinforcements were brought in by the Interahamwe. One orphan survivor said, "Some people used stones and sticks to defend themselves against people who had guns and grenades," but then said, "Of course they were defeated." And in at least one instance, "Women gathered stones and men threw them," in an effort to defend themselves. Another orphan said that the older people were in front, throwing stones, and the children were in back of them, giving them stones to throw. But they were no match for armed killers. "We were overcome then and started running." Another orphan said that the men who were trying to fight were weak because of lack of food and quickly succumbed. There was no evidence in our interviews that the local Tutsi population possessed guns or other armaments with which to fight. Rather, resistance was measured in the form of stones versus guns and grenades, which led to a very uneven fight.

ORPHAN REUNIONS

There was something bittersweet about the reunions that orphans had after the genocide with surviving siblings and other relatives. In many cases survivors were under the impression that everyone in their family had been killed. Then, sometimes by chance, and sometimes through messages on the radio and other means, children started to reconnect with brothers and sisters, cousins, as well as aunts and uncles. On first meeting each other, individuals often cried; sometimes they were speechless; and other times they simply laughed and hugged. They couldn't believe that anyone else had survived.

One orphan said that when he met some of his siblings, "We hugged each other asking if it was you or your spirit." Another orphan said, "My youngest sister was not able to talk, she only wept. I thought she had gone mad." Another orphan said, "When I saw her, I just fell down and wept. She also wept; we could not even greet each other." And another orphan reported that she and a sister could not talk for several days, saying it was "like a miracle" that they had both survived.

When they finally could talk, they asked each other questions about how they had survived. An orphan said, "We talked about our experiences, how we survived and our life during that time. But we were very much grieved, and it was not easy to talk about what had happened." Over time, the stories came tumbling out. "They told me the names of those who killed them, those who destroyed our house." Another orphan said he met his brother in Kigali, "He showed how he was cut on his neck and his chest," and then commented, "We were happy anyway for meeting each other. We shared how we survived." Another orphan said, "When we met for the first time after the genocide, I told him how all my people were killed, how I spent days running for my life. He also told me what had happened to his people."

Another orphan said that he and his siblings did not immediately recognize one of their siblings: "We cried first and then we talked about our experiences. But one of them was disfigured; it took us time to recognize him." Orphans tried to comfort each other, but it was not always easy. "As one of the eldest, we tried to comfort them [referring to the younger siblings]. We told them that there are some families where no one survived or only one child survived. We decided to be courageous and patient, though the situation was not easy." Another orphan said that after the genocide, "I used to rejoice whenever I could meet those I knew, but immediately the problem was there, how will I live?"

Indeed, not only did they have the problem of food and shelter, but also several orphans reported that a brother or sister had gone mad, suffering severe PTSD. Furthermore, orphans said that aunts and uncles who had survived were not always in a position to take them into their household, and in one instance where they were accommodated, the uncle then married but the new wife did not want this adopted child. Another orphan said that her brother was shocked when he met her a year or so after the genocide. She had given birth to a child from the RPA soldier who had rescued her.

But perhaps most poignant were comments from orphans who connected with one another immediately after the genocide. "When we met, we hugged each other, then we wept. The first thing she asked was, 'Where is mummy?' I said, 'I don't know.' We went to look for them [referring to the parents] but we couldn't find them."

CONCLUSION

Although the accounts in this chapter echo the stories of adults interviewed, they contain important elements that remind us that we are reading the memories of genocide from the perspective of children, and that their viewpoint and experience is different from that of adults. Often, orphans did not have a larger frame of analysis or big-picture thinking about survival strategies. As the sections on parents' last words and children's modes of escape remind us, we are not only reading accounts of survival but also accounts of children who witnessed the killing of the people who they most counted on to protect them. As they escaped, they often escaped alone, sent off into the fields and forests by their own caregivers. They diligently obeyed their parents, as mothers stayed behind with younger siblings, and fathers broke off from the family with the hope that their absence would save his wife and children.

Children survived rape and killing, but they also survived hunger, thirst, loneliness, terror, and wounds, sometimes following in the path of a totally unknown adult with the hope this individual might lead them to safety. Also, naive to the fact that this was a genocide, they often first sought out a Hutu neighbor, friend, or relative. The element of "shock" and disbelief that we will witness in the following chapter on women is somewhat absent in these interviews with children; their accounts are of moment-to-moment survival with little philosophical reflection. And as painfully recounted in Mama Lambert's opening story in chapter 1, often children did not even understand why they were targeted, apologizing to killers for very innocent things, such as urinating in their bed, and promising to "never be a Tutsi."

While it is easy to forget the age of these interviewees as we read their accounts of survival, it is sometimes in the mundane interactions they shared that we are reminded of just how young they were. When a child recounts a final memory of a mother reminding her to wear her coat, it is in those moments that we can begin to grasp the enormity of decisions parents had to make as well as how young these children were and how miraculous that they survived.

In the next chapter, we will focus on the experience of the genocide from the perspective of women who survived. They add an important dimension to our understanding of the genocide since they were older and often referenced previous massacres against Tutsis that they, their parents, and grandparents had experienced. Also, their accounts are filled with constant references to rape, being infected with AIDS, and the utter loneliness that they felt having lost their husbands, children, and in many instances, most of their extended family network. In the second half of this book we deal more explicitly with the issue of survivor trauma and the process of healing. We also address the issues of forgiveness, reconciliation, and commemoration of the genocide. While reading the accounts of genocide in this chapter and the next may be gut-wrenching, the accounts provide the context for examining the healing process and the challenge of forgiving and reconciling with perpetrators of the genocide.[13]

CHAPTER 4

The Experience of Women

A young woman had twin boys who were one-and-a-half-years-old at the time of the genocide. Her instinct was to flee with the children to her brother-in-law's house, since he was Hutu. However, other Tutsis relatives had the same idea, and she was told, "There are too many of you here; you need to spread out, so they don't kill me." This brother-in-law helped her to find a safe hiding place near a bridge. The next morning, she connected with her husband. Together with the children they hid in a banana plantation. But they were attacked that night. The husband took one child and she kept the other. When they found each other the next day the children were hungry from not having eaten. Suddenly they were attacked again, and her husband fled, leaving her with the two children. The killers apparently were only interested in men at this point, and when they found her and the children they said, "Leave her with the twins; it's a heavy burden for her. It's her death."

Not knowing what to do, she returned to the brother-in-law's house but was told, "Why do you return when the others are already dead?" Even her request of blankets for the two boys was refused. So, she fled to the local parish church where she found her husband. Shortly after she arrived the Interahamwe forced all of the men in the church to get into a truck. According to a man who escaped and made his way back to the church, they were transported a short distance away and killed. He returned to the women telling them what had happened and informing them that they were next and should escape.

Again, not knowing what to do, she returned to the brother-in-law's house, but again she and the children were chased away. Once back on the main road she encountered her husband where the men had been killed. "Arriving on the road, I saw my husband who was almost dead, cut up all over, covered with blood, and missing his right arm. He had spent the night. I called to him, but he didn't answer. When I approached him, he told me quietly, 'Take my children out of the road.'" He told her that he was going to try to return to their house.

Uncertain of where to turn, a day later she went to their home with the children. When she arrived, a neighbor said, "Where are you going? Your husband is dead. What are you going to do with your children?" The neighbor told her that all males were being killed, including young children. "I asked him for baby cereal. He took the children and me into his house. There were two other Tutsi female neighbors in this house with their little boys. . . . They gave us cereal and told us that their councilor had given the order to kill all little boys and even those who were only one month old, because they said that even Kagame [leader of the rebel RPF] had left Rwanda at that age." That night they were all locked inside of this Hutu's house. No one could leave, not even to urinate, she said.

The next afternoon a group of killers came, took them from the house, and dug a ditch for disposal of the bodies. "When we arrived in front of the ditches, they told us that they wanted to kill only the children and leave the women. They ordered us to return to the house, but I resisted because I had these twins." They then started to kill the other children who had been in the house. "They pierced their eyes with pins and beat them on their little heads with clubs and threw them into the ditches."

When they approached her twin boys, she resisted. "I refused to let them take both of them. I begged them to kill one and leave the other, or to kill at another time. I begged an older man who had killed the children to at least leave one, but he told me that they had decided to kill all the young boys, even the little ones. He told me that mine were not special. With one blow, they snatched the first one, named Gilbert. He was very weak and hungry, and I remained holding Yves by the hand." One of the killers came and began hitting her hand to loosen her grip so that he could take the other child. "He began with Gilbert. He kicked him in the chest and hit his head with a club. The child died immediately, with his mouth wide open, and he threw him in the ditch. They came back to me and snatched Yves, but I again resisted." Unable to protect her second child, whom they killed, she simply said, "I left and went away." But a few minutes later she returned to place a cloth on each of the bodies as a sign of respect. The killers laughed at her and put the cloth around their own necks.

THE PERSPECTIVE OF WOMEN SURVIVORS

Women and children had many shared experiences during the genocide, but their perspectives were different.[1] In this chapter, many patterns and themes are repeated from chapter 3, but the examples are drawn exclusively from the experience of women survivors. The efforts of mothers to flee killers while carrying small children, the terrible indignity of rape, the anguish of seeing children killed, and the sense of rejection by neighbors who had previously been friends were all experiences directly informed by their social location as women and mothers. Women survivors also had a much stronger sense of historical context than orphan survivors, being aware of previous massacres of Tutsis, including the deaths of relatives.

As previously stated, in some areas, and particularly at the beginning of the genocide, men were targeted first for death. The killers worked from lists of Tutsis and often only after the man of the house was killed did they then kill the wife and children. Consequently, women had the task of fleeing alone with children. But in addition to fleeing, mothers were preoccupied during the three months of the genocide with finding food and water for their starving and severely dehydrated children. Sometimes they would collect water off the leaves of bushes and trees. Nursing mothers would feed their children until their milk supply diminished. Many times, they were going days without food and water.

It is almost impossible to imagine what these women felt when they survived an attack, often left for dead, having witnessed the brutal killing of their infant or children, and then attempting to carry on by themselves. Women sometimes contemplated suicide once left alone. Much of the meaning in their lives was tied to their relationships and roles—the companionship of their husbands and nurture of their children. For widows with a surviving child, there was a reason to push on, seeking safety from the killers, but when they were the only survivor it was another story. They lacked the support of a husband to share their burden; they were often fleeing alone, without the strength that comes from networks of caring relatives and friends. The question of why one should continue the struggle for existence was a recurring thought for many widows.

Many women, even when accompanied by their children, were raped. Some were raped while their children looked on. Others were raped and then violated with sticks. Others were taken as sex slaves, imprisoned for days, then left for dead. Several women described how their genitals oozed pus from infection after these sexual assaults. One woman said that she smelled so putrid that only some boys in their early teens kept raping her.

Women who survived rape were often wounded and left for dead. They crawled out of latrines where they had been thrown; they came to consciousness in churches where everyone else had been laid to waste, including their own child next to them, sometimes with severed body parts on top of them. It is not surprising that some women sought out Interahamwe and begged to be killed. To their disappointment, the response was often, "Don't bother, she is going to die anyway."

Not only did women feel dehumanized from rape, they often were rejected by Hutu neighbors to whom they fled and by Hutu relatives and in-laws to whom they turned. Like the orphans in the last chapter, women were sometimes sheltered for a day or two and then turned out, with their host saying that they would themselves be killed if the Interahamwe discovered they were hiding a Tutsi. And in a few instances, survivors said their protectors feared that they would be required to kill the people they had been sheltering. The most sympathetic Hutus were often older women. Perhaps they felt they had already lived their lives and were willing to take a chance on sheltering a Tutsi; perhaps they had a more acute historical memory of intergenerational relationships with Tutsi neighbors and friends.

GAUDENCE'S EXPERIENCE

We could illustrate the experience of women through many different examples, but Gaudence is someone we got to know very well over a decade of seeing her at Solace Ministries. In addition to interviewing her, we visited her home, and we also witnessed the ways in which Solace Ministries intervened medically for her after the genocide. She is a woman of remarkable good cheer given the horrific things that she experienced.

Gaudence was newly married and had a six-week-old baby when she heard that President Habyarimana's plane had been shot down. Normally she turned on the radio around 5:00 A.M., but on April 7 the radio was silent. Then a half hour later the announcement came that the president was dead. Gaudence's immediate response was sorrow for his family, and she assumed there would be another election. But her husband, Alphonse, was alarmed.

Around 6:00 A.M., the neighbors started to gather, talking about the announcement. She looked out the window and saw the crowd lift a young man in the air and throw him to the ground. She said, "I had never thought about someone dying before then." And, in fact, the troubles they had experienced in 1990 when the RPF first invaded Rwanda had passed and had not affected them personally. So, she did not take the announcement regarding the president very seriously. She was on very friendly terms with her Hutu neighbors and could not imagine that they would do her family any harm.

However, a short time later an order was given that all men should stand outside their houses. Gaudence said it was a trick so that the killers would not need to search individual homes. Her husband turned to her and said that he felt this might be the last time he would see her. When her husband was led away, Gaudence took her baby and went to a friendly neighbor's house. "At the same moment we were talking, there came a big group of militias, holding weapons, such as clubs and machetes. I did not know what to do and finally I put my baby on my back and left that house."

The killers started asking, "Where is Alphonse's wife?" Once they spotted her, they rudely ordered her to follow them, saying that she was going to meet her husband. A few meters later they encountered a roadblock where the husband of the woman she had been visiting was stationed. "I asked him if he could keep my child, because I was not sure what was going to happen to me, but I was almost sure that I was going to be killed. I wanted my child to survive. But at the moment when he was about to take the child, one of the militias hit the man and forbid him to take the child and told him that if he wanted a child, he had to have one of his own."

With the baby on her back, Gaudence was escorted back to a large house. "They pushed me through the gate and there were like thirty militiamen there." They started hitting her with various weapons, on her head, back, and legs. She still had her baby on her back when she fell to the ground and heard the attackers say, "Hit that ugly baby so that it stops crying." With an ax someone struck her baby on the head and also hit Gaudence. "I had lost sense of what was happening, the sense of time, the sense of life, the sense of everything. And I was asking myself whether I was still alive or dead." She saw her husband lying nearby. "I kept on calling him, saying, 'Alphonse! Alphonse!' But he was already dead, and I did not know that."

She then called to other people that she knew, saying, "Why don't you answer me? Are you not hearing me?" When no one responded, she took her baby and tried to put him on her back, but he was not responding. "I will never forget what I saw. They had hit him here [motioning to her head] and he was all covered with blood. I put him back on the ground. He was so handsome, with nice hair. I covered him with a piece of cloth and put him beside his dad's dead body. I tried to stand on my feet and started moving because I knew that if I stayed there, they would kill me, but this time for good."

When she ventured to the gate of the house, she saw that the militia had departed, looking for other people to kill. "I walked slowly holding onto the walls. I walked but I was getting really weak because I had lost a lot of quantity of blood." She then encountered a boy whose mother was Tutsi, but his father was Hutu and he helped her go to his house where a number of people had gathered, seeking refuge. Her sojourn there was short-lived. In spite of the fact that the man was wealthy, the militia had found out that he was hiding people in his house. "So, all the people left except me, because I was too weak to move." When the man's two sons saw her, they asked what she was still doing there, and she said that she was too weak to move. "I begged them to let me stay there, but they refused."

"I continued walking and reached a place where an old woman lived. She looked at me and told me to get in her house. She looked for warm water and started washing me. . . . I was full of wounds at that time. I had injuries here, here, and on my head. Around 10:00 A.M., she tried to feed me, but I was refusing because I also had a wound in my mouth. She looked for butter and put a large piece of butter in my wound where they had hit me with an ax. She was hoping that the butter would make me feel better soon." After several days the lady said that Gaudence needed to go to the hospital. "I begged the old woman to let me stay in her house, but she refused, saying that if I stayed there, I would die for sure." So, the elderly woman put clothes on Gaudence, stuffing some around her stomach so that she would look pregnant, and took her personally through various roadblocks, saying that she was about to give birth and needed to go to the hospital.

Somewhat miraculously Gaudence reached the hospital with the aid of this old Hutu woman who knew many people at the various roadblocks. The woman gave the doctor some money to care for her, but she was largely ignored except by the watchman. Maggots had filled Gaudence's wounds, including her head where she had been hit by the ax. For the rest of April, she lived with the maggots infesting her wounds. The watchman would come and sweep them off the floor where they would fall. No one bothered to kill her, saying that she would soon die anyway. But finally, someone decided to start putting Mercurochrome on the wounds. They even washed and shaved her head, although Gaudence said that maggots continued to live inside her skull. She was such a curiosity that the watchman actually was calling people to come and look at the woman with maggots.

In anger at the way she was being treated, Gaudence decided to leave the hospital sometime in May. However, she was partially paralyzed from the wounds to her head and could not walk, so she literally crawled for an hour to reach the road. At the roadblock, the militia didn't bother to kill her, saying that she was already dead. Somehow, she managed to crawl to a nearby house. She said the Hutu woman there was kind, and even offered her food, but they would not allow her to sleep in their house. So she crawled to an outdoor kitchen room where she slept. But at four in the morning, the man of the house said that she had to leave. Slithering like a snake on the ground, because one of her legs was completely paralyzed, she reached the road where eventually two girls took her to one of their homes. The one girl was a Tutsi married to a Hutu. "They washed me and hid me, but she refused to tell her husband. I stayed there for one week, but the lady was very scared. Nevertheless, she really took care of me. She used to bring me tea in the morning and at noon wash me." In June, she was transported to another house where people would come and wash her early in the morning, as well as bring her tea.

Eventually Gaudence was rescued when the RPA arrived in Kigali, although this began a very long period of recovery from her injuries. "So, I was taken to the hospital by the Inkotanyi. I was treated and they discovered that my head was severely damaged. The maggots in my head were still inside. So, I went into coma and finally became conscious in 1995." After she regained consciousness, she could not walk, talk, recognize people (including former classmates who came to visit her), or read. She said that she didn't even know her name. Through the intervention of some good-willed people after the genocide, she was sent to South Africa for surgery.

When we met Gaudence for the first time several years later, she was able to walk, although with a noticeable limp. During our interview, she got out of her chair and illustrated how she had slithered on the ground like a snake. But where we really saw her vitality was during the meetings at Solace when women and orphans would dance to the beat of a drum, celebrating the gift of life. There was Gaudence, dancing with a huge smile on her face. And when we visited a home that Solace had provided for her, she proudly showed us her cow. She had named the cow "Hope"—the source of her livelihood since she was able to sell the milk that exceeded her own personal need.

Gaudence's account is valuable because it is clear that a number of Hutus assisted her, although in several instances it was because of mixed marriages between Hutus and Tutsis. It is also apparent that Gaudence was not politically aware and simply assumed that her longtime neighborhood friendships would continue after the president's plane was shot down. What is not obvious from the preceding account is the attitude of gratitude that she currently exudes in her relationships with other people. Here is a woman who lost her baby, her husband, and use of some of her limbs, yet she radiates a cheerfulness that is quite inexplicable. In chapter 6 we will return to her story, addressing the healing process that some survivors have undergone.

THE EARLY DAYS OF THE GENOCIDE

One striking difference between our interviews with orphans and widows is that adult women were often able to provide detailed historical context to the genocide in ways that children could not. Many of them recalled husbands, parents, and grandparents being killed or arrested in 1959 when the political tables turned with Hutus taking power. They also recalled other important dates of political turmoil for Tutsis, for example, 1963 and 1973. The scenario during these earlier attacks was often the same: Tutsi leaders would be killed; houses would be burned; sometimes people would flee to Zaire or Burundi; but then peace would prevail, and Tutsis would put their lives back together again.

This statement by a widow describes a pattern that many Tutsis had experienced: "In 1959 they burned our houses; we fled; we hid in the bush, but not far from our houses; and others left for other countries—Uganda, Burundi. Afterward we returned to our houses; we repaired them, because they told us that it was finished. There would be peace. In 1973, they again prepared for war. They took up machetes to kill the Tutsi, to exterminate them all. We didn't take it seriously. We wondered how they could exterminate all the Tutsis. They took our cows, cut them up; they again burned down our houses, and they began to beat and kill people. We left, went far away. After a while, returned and rebuilt again."

What made April 1994 different is that women survivors noticed a more organized set of activities. As was described by some of the orphans we interviewed, the radio station RTLM was blaring out more frequent hate messages. Hutus were having secret meetings that excluded Tutsis. And there was training of militia at a scale that had not previously occurred. Also, the RPF was experiencing some success in their invasions of Rwanda, which created a highly charged political context in which the older sons as well as husbands were suspected of being RPF accomplices.

For example, one woman remembers that in March 1994, Hutus came to her demanding that she give them the radio that broadcasts the RPF station. She didn't have one, but they beat her anyway. They even took her small child and placed her on top of the barbecue, threatening to burn the child if she didn't tell them where Radio Muhabura was [the RPF radio]. She then graphically described what happened: "My child cried and at last they let her go. They came toward me, I was at the end of the courtyard, and they pinned me on the ground, on my back, and put a knife to my throat. They threatened to cut it if I didn't show them where the Inkotanyi radio was. I told them that we didn't have it. I didn't even know about it. They spit on my face, kicked me, and left me there."

Another woman said that her husband was imprisoned, accused of being an accomplice. "There was a priest who mistreated me when my husband was in prison. He said during mass, 'Here in the church there are people who hide the Inkotanyi and weapons, but who bring their rosaries and disguise themselves as Christians, like Josephine.' He said it every time he saw me during mass until the other Christians asked me not to participate in the mass, but I refused, saying, 'I don't come here for this priest, I come here to pray to God.'" Hence, while orphans may have experienced discrimination in their school for being Tutsis, this account is a good example of what a woman experienced in her own church—from her priest.

The Interahamwe were overheard singing and chanting about the deaths of the Tutsis, well before April 7. Neighbors were sometimes overtly telling Tutsis that they were going to take over their house, and also bluntly stating, "You are going to die soon." One woman recalls that there were carpenters who were making clubs and putting nails in them to give to the militia. Another woman said, "The training of the Interahamwe was done in full view of everyone. Most of them were young boys who got weapons, guns, grenades and swords. . . . Everywhere, at our neighbors and on the hills, there were machetes, hammers, spears that had not existed before in such large numbers, but all of a sudden, we saw them in every house. We Tutsis thought that they were for domestic use."

Discrimination was also experienced in the workplace, similar to what occurred for children in school. "They persecuted us every day when we went to work, separating us. Tutsis worked on one side and the Hutus on another. When someone was late to work, the authority in charge implied that Tutsis were slow, used to dragging themselves." This same woman said that they also experienced discrimination after work. "When you went into their cafés, there were separate cafés for Tutsis and Hutus, and even for political parties. If you made a mistake and went into one of their cafés to buy salt, for example, they beat you, insulted you under the pretext that you were there to listen to their secrets." One woman said that prior to the genocide her son went to a meeting at the communal office where he was chased away by the burgomaster, who said, "Go and have your own meetings, because the fate of the Tutsis is finished." She said, "My son came back, traumatized by these extremist words, and after a few weeks, the genocide began."

Hence, it is not surprising that some Tutsis started sleeping at night in the bushes, even before the slaughter had advanced to their town. The pattern described by orphans was echoed in the accounts of widows. Neighbors whom Tutsis had known for years turned hostile, as if they knew that something was about to happen. And then after April 7, the burning and looting of houses began. Houses with thatched roofs were easily set on fire. For houses with metal roofs, care was taken by neighboring Hutus to remove the metal sheets before destroying the house. As the children recounted, women also saw this occurring under their noses as they were hiding in nearby locations. Houses were not only burned, often ignited by kerosene or gasoline, walls also were pushed down—communicating the message that no one will return to reoccupy this house.

CHURCHES AS KILLING SITES

Every survivor we interviewed had a story to tell about what they experienced in the early days of the genocide. And each one was unique, even though there were common patterns, such as running to churches for safety, where more people died than in any other single location.[2] Agnes's account is typical.

She remembers her brother coming home after he received news of the plane's crash saying that they were surely going to all die. On the urging of friends, the family ran away during the day but at night came back to their home to sleep. They repeated this pattern until April 10 when policemen found them hiding in the forest and told them to return home, which they did until April 13. That night they heard people screaming, and so they headed to a Catholic church where they slept with many other Tutsis. On April 14, around 9:00 A.M., soldiers entered the church and asked for the pastor of the church to present his identity card. He was a Tutsi.

The soldiers then opened fire on the people who had gathered in the church-yard. Her brother tried to run out and was shot by soldiers along with other men in the church compound who tried to escape. The soldiers then called in the Interahamwe saying that all the "strong" people are dead and therefore it will be easy to kill the rest. With her sister, Agnes ran into one of the side rooms in the church, holding her brother's young child. In this room, a mem-ber of the Interahamwe cut her sister's feet while she begged, "Please forgive me; I am not a Tutsi." He replied saying, "I know you are a snake." He then hit Agnes with his machete and killed the two-year-old child that she was holding, leaving them both for dead. And then he finished off the sister whose feet he had cut. As he was leaving the room, Agnes heard him say to another Interahamwe that he had only twelve more people to kill to fulfill his mission.

Agnes remained in the church amid the dead bodies for another hour or two while the Interahamwe went to feast on some of the Tutsi cows they had stolen. During this interlude, two boys entered the church. "I was still alive but did not care if I would die or not because I felt there was no reason to survive. I had already seen all my children killed earlier. So, I said to these boys, 'Come and kill me too.' These boys told me, 'We are not going to kill you. Instead, wake up and go before they come back and kill you.'"

She left the church compound and found some of her relatives who had survived, including her mother. On her mother's instructions, she went to one of her father's friend's house. She was rejected at this household, but as she was waiting nearby someone came and told her to sit down so that he could kill her. "So, I sat down, my legs straight. When he was going to kill me, he looked at me and said, 'She is already half dead.' He told the other Interaha-mwe, 'Let her go. Dogs will eat her.'"

Churches were convenient places to kill Tutsis. Sometimes thousands of people would flee to them for safety. Churches often had walled enclosures that penned people in so that it was difficult to escape. In Agnes's account, it appears that soldiers first killed the "strong" men and then invited in the Interahamwe to kill everyone else. In other accounts, the killers first threw grenades into the church before entering. In fact, in one account a survivor stated that body parts were falling on her as a result of the grenades that had exploded, and she escaped death by being covered by the blood of others, deceiving the killers who thought she was already dead. In another instance, the killers flooded the church with some sort of noxious gas that subdued those inside.

In Nyamata, children were literally sacrificed on the altar that otherwise held the communion elements for celebration of the Eucharist. For a country that was more than 90 percent Christian, it is difficult to understand such sacrilege, except that priests were sometimes sympathetic to the Hutu Power movement and a collective fervor had consumed the killers. Indeed, in one instance a priest locked fleeing Tutsis inside the church until the killers could arrive to do their work. And in Saint Famile Church in Kigali, a survivor told us that a priest was trading sexual favors with women for their survival.

Not only were churches a site for killing, but clergy too were sometimes part of the propaganda machine. One of the first individuals we interviewed is a very sophisticated and well-educated man who was working for USAID in Rwanda. He said that his local Hutu priest refused to serve communion to him, saying, "I don't give the body and blood of Christ to cockroaches." As one might imagine, the participation of clergy in the genocide later created disillusionment with religion.

RAPE AND SEXUAL VIOLENCE

While orphans sometimes referred to rapes they had observed, and in a few instances orphan girls were raped themselves, in the accounts of widows the references to rape were pervasive. Not only were women physically injured, especially when they were gang raped and taken as sex slaves, but their dignity was stripped from them. They were left feeling worthless, violated, not fully human. And numerous women continued to live with the legacy of these rapes, having been infected with HIV.

In addition to the word "rape," women used a variety of euphemisms to refer to being sexually violated. For example, "they did what they wanted," "they did bad things to me," "they used me," and "he took me as a wife." One woman, in the midst of describing how she was taken as a sex slave, paused for a long time and then said, "I must continue my account, but know that this is like a knife churning inside, wounding us; it causes grief that never ceases.

But we must get used to it." Another woman who was raped in front of her children said, "Okay, I will tell everything this time, even things I was ashamed to tell. When they beat me, they finished by undressing me and raping me there in front of my kids, who were standing at a distance, after beating them also. Such a thing at my age; it was really shameful for an old woman like me. That's why I didn't want to reveal it at first."

The fact that children were present did not seem to deter rapists. A woman pleaded with her attacker to please forgive her—that is, forgive her for being a Tutsi. "He refused and said I am not negotiating with you. So I stood up to take off the child on my back. . . . He said to the child that if he keeps on crying he will cut him. So, he came and grabbed the cloth which I used to cover that child on my back and said if I don't willingly allow him to rape me, he will tie me up. I told him to forgive me; I kept on asking him to forgive me. . . . But even though I kept on saying 'forgive me,' he threw me down and he raped me." At this point in the interview she started crying very noticeably and we stopped to comfort her.

Many women were not raped once; they were violated multiple times. For example, if a woman was stopped by three militiamen, they might strip her naked and each would take turns raping her. According to the accounts of survivors, they would then kill the woman or sometimes they simply left her for dead and went on their way. If she was able to continue fleeing after the rapes, it was not unusual for a woman to be raped again by another person or group. One survivor said, "Our neighbor women were raped as though this was the normal thing to do." Another survivor described how she encountered a soldier while she was fleeing. In a matter-of-fact way, he gathered some banana leaves, ordered her to lie down, raped her, and then actually gave her a ride in his car to the location she was pursuing. Tutsi women had lost all rights; their bodies were not their own. They existed to be abused.

A survivor said that she actually felt fortunate compared to other women. "Those whose genital parts always had pus because they had infection resulting from raping them with cow horns. They were badly off. Some had gone crazy because they had been pierced with knives everywhere. So, compared to myself, I was far better than them. I found those whose arms had been cut off, so although I was internally hurt, I was better than them because I was able to do something."

Even local Hutu youth humiliated women. "Young boys came from the streets, very dirty and they said to me, 'Teach us.' They spit all over me since

I was lying down; pissed on me and the urine got into my wounds and made me very sick and I felt like they were pouring pepper into them." Another woman said, "I was lucky that I wasn't raped by adults [who might have had AIDS]. They were kids from the street, adolescents. No adult dared approach me, such as a soldier or a man worthy of his name. As a result of the beating that I got, I was putrid."

This physical suffering from rape was compounded by the need for women to care for their children. A survivor recalled returning to her children after being raped. "I spent a whole week in that ditch and found my youngest child who was by then four months old with the older sibling on top of a hill. I was getting rotten and actually the skin was coming off my genitals and they were white. I don't know what they had poured in my private parts. Then I found the elder child sleeping next to the young one while ants were running over this baby."

It is obvious that degradation and humiliation—not sexual pleasure—was the motive behind rape. A survivor said, "They would get the useless people to rape. Men who were important were spectators to rapes by those street people, very poor people. The nobodies who were not recognized in the society would rape women so that they take away our value." Another survivor said, "The most traumatizing thing that happened to me was being raped by lots of people, one giving me to the other. But the most hurtful thing was being raped by an old man, the age of my father, and being raped in front of my father." And for others, rape was almost a sport. A woman said, "They often undressed me to see the height of Tutsi women," and "they even called teenagers to rape me to learn what Tutsi women were like."

In at least one instance, even young children were not spared. A woman who was four months pregnant said, "It was there they raped me. They took my little girl, put her on the ground to rape her, and she was a baby! As I was raped, I told myself that the world is evil; that it would be better to die than live like this."

Young women in their early teens were also raped, including a thirteen-year-old who was repeatedly raped by two neighbor boys. They told her, "There is no Tutsi of my age with breasts that hadn't played sex, so we will play sex with you." Another woman said that she escaped being raped, but two young girls were not spared who had come to visit her. "They took them and raped them. They wanted to rape me too, but I told them, 'Can you really rape a person without shame, who has just given birth a week ago, who still has problems after just having delivered such a short time ago?' So, they left me alone and they took these young girls."

Repeatedly, women said that they could barely walk after being gang raped. One woman said, "I was constrained by force, as if it was their 'work.' Twenty men raped me." Another woman described the fate of her niece: "She had just finished her studies. Everyone in the village took turns on her until she died. Worse still, after having intercourse with her, they shoved sharp objects into her genitals. It was because of this that she died." Another survivor described a young teacher: "They took her and tied her arms; they put her in the bush and every day they came and raped her; they took turns raping her; it was horrible." And a mother said, "They took me aside, so they could take my daughter; there were thirty of them, who took turns raping her."

The fact that a woman had already been raped did not seem to deter other men from violating her again, even if the woman was nearly unconscious. For example, a survivor said: "After those men raped me, I tried to look for water to drink, but couldn't find any, so I had to lie there like a zombie and spend the night. The next day I was bleeding to death. At around 1:00 P.M., two other men came and raped me again, but a third man came and said he can't rape a Tutsi, but instead he beat me with a machete. I spent three days unconscious, like a dead person."

Some women were simply discarded after being raped; they had been so abused that their perpetrators didn't think it was worth the effort to kill them. For example, a survivor said that they were fleeing as a group. When they would encounter Interahamwe or soldiers, "They would choose a young girl and take her away from the group so that they may easily rape her. Then after raping her, they would tell her to get away from their sight and go die elsewhere."

When we asked survivors whether they could identify their rapist(s), we had mixed answers. In some instances, the perpetrator was in prison and they had given testimony against him. In other cases, so many men had raped them that they had lost track of their identities. For example, one woman said that every man in her village had known her body. In other instances, the rapists were Interahamwe from other regions and their victims did not recognize them. On the other hand, women were sometimes very specific and said that their rapist had escaped to Zaire or was living in Europe and therefore had not been brought to justice.

The enduring legacy of rape for many women is that many are currently HIV positive, and a number of survivors said that on a daily basis they are reminded of being raped because of their struggle to deal with the AIDS virus and its implications. In addition to taking medication, a woman said that AIDS has left her so weak that she can no longer till the soil and therefore has lost her means of livelihood. Another survivor said that various employers have discriminated against her, including being terminated from her position, once they found out that she was infected. "Because I am HIV positive, my bosses fired me because they were afraid I could contaminate their children. Even now where I am working they have a problem with me because of the same issue."

Tragically, women who married after the genocide and unknowingly were HIV positive ended up transmitting the virus to their husbands. Several women said that their husbands had died from AIDS and they felt responsible, and in several other instances husbands had divorced their wives when they discovered that they had AIDS. Sometimes the children born of these marriages were also infected by their mothers, although this was only true in a few instances in our interviews.

Other times it appears that husbands may have infected their wives. "So, the time came and we went for tests at the hospital and found out that we were infected. We were living together before we made the tests. We continued living together in that manner, but he went on getting worse. He died before he could take the medication, but I took the medicine." Another survivor said, "He got symptoms before me, but honestly I think I infected him."

Women who have been raped are strongly encouraged by the government and NGOs, such as Solace Ministries and AVEGA, to be tested—along with their children. Women inevitably dread receiving the results, and therefore it is a major turning point for them to agree to be tested. One woman said that she could not believe that she tested positive, even though she had been raped three times. "I could not believe it. I even almost fought with the doctor and went home. The doctor sent one of the health workers to be on guard at my house because I wanted to commit suicide."

In response to the tests, several survivors said that their children wanted to know why their mother has AIDS, and this raised the dilemma of whether to tell the truth or not. In one instance, the child actually witnessed his mother being raped during the genocide and, along with the doctor who did the test, played a major role in comforting the woman after she received results that she tested positive for the AIDS virus. And in one particularly poignant case, the child was born as the result of a rape and has repeatedly questioned his mother about his father, leading her to lie, saying that he was killed during the genocide. In fact, she didn't even know the identity of the father: "I never knew who got me pregnant, for I was raped in the forest."

SURVIVAL EXPERIENCES

In addition to the pattern of sexual assault, women faced another highly gendered predicament—the need to survive while hiding, caring for, and comforting small children. One mother with several children remembers that after the president's plane was shot down, they became very concerned about their safety and, on April 15, they left their house for good and for six days hid in a sorghum field. Then, she recalled that they were attacked. "The soldiers fell on us and started to kill. It was the same day that I got separated from my husband and the children scattered. I had six children; each went their own way. I was left with a child I was carrying on my back, and in front I was holding my youngest. We continued to hide not far from our house, in the woods."

She remembered the comments of some soldiers who passed within earshot of where she was hiding. "They were quarreling about who they were going to kill, and my neighbors were among them." She was then discovered. "Some of them were arguing about who should kill me and the others asked for my identity card to see if I was a Hutu woman, but I told them that I hadn't brought it with me. Others asked me for money and I gave them the money I had. It went on like this until nighttime." For whatever reason, they didn't kill her and she went down the hill to where they were burning Tutsi houses. "I left and arrived down there, but I didn't find anyone to kill me. Later, I met someone, a good person, who showed me where to find members of my family. He told me that they had crossed to the other side of the river."

So, she went in search of her family, carrying two of her small children and also dragging along the wounded child of her brother-in-law. She was able to reunite with some of her family after crossing the river. "We slept outdoors. The next day, the soldiers pursued us. We again spent the day hiding, and at night I found two of my children. The oldest was carrying the other on her back. We continued to hide, and we again spent the night outside." They then heard that the RPA soldiers were advancing in their direction and were not too far away. "We continued to walk, my four children and me, and the other one who was wounded." The poignancy of this story is not that this woman survived, but the fact that she was carrying two children—one in front and one on her back as she fled—and that an older daughter was also carrying one of her siblings on her back.

Another survivor said that she survived by pretending that she was dead. She was in advanced pregnancy and was unable to run, in part because she also was carrying her youngest child. She saw many dead people along the road and this gave her an idea. "It occurred to me to lie down on the ground among the dead bodies on the road. The child I was carrying on my back, I put down also among the dead. Later my husband passed near me with our oldest child and pointed at me, saying, "Look there, your mother is dead. You must not ask me anymore where she is." He continued on the road and was spotted and shot on the spot. He was going to save himself by running, but the child he had just put on the ground called for help and he came back to him. "So, they got him. He was killed by one of my teacher colleagues, and they also cut off his hands."

This woman heard the report of her husband's death by an Interahamwe who came back a little later and was rummaging around among the dead bodies looking for money. To her shock, "I saw that he was wearing my husband's pants and jacket, and I realized that it was over for my husband." When this man and others who were scavenging got to her and nudged her, she said, "Don't search me. I am alive." And they responded, "Don't do anything, we only want money," and then left. But she also heard one of the men say, "Why don't you finish her off, the one you are talking with?" and he answered, "It's not worth it. Look at her head." She had cleverly put some of the extruding brain matter from a nearby person on her own head.

Later, another group came looking for money on the bodies of the deceased. To this group she said, "Kill me," but they answered, "Get up, we will take you to our house so that you can become our wife." So, she said, "I got up. I was half naked. I only had a slip on. The robbers had taken the rest of my clothes. My child, who was still alive, I put him on my back with the help of a scarf that they had forgotten to take and I followed them." When they arrived at their house, an old man said, "This miserable wet woman, at one o'clock in the morning with a child on her back, let her leave so she can die elsewhere." They let her leave after slapping her several times. She then walked until it began to get light, not knowing where she was. "I arrived at a house and said under my breath, "I am going to take a chance here and they are going to kill me." The woman answered the door and asked who she was. When she said that she was a refugee, the woman said, "Continue on your way; my husband is going to kill you. He has gone out, and on his way back he will kill you. I assure you." She continued saying how she was rejected from place to place until finally she encountered the pastor of a church who helped her.

Women's stories are scattered with detailed accounts of how they scavenged for food and water to keep their infants and toddlers alive. Women recounted opening their mouths to catch rain water, attempting to give their very young children the droplets of water from banana leaves, and even resorting to drinking or giving their children urine in an attempt to save them from dehydration. Many infants were reported as being weak, silent, and on the brink of death while being carried on their mother's back. One woman described chewing raw bananas and spitting the partially digested food into her child's mouth with the hope of getting him some nourishment.

After husbands scattered, mothers were presented with the awful decision of having to decide which child to save, which child they would carry, and which children they would abandon or—if old enough at four or five years of age—which children to send off to survive on their own. As noted, it was extremely common for families to separate in this way with the hope of increasing the survival of just one or two family members.

By contrast, an elderly woman described her survival. She said how she was separated from her husband, older children, and other relatives and never saw them again. She said everyone went a different direction. When she returned to her home, she found everyone dead. It was raining hard, in fact pouring. "I told myself, why not die instead of suffering like this? I wanted to die, but I didn't find death. By chance, I found eggplants in the field and I collected them to put them in a sweater I had. Everywhere I went, I took one and I ate it." After three days, early in the morning, she said, "I found a house where there were Hutu women, but who had Tutsi husbands. They welcomed me. I spent the night with them."

The next morning these women prepared food for her and another twenty or so individuals who were hiding there. At midnight the next day they were attacked. "The others ran, but I stayed there with my cane. I was afraid. They returned and said as they insulted me, 'Where does this old woman come from?' . . . One of them said, 'Why do you want to kill this old woman since she is almost dead?'" They then killed eight individuals who had not fled. But rather than kill this older woman they simply struck her on the head. "I remained there in despair. At 3:00 P.M., I was attacked again. They forced me to leave and I was sitting on the ground. One of them came by and spat on me and told me, 'You are not going to get away. You are going to die like this.' They entered this house where we were, and they stole everything there."

WIDOW REUNIONS

After the genocide ended, the experiences of mothers finding children were particularly poignant, and sometimes troubling. One widow said that her child was three years and seven months old when they were separated. The Interahamwe had fled with this child during the genocide. "When there was a bit of a lull in the fighting, the Inkotanyi accompanied me and we found him in Murambi. At my arrival, seeing the condition I was in, walking barefoot, wearing grubby clothes, he didn't recognize me and said, 'You are not my mother!' After some explanation, he ended up recognizing me. He didn't understand anything. He was still young, but for me to find this child I thought had died was a miracle."

Another survivor described finding her children after the genocide ended. "When I found them, they were very dirty. They were wearing the same clothes they had on at the beginning of the genocide [three months before]. Their hair was long and dirty. I suffered a lot. The older one cried a lot. She asked me where the others were. I told her that I didn't know where they were, that we had been separated at the beginning of the genocide." From this reunion, a fractured family was formed, but missing a father and many of the children.

Widows also connected, on occasion, with adult relatives. One woman said, "At the reunion, we all cried, because we didn't know who was dead and who had survived. But afterward, the adults tried to console the children, comforting them, saying that life must go on in spite of what we had endured." Another widow said, on meeting her cousin, "He collapsed, and I collapsed. We stayed for three hours glued to each other. We didn't want to separate." And then she said with a twist of irony, "He died in 1998," after having survived the ordeal of the genocide.

On rare occasions, reunions were also mixed with grief. When one widow saw her younger sister, she said that she was afraid to meet her. "Seeing me, she went inside the house and started to cry. I also cried. We took leave of each other after two days and I asked her why she had not come to see me since she had found out that I was alive. She answered that she was ashamed to see me because of the fact that she had not been able to save my children, since I had left them in her care." Therefore, reunions were not always happy occasions. They were multifaceted and complex. A survivor said these reunions were full of anger, sorrow, and tears. Reunions prompted stories of the genocide, and there was little joy to be found in them.

CONCLUSION

It was one thing to survive the excruciating one hundred days of the genocide. The challenge now was to make a new life. That is the focus of the next chapter. How does one live with recirculating memories of the horrific things one experienced? How does one reknit a family when many of the members are missing, or in the case of some orphans, not a single adult relative survived? What is the daily experience of living with shattered and missing limbs? Headaches? Insomnia? HIV? And at a very primal level, how does one survive with a lack of shelter and food, and the total destruction of one's economic means of survival?

If life is to have meaning, it must have purpose. But for many survivors, the support structures, institutions, and relationships that enabled them to flourish before the genocide were now completely eradicated. Survivors had experienced the moral rupture of their world. In chapter 6, when we discuss the symptoms of trauma, the issue of rupture—morally, spiritually, socially, and politically—is identified as the root cause of trauma. The world no longer makes sense. One has lost the categories to explain, rationalize, and/or interpret one's experience. Healing requires a rebirth of the meaning structures of life and, in our view, this is best done in community where one can grow a new soul and find comfort as well as social roles and affirmation to replace what has been lost.

As one reads the next chapter, it is important to keep the roadmap of this book in mind. After the chapter on trauma, in chapter 7 we describe a model of holistic healing, and in chapter 8 we tackle the complexities surrounding forgiveness, which survivors identify as having the potential to liberate one from the revolving memories of the horrors of genocide. Then in chapter 9, we move from the individual level of analysis to the social and political level, looking at survivors' experiences of the *gacaca* courts and commemorations. But, first, we examine the experience of survivors immediately after the genocide.

CHAPTER 5

Coping after Genocide

If surviving the genocide was an ordeal, the weeks and months after the genocide were filled with deep uncertainty and practically insurmountable challenges. People began to come out of hiding. Children were roaming the streets
having lost their parents, fending on their own for food and shelter. Widows
were filled with grief over the deaths of their spouse and children. Survivors
were nursing wounds. Many were malnourished, wearing ragged clothing after
months of hiding in the bush. And yet they still needed to eat. They needed
shelter. Dealing with their psychological trauma was a task for later; first, they
had to answer the question, "How will I live?"[1]

As the RPA occupied territory, thousands of Hutu perpetrators fled with
their families. As stated in a previous chapter, it is to these empty houses that
survivors sometimes turned to find shelter, since their own homes were
destroyed. In these homes were often provisions, including food that they
could eat. There were also fields that could be harvested. Some areas had been
almost completely evacuated, and so there were provisions in stores that survivors could use. In many ways, it was a strange irony—the perpetrators of
genocide had destroyed homes and killed countless cows. But now they were
refugees, and the few survivors who remained were living in their houses and
feeding themselves from their fields.

This solution to shelter and food was temporary, however. In time, Hutu
refugees began to return to their homes. Survivors were displaced once again.
They were living in the midst of the very people who had killed their family
members. Some Hutus were ashamed. Others could not believe that anyone

had survived the extermination process. And the inevitable happened. The perpetrators of genocide began to blame the victims, especially as those victims reported to the police individuals who had participated in the genocide, sometimes leading to imprisonment and the fracturing of returning Hutu refugee families. However, many of the men who participated in the genocide remained in Zaire or other countries, fearing imprisonment, even if their families returned.

Surviving orphans living on the streets were sometimes gathered into orphanages; other orphan-headed households tried to reconstitute a sense of being "family" with the children that remained. The eldest member of the family became the parent, even if these "parents" were sometimes in their preteens. They collected surviving brothers and sisters, and sometimes there were orphans with no surviving siblings who were adopted by default. Heroically, widows also often took on the responsibility of caring for extended family members, nephews and nieces, and neighbor children. Initially, survivors shared whatever means they had, although eventually these family units had to exist on their own, as stated by this orphan head of household: "We were young but depending on our age we became responsible for those who were under us. Life was very difficult, but we put together with our neighbors and shared whatever we had."

ORPHANS

Eight years after the genocide, when orphan heads of household were asked how they felt about becoming parents to their younger siblings, the answers were nearly all the same—we had no choice, it was our responsibility. Here's a typical response: "After the death of my parents, I told myself that I have to help my brothers; they will eat what I eat and live as I live, because they don't have those who were supposed to look after them." Another orphan said about his role as a surrogate parent, "I had no other option; being the eldest of them, I felt I had to take up the responsibility." And a third survivor said, "It just comes naturally when you are the eldest."

Parenting their surviving siblings carried substantial responsibilities. Repeatedly orphan heads of households said that they worried, almost constantly, about how they could feed their siblings. Many orphans also had very precarious housing situations, and, no longer living on the land of their families, they worried if they could pay the next month's rent. In addition, they said repeatedly that they struggled to clothe their siblings. And while the government paid school fees for orphans, the orphans often could not afford to pay for school supplies, such as pens, notebooks, uniforms, shoes, socks, soap, and so on. Furthermore, some orphans did not see the merit of going to school, such as this individual: "After the genocide, I felt useless and wanted to do nothing because I knew many people who were highly educated who died like dogs." It was also typical for many orphans to stay out of school for a year or two after the genocide, even if they eventually returned, although some orphans reported restarting school as early as September 1994.

The challenges facing orphans were enormous, and for most, school was not their immediate priority, even long after the genocide ended. Typical statements by orphan heads of households include the following: "I find it difficult to face day-to-day life; to find school materials for my children." "I have no permanent job, and whenever I have a job, I get very little money because of my educational level. The way we live is very difficult." "It is not easy to find a job these days. Money for rent and to find food are my biggest problems." "The difficulties are many, like not getting school materials, money for housing. If we could get one more goat—we have only one—it would be helpful." Nevertheless, orphan heads of household made every effort to care for their children. One twelve-year-old boy said that he was paid a small amount on Sundays to plow the fields of neighbors. Another orphan, who is disabled, said: "I use only one leg to sew, but still I gain the bread for all of us . . . we delight in what we have, even though it is not sufficient."

Not every child-headed household shared this optimism. To the question, "What problems are you facing since the genocide?" a survivor replied: "I have income problems. To get clothes for my children, it is a problem. When I see that I am of no help to them, I become desperate. If any of them fall sick, I have no money to take them to the hospital. I have nothing in my house that I can sell to get money. I didn't dream of becoming a parent in my life, but it happened to be the case. If we had parents, we would have no problems. Actually, I am unable to return to school because I have no one to stay at home with my children or place to leave them. How would they get food? Even if I could get someone to pay my school fees, I could not get school materials. "

Many orphan survivors reported that they had to forego their own education in order to care for their children, taking away their hope and future-oriented thinking. As evident in the previous paragraph, when queried about this they simply asked, who else would feed their siblings if they did not work?

Some of these orphans said they still had the goal of returning to school, but this is doubtful, since after skipping years of school they would be entering primary or secondary school in their late teens or as adults. To the question, "Can you return to school?" a survivor bluntly replied, "No. If I return to school, how can my siblings live?" While sacrificing their education for the good of their younger siblings sounds heroic from a distance, in fact, they felt they had no other choice.

As parents, orphan heads of households also had to deal with the immediate emotional needs of their children. In response to the question, "How did you comfort your siblings?" a survivor said: "I was not so mature, but anyway, I told them to be patient and courageous. They used to spend the whole day crying, but I asked them to be quiet. By God's grace, as days went by, they understood." In response to the same question, another survivor said, "First of all, I told them that we have to thank God that we survived. It was by God's grace only. I told them also that we have to love each other, to help each other so that our beloved parents who passed away will be pleased where they are. That's how we comforted each other."

Orphan heads of household experienced multiple emotional challenges with their children. For example, one survivor said that his oldest brother has mental problems. This child was with their mother when she was killed. He rescued his infant sibling who was on their mother's back, but the child then died. He also witnessed his father being killed. This child was struggling to finish secondary school at the time of the interview, having already failed once.

Another survivor said that one of his siblings is totally disabled and sits at home all day without doing anything. Several of his other children refused to go to school. He does not have any physical problems and said he used to go to the fields to plow in order to get food for the family. When he was interviewed, he said, "As I told you, I am jobless and have no other sources to support them. I just tell them to be courageous and that we are together." Another survivor responded to a question of how she comforts her sister, saying: "I told her that she had to be strong because we had no choice. Hutus killed our parents and I became disabled, but we had to live!"

The emotional burden orphans felt caring for their siblings cannot be overstated. Repeatedly orphans said that they would not be in this plight if they had parents. Perhaps they romanticized the past, but they all said that they had plenty to eat prior to the genocide. Yet despite these material needs, orphans frequently said that what they miss most is that they now have no one to offer them advice and given them guidance. One survivor summed it up succinctly, "Not having parents is a very big problem, because parents are people who you are certain will love you. But now it is hard to find people who can really love you."

When we interacted informally with orphans, we were often surprised that they first and foremost wanted our counsel on issues. Rather than fleeing authority, orphans genuinely wanted guidance on their lives and future plans. They were not asking for handouts; they needed parental counsel in the absence of having anyone to whom they could turn. It is easy to lose sight of the fact that many orphans not only lost parents but oftentimes all living relatives, including grandparents and aunts and uncles; they lacked an "elder" with whom they could talk things over.

On occasion, orphans remembered the counsel of a parent. "My father told me to be a man. Therefore, whatever I do, I do it with that in view." But a more frequent reflection on parents was one that stated a sense of loss. "When I think about them, and when I think that I will never meet them again, I feel very much grieved. I try to be courageous, but there is no peace in my heart." Another survivor said, "When I see other children with their parents, especially their mothers, I feel very grieved and I remember what I passed through."

Courage and patience are words that frequented the interviews with orphan heads of households. For example, one survivor said, "Concerning food, we eat when it is available; otherwise we have to be patient." Another survivor said, "You see, I am studying and my siblings too. This makes our living a problem. At times, some temporary job helps. But when we don't have any, we have no choice but to be patient." This sentiment was echoed in the statement of another survivor: "It is not easy, but once you see that you have no other choice, you just have to be courageous. I, at times, get temporary jobs, but the money I get doesn't last for long." Another orphan head of household rationalized, "When I saw those who had more problems than me, I chose to be courageous."

Other youth who headed households seemed to have lost hope, mired down in worry over the problems of caring for siblings: "At times I think it would be better if I were no more." On the other hand, most orphan heads of household persevere in spite of the obstacles, as stated by this survivor: "Yes, a time came when it was too much. I wanted to study but could not. Our toilet needed repair. Children needed to eat and to study. And there was no money for school fees. So, it was too much. But I never tried to commit suicide because I thought that if I tried to do so, my siblings would go mad, as I had done. I thought it wise to stay, pray, and commit everything to God, because there was no other way."

The one form of assistance for school fees and medical assistance mentioned frequently by orphans was FARG (Fond d' Assistance aux Rescapes du Genocide). Although FARG assists orphans with school fees, and one orphan even said that FARG helped them rebuild their house, FARG does not pay for university tuition or many other expenses. Very few orphans mentioned getting assistance from NGOs, with the exception of occasional references to the Red Cross, ARDA (Adventist Relief and Development), Caritas (Catholic Charities), and the IRC (International Rescue Committee). As previously stated, many of the relief efforts by NGOs immediately after the genocide seemed to be directed to Hutu refugees who were fleeing the killing fields.

Some survivors ended up in orphanages, but they did not have good things to say about them. One survivor said, "Life was bad. We just lived there because we had nowhere else to go." Another survivor described the scene in an orphanage: "When I first came, many of the children were always silent, never talking. Some were always crying, and others were constantly sick. They would pray for us and teach us. That way these [sad] feelings started to decrease and go." Another survivor said that they were actively discouraged from talking with one another about their experiences during the genocide. "We used to talk about the genocide. Our teachers wanted us to forget about it, but we couldn't." Another survivor simply said, "I lived in an orphanage where I was depressed."

WIDOWS

Widows interviewed through the organization AVEGA brought a somewhat different set of issues to the immediate postgenocide period when compared with orphans. Many had been raped. Many were injured. In some ways, their life experience and larger frame of reference created a different perspective. They were faced with cohabiting with Hutus whom they had known for a long time and whose husbands and sons were responsible for the deaths of their children and spouses. It would be inappropriate to say that their suffering was worse than that of orphans, but their feelings and internal thought processes differed. Children had lost their provider and protector; widows had lost their life partners, an extended family network, and the children they had nurtured.

One woman asked, "How can I not be reminded of my husband? The person with whom I lived for twenty years! With whom I had children! First, what I remember about him is that I am alone. While he was alive, we shared everything, all the problems. Now I have to do everything and sometimes it is impossible for me. I had grown children. They were going to finish their studies. They were young men and women. I should have grandchildren now. I should have people to help me." Then she recalled the events of the genocide. "What I remember about them is the conversations we used to have. When the Interahamwe came to kill us, I was close by my daughter Olive. They killed her with machetes while I was holding her hand. It was she who told me to get up, telling me, 'Don't be afraid, Mama, we are going to be in heaven soon.'"

About her husband, she fondly recalled, "He often told me, 'Be gentle with everyone.' When he found a mentally ill person, he helped him as much as he could. He told me also, 'We only die once. We must never harm anyone.'" And about her children she reminisced that when they came home for their vacations from school they used to say, "Mama, give the servants time off so we can do all the housework early and can have time to chat and play. The servants bother us when they are here." She also recalled her paternal uncle who was a priest. "He loved me very much. He often told me, 'My daughter, you have suffered a lot as an orphan, but hatred must be vanquished by love.'" These are the philosophical reflections of an adult.

Widows sought out housing, much of it temporary. However, sometimes they found indisputable evidence of the genocide. One widow was given the home of a former Interahamwe in which to live. "I still have the machetes I found in this house. We found six machetes, two of which had traces of blood on them and four of them had never been used." Another woman said, "We settled in the houses of the Interahamwe who had already left because of the fear of what they had done. They mostly went to Zaire. We found food and water in the houses they had left behind; in the fields there were manioc, beans, bananas. Sometimes we sold these to get money to buy other things—clothes and other things. It was at the beginning of September 1994 that we took up our normal life to cultivate, harvest, and return to our jobs. Some schools started to open. The hospitals were back in service. Little by little we left these houses because the owners returned, and we rented houses in the city." But other survivors faced the prospect of living in the remnants of their destroyed houses, according to one survivor, living like animals.

For many widows, the transition to "normal" life was not easy. They did not have jobs, their house had been destroyed, they had often lost their land and their cows or means of economic survival, and they were grieving over the loss of family members and relatives. For example, one widow said: "The life we had was not good. I remember that we lived in houses in which we found dead people and we were the ones who had to remove their corpses out of these houses. I remember that I never ate meat for a long time because the corpses smelled like meat and blood. We could not easily find food, so sometimes the soldiers would bring things for us, but mostly we ate food that we found in the houses or in the field. Food was very rare; some even died of hunger." Nevertheless, survivors worked together to find a new life. A widow said, "We tried to share the little we had. Those who had more gave them to the poor, clothes, building materials. We loved one another a lot."

Widows also began to deal with the physical effects of rape, particularly HIV. A number of survivors said that on a daily basis they are reminded of being raped because of their struggle to deal with the AIDS virus and its implications. In addition to taking medication, a woman said that AIDS has left her so weak that she can no longer till the soil and therefore has lost her means of livelihood.

Additionally, relationships between survivors and Hutu neighbors were often strained—something we return to at length in the coming chapters on trauma, forgiveness, and reconciliation. Even if a neighbor had not participated directly in the genocide, he was aware of the attempt to exterminate the Tutsis. Some widows said that their neighbors were ashamed of what had occurred and rationalized that they were not the ones who did the killing. One survivor said, "They were shocked to see me. They wanted to know what I was thinking toward them, but I couldn't reveal that. They used to tell me empty words, accusing absent people. Personally, I didn't want to listen to them." Another survivor said, "The people who had killed had fled and those who were still around were afraid and would come and tell us that they didn't take part in the killings of our families, but so and so did, and therefore they had fled."

There did seem to be regret by some Hutu neighbors regarding what had happened, or at least shame. Referring to a Hutu neighbor who refused to hide her during the genocide, a widow said, "He is ashamed of what he did and whenever we meet he tries to show me that he feels sorry for me and once he wanted to give me money, but I refused." Another widow said more generically and ironically about her Hutu neighbors, "They seemed to be ashamed of what they did because they thought that we all were killed." Another widow stated that neighbors were so ashamed "they can't even greet you." But some widows said the mood was not shame, but hostility. "Our neighbors took refuge in Zaire. On their return, they had fear mixed in with hatred for us. They believed we would denounce them and they detested us for that."

One widow said that some of her neighbors were "afraid to see us" and avoided direct contact. When widows asked about the fate of their relatives, Hutu neighbors would either avoid the question or would say, "They were killed by so and so," but would not take direct responsibility for what occurred. One widow summed it up succinctly saying that there was a "kind of hypocrisy" that existed between Tutsis and Hutus after the genocide, with a survivor bluntly stating that Hutus sometimes pretended that nothing had happened. Another survivor said, "We used to smile, though not being happy," when they passed Hutus on the streets or in the market. And one widow put a positive spin on their hypocrisy, saying, "We tried to pretend that there was no problem between us in order to live in peace with others." However, another survivor said, "It was hard for me. For them, it was as if nothing happened. They had no problem. But for me, I didn't understand how a man could kill others without a reason and after that take it as a normal thing. Really, it was hard to me!" With regret, a widow said, "The neighbors never came to give me their condolences. We meet on the street. We say 'hello' and go our way."

One thing that inflamed relationships between survivors and Hutu neighbors is that widows began identifying individuals to the authorities that they had witnessed participating in the genocide. For example, a widow stated: "When they [Hutus] came back from the Zaire, we reported them to the police and they took them to jail." Another survivor said that her neighbors called her "Satan" because she accused individuals who had killed her family. In one case, a widow said that her neighbor preemptively returned some of the goods they had stolen from her house, but she reported them to the police anyway.

As one can imagine, Hutu neighbors did not accept these acts of justice gracefully. One survivor said that her neighbor accused her of unjustly identifying Hutus who were imprisoned. Nevertheless, survivors held their ground in most cases, such as this widow: "We know that they killed our family members and they know that we put their family members in jail." Over time, however, relationships seemed to ease, as stated by one widow: "After coming back from exile we were very angry with them because they were the source of everything, but now the relations are becoming more and more normal."

CONSEQUENCES OF GENOCIDE FOR SURVIVORS

When many of us face a challenge, it is singular in focus. A spouse dies, a child is killed in an accident, we contract a serious disease, our house is destroyed in a natural disaster, we lose a job and are unemployed. For many survivors of the genocide, all of these elements and more confronted them simultaneously. They were homeless and landless, they had lost multiple family members and had witnessed horrific acts, they were physically injured and/or sick, they were hungry and had no source of income. The relationships that knit people together in community were shattered, including connections to churches and other institutions, and an entire generation of elders that could pass on wisdom, know-how, and leadership had been eliminated.

Indeed, while each circumstance was unique, what was common to all survivors was poverty. While survivors were temporarily helped by the RPF and may have been able to live in the houses of Hutus who fled, as well as eat their food and harvest their fields, within a few months they often found themselves with nothing. The economic infrastructure of everyday life had been destroyed. Not only were they traumatized, but many survivors had also lost their land in addition to their homes; widows could not rely on husbands for support; and employment was difficult in a country that had gone through a civil war. Plus, how were children to support themselves without skills? At most they could do temporary jobs related to manual labor. When survivors were interviewed years later, many of them were still acutely suffering from the consequences of poverty.

In a few instances, survivors' homes had been rebuilt or a charitable organization had helped them construct a new one, but in most instances, they had gone from being landowners—where they could grow food and live off the land—to living in rented quarters. Paying rent was a constant struggle. Very few survivors had permanent, well-paying jobs. And it was very common for survivors to say that they only had one meal a day and oftentimes, within a week, they would skip any sort of substantive meal for one or two days. Evidence of minimal caloric intake was evident in the thin arms and legs of survivors, especially orphans.

Regardless of their degree of personal psychological trauma, the immediate daily grind was finding food and shelter. Moreover, survivors explained that their ongoing poverty was a constant reminder of the genocide, of the way their lives and livelihoods had been disrupted. Orphans heading households and widows with children said that they were constantly worrying about what to feed their children that day. Widows sometimes said that they sold items on the street, earning a small return as a vendor. Orphans sometimes did odd jobs, such as carrying bricks for construction projects. But these jobs were intermittent and did not provide a regular income.

Loneliness was another major problem cited by survivors, and especially widows. They were used to having family around them. Prior to the genocide, if they were to lose their spouse through death, they were taken into the extended family network and cared for. Now, the extended family no longer existed. They spent long days and nights alone. Many widows reported crying day after day. Some called out to God, seeking some sort of companionship—as well as deliverance from their problems. For some survivors, adopting children or caring for their own was a form of solace, even if they then had to worry about feeding, sheltering, and providing school materials. In fact, one widow said that as soon as one of her children came of age and left the household, she took in another orphan.

Both widows and orphans complained of a "lack of love" after the genocide, but it typically was with reference to the relationship with neighbors. The spirit of compassion and collegiality that existed among people prior to the genocide was gone. Frequently survivors said that there was a lack of trust between people, which is an essential ingredient for any well-functioning community. Some survivors said they feared that killing would break out again. Ironically, survivors said that their Hutu neighbors were frequently angrier at them than were the neighbors who had been violated. Over time, some of these feelings abated, but nevertheless it is fair to say that genocide does not only involve loss of life, it also destroys compassion toward other people, which is the basis for human community. Community requires people to feel empathy for others, loving others as one would wish to be loved.

As stated, widows felt the loss of husbands who could hear their problems, sympathize, and help with the stresses and challenges of raising children and managing a household. Child-headed households experienced the same absence—the guidance and empathy of parents. In addition, many widows worried about the future of their surviving children, especially since some of our interviewees were disabled and many had AIDS and were not yet taking antiretroviral drugs when they were interviewed. They feared that they would die and then who would care for their children?

And then as time passed, more and more widows, as well as orphans heading households, were concerned about the mental status of their children. For example, one widow said that her child had been thrown in a latrine and had been there for a long time; he never recovered emotionally from this incident. And we vividly remember sitting in the home of an orphan whose sister had recently broken out all the windows during a psychotic episode. We could see the worried look on her face as we sat across from each other. The fact that this young woman was nicely dressed and was attending school did not cover over the deep anxiety that she felt internally, wondering how she was going to deal with a traumatized sister.

A widow we interviewed turned from thinking about her own problems to expressing concern about female orphans that she knew. She said that too many young women were turning to prostitution as a way to have a little spending money. She said that some orphan girls were getting AIDS from these encounters as well as giving birth to children. But she also understood their motives. They had no one to care for them, to teach them responsible behavior, nor did they have a source of income to buy the things that help to give girls pride and dignity. One young woman said, "Life was difficult. I would think and hate myself. I thought of being a prostitute. I thought of what to do with my children." And then crying, she said, "But God created a way for me and I got a job as a road sweeper." Another woman recalled her own lifestyle prior to coming to Solace Ministries. She was working in a bar and said that she would sell her body, pray, and then go back to work. It is for this reason that some NGOs, such as Solace Ministries, have an explicit commitment to buy girls clothes, lotions, and toiletries that honor their bodies.

Both orphans and widows talked about their disabilities. Many survivors were severely beaten, and some have amputated limbs that make it difficult, if not impossible, to do manual labor. Survivors also complained about having severe headaches and that it is nearly impossible to carry things on their head, which is a common practice in Rwanda. Teamed with various manifestations of trauma, it is not surprising that employment is a challenge for many survivors. They had lost the infrastructure of support that assists people to meet challenges, such as mentoring by parents, family lands to till, and connections that lead to job opportunities. Nevertheless, we found substantial numbers of orphans wanting to go to university, and many who were not able to finish secondary school stated this fact with regret.

What pervaded many of the early testimonies by survivors, both orphans and widows, was a spirit of resignation and sadness. One orphan heading a household said that it makes her sad when her children ask her for something and she can't provide it, since she is barely able to feed and shelter them. Another orphan, who is caring for her siblings but also is attending university, said that she is pained by the fact that she cannot rent a computer to type her papers and final dissertation. In spite of her will power to study, she feels handicapped by her poverty compared to her fellow students who were not victims of the genocide.

Nevertheless, survivors emphasized in interviews the need to have dignity. Several survivors said how they hate to beg, even though that is sometimes the only way that they can get food. At meetings with survivors, we were always impressed with how clean their clothes were, even if it was often their only outfit. They carried themselves with dignity. On the other hand, there was oftentimes a profound sadness in their expressions. Behind the polite verbal exchanges, there was grief waiting to spill out, held in check by the need to be proper, especially in a public place.

Finally, the social structures at every level, from schools to churches to the courts and other government institutions, had to be rebuilt. In the interim, organizations such as AOCM, AVEGA, and Solace emerged to meet not only the physical and emotional needs of survivors but also to help survivors begin to rebuild social relationships, trust, and meaning. We will have more to say about this in subsequent chapters.

CONCLUDING REFLECTIONS

As we address the issue of trauma and healing in the next chapters, it is important to contextualize trauma as being not simply a psychological state of being. For survivors of the Tutsi genocide, trauma is enveloped in poverty, physical disabilities, illness, and sometimes hostility by neighbors. Hence, any attempt to address trauma within a narrow paradigm of psychological intervention is not adequate. Indeed, it may not even be the first step in addressing the needs of survivors. The struggle for daily survival and sustenance was all consuming; it left survivors depleted and drained without resources or time to work on psychological healing. For people to heal, they first need to eat, they need to have shelter, they need to have a degree of physical well-being and security before they can move forward. As one orphan put it, "When you have nowhere to live or have no food to give your children, how can you forget? Grief follows you everywhere. We try to forget, but we can't."

The following statement by a widow reveals the realism with which some survivors confronted their circumstances. Reflecting on the fact that her husband was killed, she said: "You know yourself [motioning to the interviewer who was also a widow] that it is very difficult to live without your partner, with whom you shared everything. It's an insoluble problem. Especially since I am handicapped. I don't have an arm and I am responsible for my family that remains, and I no longer have anything. This confirms for me how important and crucial a role a partner plays. But since I am not the only one who endures this, I have resigned myself to it. There are other widows, and that comforts me. . . . What I have noticed is that we have become father and mother at the same time. I hope we can overcome it. We do what is possible and leave the impossible because you can waste your time over the impossible. You can even become traumatized. We must watch out for this and calm ourselves."

NGOs like those noted above can play an important role in mediating the loneliness and suffering of survivors, although this intervention may be perceived as temporary. For example, a widow said, "It's fortunate that when I am at AVEGA I forget all my sadness, but when I return home the sorrow comes back as I think of my family and everything that has happened to me." When asked how she deals with the children and orphans she supports, she immediately cited the problem of feeding and educating them, and then said, "When children lose their loved ones, they are troubled; they compare themselves with others and they are not happy because I am incapable of satisfying them." Another widow reflected on her personal situation: "The consequence of poverty is that it contributes to loneliness, because if one is well, he can come out of loneliness, but when one is poor and has nothing to eat, he begins to have unhealthy thoughts, and that's bad."

Nevertheless, there were individuals who had a remarkable ability to confront the challenges survivors experienced, such as this widow: "After realizing that I was going to be a widow the rest of my life, I tried to strengthen myself. I compared myself with other widows who were very young, at least thirty years younger, who didn't have a single child, and I thanked God. I saw how strong they were and wondered how they could be. I could cry in front of them because they had suffered more than I. Later, I tried to comfort them, always being at their side, to give them advice as an older person. I told them that they were still young, that they could still remarry. I promised to be faithful to them and they promised me the same."

SUMMING UP PART I

In the first half of this book, especially chapters 3 and 4, we felt it important to take the reader through the extreme trauma and details of the period of killing and survival. Only by absorbing those details can the reader achieve a baseline understanding of survivors' experience of genocide. What the interviews taught us, however, is that looking at those three months of killing and survival—the official period of "genocide"—is not enough. In order to grasp the lived experience of genocide's total destruction—the social, emotional, communal, material, and existential challenges—one must examine the immediate aftermath of the genocide as well.

It is our hope that the first half of this book has given readers a broader understanding of genocide, as orphans and widows came out of hiding, reunited, and searched to find a way to live. The layers of immediate post-genocide suffering are multiple and deeply revealing: the loss of studies, careers, homes, land, and thereby the means of production and sustenance; the loss of relationships, social roles, community, and trust; the loss of physical and mental health, dignity and confidence, and the ability to think hopefully into the future; and the loss of basic institutions and social networks for the sharing of social and cultural capital.

In the next half of the book, we continue our exploration of the aftermath of genocide, now stepping into the psychological, spiritual, moral, and existential realms. In what follows, we focus on our interviewees' experiences of trauma, healing, forgiveness, justice, and reconciliation—all of which are ongoing processes that are not always linear and may never be fully complete.

PART II

Postgenocide Experiences

CHAPTER 6

Trauma as Moral Rupture

We believe that the root of the various symptoms of survivor trauma is a collapse of the meaning structures that make sense out of life, which leaves survivors hopeless, untrusting, confused, and disoriented. For genocide survivors, this social and moral rupture that began prior to the genocide in response to propaganda and exclusionary policies was intensified during the one hundred days of killing and was exacerbated with the collapse of social institutions and political structures in the immediate postgenocide period. Repeatedly, survivors told us that they could not believe that people they knew and trusted would not assist them or would even participate in the killing itself. These were Hutus that they had known as neighbors, whose weddings they had attended, and whose offspring were their godchildren. The most basic element of our common humanity, trust, had completely broken down and with it the moral order that gives structure to life.

For some, this moral order was symbolized in God. Where was he? Why didn't he intervene? The moral rupture was further dramatized when people were killed in churches and, in some cases, when clergy were complicit or actually participated in the killing—ideologically through propaganda or by being bystanders to what was occurring. After the genocide ended, many people had difficulty returning to their church. Religion had lost its claim on their conscience. It was no longer an institution that represented hope, justice, fairness, and a divinely inspired moral order. Genocide represented a spiritual crisis of meaning, especially in a country where more than 95 percent of the population was Christian.

Trust is one of the earliest stages of personal and social development. Infants learn to trust when they cry and their mother nurses them, when they fuss and their diaper is changed, when parents and caregivers create a nurturing environment that is predictable. Genocide, car accidents that kill and maim, loved ones who die early from disease, these are senseless acts. People rightly ask: Why? Why me? And why was no one—not government, religious institutions, neighbors, community, parent, or spouse—able to protect me?

Trauma for genocide survivors exists at two levels. One is personal and psychological; the other is social and political. At the heart of both of these levels is the idea of moral disruption. Standards of civility have been violated and, experientially, the world is no longer trustworthy. Therefore, the trauma of genocide requires healing at both an individual and a social-political level.[1]

According to the French sociologist Émile Durkheim—writing at the beginning of the last century—every society is bound together by shared values that must be renewed on a regular basis, and when this does not occur, anomie (normlessness) sets in, accompanied by rising rates of suicide and violence.[2] Although an atheist, he believed that this was one of the functions of religious ritual, to celebrate the core values of society. For Durkheim, God is not some metaphysical being; God is the collective representation of the moral values of the group. Hence, it is not surprising that during the genocide, people were losing their faith. The social order was collapsing and with it the symbol of social solidarity, God.

In this chapter, we tackle the rupture of the social order on an individual level, examining the symptoms of trauma that we see as the manifestation of a broken social order. In subsequent chapters, we view healing of trauma as a social process of reintegration into society—a society in which one is loved, cared for, and where one finds purpose and identity in contributing to the social good. In a moral rupture as severe as Rwanda in 1994, the rebuilding process requires strong, even sometimes authoritarian, action on the part of the architects of the new order, although in time one would hope that the society would evolve politically to be inclusive of political dissent.

SURVIVOR TRAUMA

In the early years of our research we were focused primarily on understanding what happened during the hundred days of the genocide and the immediate aftermath as survivors tried to reassemble their lives. Then, in 2006 we had an experience in a town outside of Stockholm that refocused our attention. We had nominated the orphan association AOCM for "The World's Children's Prize for the Rights of the Child," and, after a careful vetting process, we were informed that AOCM was one of the prizewinners, which meant that five members of the group were chosen to travel to Sweden from Rwanda, which was quite a journey that required a chaperone and purchase of warm clothes. We were also invited to accompany the group and gladly accepted, arriving a few days in advance of the actual ceremony when Her Majesty Queen Silvia would honor AOCM and several other prizewinners.[3]

Along with the president of AOCM and the founder of the organization, we took the group of survivors to an ice cream parlor to celebrate prior to the awards ceremony, including a young orphan who was the only one in her family to survive. As we were enjoying our cones, suddenly this young girl ran out the door and we found her standing on the sidewalk some distance away, with her head against the wall of a building. She was crying inconsolably. We were unsure why such a pleasant moment had turned to tears.

Finally, we persuaded her to come back to the hotel where we were staying. After an hour or more of talking, we started joking with her and eventually she smiled and regained her composure. She later explained that she was watching mothers enter the ice cream parlor with babies in strollers and young children in tow. Even though she was orphaned at two years of age, she had a flashback memory of her own mother and was faced with the reality of what it meant to be an orphan, completely alone, without any living relatives.

From that moment forward, we started paying much more attention to facial expressions, body language, and overall affect during our interviews and interactions. Especially in our videotaped interviews with Solace, we asked survivors to tell us about trauma they had experienced. The word "trauma" needed no explanation. Every survivor knew individuals who were suffering the emotional consequences of the genocide, and in some cases, they were very forthcoming about their own internal struggles.

DEFINING PTSD

It is useful, however, to look briefly at the technical definition of posttraumatic stress disorder (PTSD) before turning to some examples from our interviews. According to the Diagnostic and Statistical Manual of Mental Disorders (DSM-5), PTSD typically has varying degrees of the following symptoms, and to qualify as PTSD a minimum number of symptoms are required in each category.[4]

First, the individual who has experienced a traumatic event, such as the death of a family member or friend, sexual violation such as a rape, being a first responder to an accident or natural disaster, as well as having experienced violence in the military, may have various *intrusion symptoms*. Most common are distressing memories of the traumatic event, troubling dreams, flashbacks where one reexperiences the trauma, and physiological reactions to cues that remind one of the events.

Second, the traumatized individual will practice persistent *avoidance* of any cues or stimuli that remind them of the event, such as people, places, conversations, objects, or situations, so as to avoid having distressing feelings related to the event. In the case of genocide survivors, this might include avoidance of memorials, commemorations, and even avoiding conversation about the genocide with fellow survivors.

Third, there will be *negative alterations in cognition and mood* associated with the event, including inability to remember important aspects of what happened; negative beliefs or expectations about oneself (e.g., "I am bad," "No one can be trusted," "The world is completely dangerous."); blaming oneself for what happened; persistent negative emotions (e.g., fear, horror, anger, guilt, or shame); a diminished interest in participating in social activities; feelings of detachment or estrangement from others; and a persistent inability to experience positive emotions such as happiness, satisfaction, or loving feelings.

And, fourth, alterations in arousal and reactivity, marked by irritable behavior and angry outbursts, reckless or self-destructive behavior, hypervigilance, exaggerated startle response, problems with concentration, and sleep disturbances such as insomnia. These symptoms are often labeled as *hyperarousal*.

Whether one is classified as having PTSD depends on the number of these symptoms, whether they have lasted longer than one month, whether they are experienced as personally distressing, and/or are impairing one's functioning at work and in social relationships.[5]

Based on our interpretation of genocide-related trauma as social rupture, we see the various symptoms of PTSD as attacks on the survivor's attempt to regain a sense of moral order in his/her life. For example, intrusion symptoms, such as flashbacks, represent the chaos of the genocide and, as such, challenge the sanity that one is attempting to achieve. Avoidance of triggering cues related to the genocide can be understood as an attempt to keep a lid on memories that disrupt the fledgling moral equilibrium that one is seeking to achieve. Negative self-perceptions, including feeling that one is unlovable and unworthy, are remnants from the traumatizing period when one was violated, humiliated, and dehumanized. And the symptoms of hyperarousal are a way to guard against imagined threats to one's personhood.

During the healing process from PTSD, creating a safe, stable, moral order is the key to dealing with PTSD symptoms. The individual needs to develop a new sense of meaning and purpose, but first, survivors need to articulate the hurt, pain, and violence that they experienced. As we will convey in the next chapter, healing is best done within a community of loving, caring people where one can share unthinkable memories, and over time develop a personal narrative of life's meaning that incorporates the disruption of the trauma without it overwhelming all other aspects of one's being. As humans, we are fundamentally meaning-seeking beings, and the impact of genocide is not only the loss of life or the amputation of a limb, it is the fact that the structures of our taken-for-granted world are disrupted, our moral world has been ruptured. Identity is challenged as we no longer have social roles as mother, wife, teacher, bread earner. In the postgenocide experience, one may not be able to regain these old identities, but one must nevertheless build a new sense of purpose and meaning. And one cannot do this as an island unto oneself. One needs a stable moral, political, and social order in which to give birth to a new sense of personal meaning.

It is after some deliberation that we titled this book *Becoming Human Again*. Repeatedly, survivors told us that during the genocide they felt like they had become inhuman. Their rights as human beings had been violated. Their moral world of neighborly reciprocity had collapsed. Their sense of agency, identity, personhood was diminished. This was the context in which survivors talked about the struggle to become human again as they dealt with trauma symptoms in the process of seeking a sense of life's meaning in the present.

SURVEYS OF TRAUMA

Nearly a quarter century after the genocide, the Rwandan government did a mental health survey, comparing genocide survivors with the general population.[6] The survey found that 28 percent of the survivor population had PTSD symptoms compared to less than 4 percent of the general population. PTSD rates were much higher among the illiterate and primary-school-educated population compared with survivors who had completed university, although 18 percent of college educated survivors were classified with PTSD. Of those who fit the PTSD classification, two-thirds had had a major depressive episode. In general, survivors exhibited higher rates of psychological distress on nearly every measure compared to the general population, with education and secure employment being the major mitigating factors.

In our interviews with survivors, as well as daily interaction with survivors over a number of years, we have observed all of the various expressions of PTSD. Several years ago, we worked with a psychologist, Beth Meyerowitz at USC, and one of her graduate students, Lauren Ng, to assess the psychological symptoms that survivors were experiencing more than a decade after the genocide. Surveys were administered to orphans who had been members of AOCM as well as survivors associated with Solace Ministries. Five different areas of adjustment were assessed: posttraumatic stress reactions, emotional distress and physical symptoms, social support, coping strategies, and overall quality of life. The results of this research are described in appendix II, including references to published articles and the way to contact the researchers for more specific information on the measurement instruments.[7]

Survivors associated with AOCM and Solace scored well above the threshold for diagnosis of PTSD. They exhibited high levels of distress, with 76 percent reporting headaches in the last two months, 68 percent having difficulty falling or staying asleep, and 59 percent reported stomachaches. Other indicators of emotional distress included feeling sad and depressed (88 percent), feeling anxious and nervous (74 percent), being scared (73 percent), having nightmares (69 percent), feeling like crying (68 percent), and feeling lonely (57 percent). Further details regarding this research are available in the appendix, which we highly recommend that readers view as a supplement to the qualitative focus of this chapter and the next one on healing.

DISENGAGEMENT AND TURNING INWARD

In our interviews, survivors stated that they often felt numb; individuals would be talking around them, and while they could hear them, they were withdrawn, mute, and did not respond. They were in their own internal world of revolving thoughts about the genocide, or sometimes their minds were completely vacant. People would speak to them and they would not respond. For example, one survivor described how she would be sitting by the fire cooking for her children. The food would be burning on the stove and she would not even notice it. Her children would say, "Mum is sick and has a headache." But from her perspective, it was more than a headache; her mind was completely disengaged from what she was doing.

Another survivor said, "I would look at you and not realize I was looking at you. I would look like someone who has lost her mind. I would immediately fall sick with a high body temperature, feel a headache, and start crying." In social settings, survivors sometimes appeared to be absent. Their minds were elsewhere. Momentarily they had lost connection with ongoing reality, the reality of being engaged in a task or mentally present with other people.

We sometimes observed this behavior during an interview. Survivors would be describing some aspect of their genocide experience and then they would disengage from the conversation. We would then need to spend a few minutes focusing their attention back on the interview. This pattern was also present in everyday interaction, especially when we were first going to Rwanda. Individuals would glaze over in the middle of a conversation. It was clear that their attention was elsewhere.

Sometimes their trauma expressed itself in physical symptoms and bizarre actions. A survivor said, "Sometimes I lose my mind. I feel lost and don't know where I am. I sit down and fall over." Another survivor said that she would go to the market and collapse. Another survivor said, "I used to fall down like an epileptic." Other survivors said that they did things they never would have done in their right mind, such as defecating in public, stripping off their clothes and running naked in the streets.

Especially during periods of national commemoration, survivors said that they would physically withdraw from other people, sometimes for days. They would lock themselves in a room, sometimes crying hysterically and other times simply sit alone, unable to be with people. Social interaction demanded too much focus.

One mother said that during these episodes she ignored feeding her children and was so absent that her neighbors thought she must have a part-time job in another town. Instead, she was in her house sleeping in a near coma-like state. Another survivor said that she would isolate herself in her house, not for a few days, but for a full week. During this time, she would feel like someone had stomped on her chest; she felt completely deflated.

During these periods of isolation and depression, survivors said that they became completely self-absorbed. "Nothing interests me. I even want to give up work. I withdraw into myself with my own thoughts." Several survivors said that they hate themselves at these times and they also hate everyone else. In fact, one survivor said that at these times she doesn't feel anything at all; she is numb, without emotions. Another survivor said, "I felt like a piece of wood," and as if she were not even a person.

Complete withdrawal, alternating with screaming and crying, was commonly reported, such as in these examples: "I sit in front of my house. I feel like the next person approaching is going to kill me. So I enter the house and lock up, but even then I sit down very scared and feel like I am going crazy . . . [then] when someone talks to me, I start crying." "I would go to my room, lock the door, and cover myself up." "I used to lock myself in the house and scream." "I would go somewhere and lock the door and if I am lucky I sleep and wake up when I am normal." "I lived with trauma. It manifests itself in several ways. I sometimes fall into deep silence. At other times, I talk nonstop or cry. Other times I become completely mute and can't talk; I hear you speak, but I can't answer."

TRAUMATIC MEMORIES

Flashbacks are typically triggered by events or cues that remind one of a past trauma. For example, one survivor stated that she saw a man with a yellow shirt that had a tennis racket on it. She immediately felt traumatized, because this is how the man was dressed who stabbed her during the genocide. Another survivor said that she saw someone coming to cut the grass with a machete, and she started shouting, "We are finished," and the people around her had to hold her until she calmed down.

Sometimes there are specific associations, such as smells or taste, that triggered memories of the genocide. For example, a survivor stated: "Once my mother brought me sauce she had made from meat bones. I just started screaming, saying she was giving me human flesh." Another survivor said that the mere sight of prisoners in their pink uniforms triggers a negative emotional response. And even attending funerals of friends who died of natural causes, sometimes evokes powerful memories of the genocide. For example, a survivor said that after a funeral, "That night the genocide came back to me as a video film. Then I started weeping."

We witnessed a dramatic example of a flashback while interviewing a widow. We were sitting in a nicely furnished room in the Solace guesthouse when the rain that had been gently falling outside turned into a downpour.

All of a sudden, our interviewee froze. It was during a similar downpour of rain that she had been raped during the genocide. We paused during the interview until she was able to focus once again, and before we proceeded she told us why the rain had triggered her response.

At both the tenth and twentieth commemorations of the genocide we witnessed very emotional responses by members of a large audience in the football stadium in Kigali. Intermittently during the ceremony, people would start shrieking, shaking, and would be carried out by attendants to ambulances waiting near the stadium. During these ceremonies, there were testimonies given by survivors, and at the twentieth anniversary there was an actual reenactment of the genocide. It is little wonder that survivors in attendance relived their own experiences during the genocide.

In some ways, these examples are more dramatic than what happens on a day-to-day basis for many traumatized survivors. Memories from the genocide simply surface randomly, without any particular trigger. Intrusive thoughts contribute to their inability to focus on what is important in the moment. As a result, traumatized children and adults find it difficult to concentrate on their studies; they are "somewhere else," reexperiencing an unassimilated event from their past.

Traumatized survivors are also plagued by nightmares in which events are replayed, sometimes in literal ways and other times in dreams that are rich in terrifying symbolism. Many survivors said that they had difficulty sleeping and, when they did sleep, they were wracked by nightmares. They would startle awake, dreaming that they were being chased or cut. They would dream about children being thrown in latrines after they were killed, as well as other various atrocities they had witnessed. A survivor said, "I would have nightmares of the people who raped me coming back to do it again." Other survivors described nightmares in which they were cut or beaten with machetes. One survivor said that her head contains a videocassette of what happened during the genocide and it is frequently turned on when she falls asleep.

Sometimes survivors reported having dreams that were mixed with both negative and positive elements. For example, a widow said, "I have nightmares all the time. At other times, I dream that my husband and I are exchanging ideas to improve our family and other needs." And an orphan said, "I dream of my father milking cows . . . then when I wake up I find myself alone in the house." Similarly, an orphan said, "At times I dream of my parents telling me to be courageous. I think it is real but when I open my eyes I don't find them."

Clearly, most of the times these dreams are more disturbing than comforting, such as for this orphan who said: "I dream of being with my father and when I wake up I look for him and can't find him. This drives me crazy. When I go to the doctor, they refer me to counseling."

Other survivors said that it is not only dreams that disturb them. When night comes, a survivor said that she becomes preoccupied with the terrible ways in which her children were killed, bashed in the head so that their brains were extruding, and then dumped in a latrine. Other survivors said that they become preoccupied at night with their future life prospects. A survivor said that she complains in the middle of the night to God, questioning why she is alive. During these periods of insomnia, she said, "I don't even know if I am a human being."

People cope with these intrusive thoughts in a variety of ways. Several survivors said that they can sleep only if they drink and become intoxicated. A young widow said that she used to sleep with different men because they would treat her to alcohol and then she could sleep. And an orphan who was supporting several of his younger siblings said that he would drink to lessen the pressure he felt to feed and support his brothers and sisters.

RAGE AND AGGRESSION

According to psychiatrist Bessel van der Kolk, during traumatic events the physiological system of individuals go on "high alert," pumping extreme amounts of the stress hormones, adrenaline and cortisol, into their system.[8] This is a normal response when we confront danger, preparing our bodies to fight off attack, whether physical or verbal. For the "normal" person, when the danger subsides, their bodies return to a baseline of normal functioning. However, for traumatized people, their baseline remains elevated, making it difficult for them to relax.

As reported in a previous chapter, we remember visiting a young college student who was caring for her younger siblings. The previous day, her sister had broken out most of the windows in their house. This orphan did not know how to handle the sister's rage and, furthermore, it was distracting her from her studies. It was very painful listening to this neatly dressed young woman trying to manage a household when one of the members was out of control. She had experienced the trauma of losing her parents and now she was dealing with a traumatized sibling.

Survivors sometimes described their trauma and that of fellow survivors as a form of "madness." One moment they would be enraged and a short time later they would be completely withdrawn. Years after the genocide, they were still poised in a "fight or flight" posture, unable to relax. Their body chemistry would not allow them this luxury. Survivors routinely complained of headaches, high blood pressure, and ulcers. One treatment for PTSD is to medicate traumatized people as a way to deal with their symptoms and enable them to participate in psychotherapy. But psychiatrists such as Van der Kolk say that drugs are not the answer. They simply mask the symptoms.[9] Other approaches to dealing with hyperarousal are meditation, yoga, massage, dance, drumming, and neurofeedback. The goal is to calm the state of hyperarousal, assisting the individual to return to a normal base point. So long as one is in an elevated state, it is difficult to take in new information about the world or to engage it in creative, playful, and constructive ways.

THE ROLE OF CONTEXT

Although survivors may experience relief from their trauma, healing is not linear, it is never complete, and it is affected by the present-day context of survivors. In short, trauma and PTSD do not exist in a vacuum. The social and political reality that survivors face, the degree of poverty or illness they experience—these things interact with their original trauma, inflaming or helping to quell complex emotions in the present moment.

For example, most of our interviewees live with anger toward the killers, even those who have forgiven the perpetrators at some level. Many survivors said that they feel most angry when they visit their home areas and see Hutus prospering, including the families of the killers. Sometimes survivors meet perpetrators who were never imprisoned and roam freely; these encounters also evoke anger and resentment, especially if survivors directly witnessed their crimes. In extreme cases, survivors stated their desire to revenge perpetrators by attacking or killing them.

However, most survivors feel powerless to do anything, as illustrated by this survivor: "When I see those who killed our people, I think to kill them too, but I can't do that." Other survivors echoed the same feeling. They feel anger and sorrow, but they have no recourse but to live with the killers or else move away to an area where they are not constantly confronting perpetrators. One survivor articulated his internal struggle as follows: "When those feelings come, and I get troubled and I feel hatred coming in me, I keep quiet. I die from inside. I try to tell God, please forgive me and give me power to be patient."

Survivors said that the political and practical reality teaches them that they must be civil in their interactions with Hutus they encounter, restraining their real emotions. One survivor said that this means they have "insincere" relations with killers and their family members, which does little to deal with their nighttime terror. For example, one survivor attributed his constant insomnia as well as stomach problems to his anger. At night, he lies awake thinking about the injustice of the genocide. When he does sleep, he dreams of being chased and cut by machetes. His anger festers in the quiet of the night.

In fact, the practical need to keep peace and to coexist daily with people responsible for killing family members was reiterated by many of our interviewees. It is a unique form of trauma in and of itself—one that is replayed in almost every social interaction with Hutus. And while protecting the peace is of the utmost importance, survivors' struggles with this burden raise questions about the psychological harm, both individual and collective, that results from the suppressed anger and inauthenticity of such relationships over the long run. On the other hand, it may also be the case that a new social contract is formed in the minor hellos and greetings that occur between survivors and perpetrators—although this takes time.

Politically, the government instituted the *gacaca* courts that gave survivors an opportunity to testify against their perpetrators, although as we will see in a future chapter, this judicial process has been met with mixed results. More mundane and incremental means of dealing with the genocide are more typical. For example, survivors indicated that religious practices, such as prayer, have provided a means for them to deal with their anger and desire for revenge. Also, some survivors said that their anger decreased as their material circumstances got better, once they were able to get a job or otherwise feel that they were living a productive life.

FEAR AND SADNESS

In addition to the symptoms of PTSD described above, the survivors of genocide continue to struggle daily with a complex layering of emotions such as anger, fear, and sadness. Even as the more extreme forms of intrusion and constriction become less common or acute, difficult emotions remain just under the surface and may take a lifetime to work through. A number of survivors indicate that they carry fear around with them, just under the surface of their conscious interactions. They are fearful that the genocide might be repeated, which is one reason that they work to suppress their feelings of anger. Some survivors are anxious that the killers now living in the Congo could reenter Rwanda to finish what they had started in 1994; others feared reprisal if they testified against killers in court.

Fortunately, fear of another genocide has lessened over time, especially given the current stability of the government and the strong military presence of Rwanda on the border with the Congo. Nevertheless, the potential of another genocide may still exist at a residual level in the minds of survivors, especially given the minority status of Tutsis who are only about 15 percent of the population.

In addition to inflaming emotions of anger and fear, the consequence of feeling powerless is that many survivors at one time or another turn their emotions inward, feeling guilty for having survived and having not intervened in more strategic ways to save their loved ones. They often show little awareness of the larger political context that turned Hutus against Tutsis, and instead focus on the microcosm of their own circumstances during the genocide.

Some survivors we saw on repeated occasions were perpetually sad and withdrawn. It was as if grief had overtaken them. Sometimes it was possible to evoke a smile from them, but then they would relapse into a more primary emotion, a sort of expressionless gaze. The fight had been taken out of them, along with hope in their future. It was as if they were carrying a hundred-pound sack of burdens on their back, and, indeed, they were. They were worried about housing for the month, food for the day, disabilities, and for those orphans and widows taking care of children, there was the constant concern about their welfare. One survivor said, "I get sad . . . but never angry." While this might seem morally praiseworthy, the inability to feel the full range of emotions may be problematic. And from our interviewees' descriptions, this sadness is often correlated with survivors' poor material circumstances.

Sadness was particularly prevalent in orphans. For example, one orphan said, "When I see other children with their parents, especially their mothers, I really grieve." Repeatedly, orphans said that they miss the nurturing care of parents, even in simple things like being able to buy shoes or receive a gift on a special occasion. Another orphan said that she feels the loss of parents very acutely when teachers tell students to "bring your parents" to an event at school, and yet she has no one to be there with her. Another orphan said, "I feel the problem of not having parents, especially when I make a mistake and there is no one to correct or punish me."

In one poignant example, during a visit from several outsiders to Rwanda, a teenage orphan talked through the multiple problems she faced in caring for her younger siblings, especially the struggle to feed and clothe them. When they asked how they could help her, instead of asking for money or material aid, she simply said, "I need advice from adults. Can you give me some advice?" Similarly, another orphan said that he deeply misses the presence of parents who might help him strategize on how to solve various problems. In short, orphans miss moral boundaries—as well as the social support and wisdom— that parents provide.

Orphans also feel the material and psychological burden of being surrogate parents to their siblings. This was poignantly articulated by an orphan who said, "I look after my siblings when I need to be looked after myself." As discussed in previous chapters, sometimes there were child-headed households where the senior member had not even reached puberty. These households were headed by children who had experienced scenes that defied all boundaries of civilized humanity. Could they be expected to be exemplary role models to their younger siblings?

As we have seen, the problems of orphans are exacerbated when they were raped. For example, a girl who was sexually assaulted during the genocide said, "I hate people and don't feel loved by anyone." And survivors who contracted AIDS during the genocide carry a unique burden. Not only were they raped, but as indicated previously, these survivors also have the daily struggle of dealing with the symptoms of the disease.

During the early period of our interviewing, many women were very sick and were dying of AIDS. Recently, most victims are on antiretroviral drugs (ARVs) that they take daily, and some survivors have made remarkable recoveries. Nevertheless, they must make certain that they have an adequate diet, which is not always easy. One widow said bluntly, "You can't take the drugs when you have nothing to eat." And they are sometimes plagued with sores in their mouth and other symptoms of the medications.

Reflecting on her hopelessness prior to ARVs, a survivor said: "All I wait for is my day. I know neither the day nor hour." Another survivor said, "A widow who has nothing and is always unhealthy and ill, how can she not be discouraged?" On the other hand, we interviewed a woman whose two children were HIV positive. She lived in a house that Solace Ministries was helping her rent. Solace had given her a cow that provided milk for the children, and she was able to sell the remaining milk that they didn't drink. She had an optimistic spirit and the children were neatly dressed and sat next to her as she explained their regimen of medications. As her material circumstances improved, she was better able to move through her sorrow and envision a future for her family.

CRYING AND LONELINESS

Crying was previously mentioned, but it was cited so often by interviewees that it merits further discussion. Crying was continuously cited as a coping mechanism, especially after the genocide ended. Survivors would isolate themselves in a room and weep, sometimes for hours. One young man said that at night his bed would be wet with tears, "as if a bucket filled with water was poured there." Another orphan said that he would cry with his sisters, "because I was powerless to change anything, so we would all cry together." In extreme cases, survivors might cry for several days, isolating themselves from others. But more frequently, a survivor would feel overwhelmed with his or her circumstances, as well as grief over the loss of loved ones, and would cry alone for a few hours and then feel better.

At one level, crying seemed to have a beneficial effect for survivors. It was a positive step beyond the numb state of not being able to feel anything. Several survivors said that when they first tried to cry, there were no tears. Only dry sobbing. But in time the tears began to flow, especially as they could articulate to others what they had experienced.

Regarding the benefits of crying, one survivor said, "When I cry, my heart feels released." Another survivor said, "When I cry, everything goes away." A different survivor said that she used to run away and isolate herself, but now she can cry at home, which in her view was a positive step. Another survivor said, "When you cry you are set free," and then followed this statement by saying, "I was only able to accept what happened after crying."

Mama Lambert, described further in the next chapter, said that, initially, survivors would gather at Solace Ministries and cry together, sharing their burdens with one another. She said, "Through crying, comfort is found." Even today, she says that one of her gifts in comforting people is to cry with them when they first visit her office at Solace. These tears let survivors know that she understands their pain, and it may also be a way for Mama Lambert to continue her own healing process.

FACING REALITY, FACING THE FUTURE

One thing that impressed us in our interviews is that, despite their high levels of trauma, many survivors were exerting their will power to not be victims, to make the best of their circumstances. For example, one survivor said resolutely: "All these problems are there but I try not to make them a big deal. I try to adjust my attitude so as to not be angry. As for anxiety, we have no one to tell our problems; therefore, we try to be patient. Nevertheless, during the night I dream about all I have been through in the genocide." One can frame this statement as denial or one can see it as the attempt to face reality and move forward despite one's circumstances.

Some of the proactive actions of survivors are relatively small. For example, a widow decided to act on her isolation: "I told myself that I must not feel lonely, live in endless solitude, because it will have negative consequences for me. So, I started to sell charcoal. It helps me live. I make 100 Rwandan francs per day and I buy food." Other times, the resolution has more to do with attitude than behavioral actions, although oftentimes these statements are mixed with a degree of realism: "I try to be courageous and cry only in my heart." Or, "I try to be courageous, but there is no peace in my heart." And other times a degree of future optimism is projected, even if things are not currently particularly positive, such as in this statement: "There will be a day when things will change." Or, "I have all these problems, but I try to come out from them."

Prayer is a nearly universal resource that survivors use to cope with their problems—one that is explored in depth in the next chapter. In some ways, it has a dual function. When survivors are alone without anyone to talk to, they pray to God whom they believe to be personal, real, and all-powerful. Emphasizing the role of prayer, a survivor said, "Knowing how to pray was the only thing that helped me to be happy again." Another survivor emphasized the importance of being able to pray at night when she is alone and anxious. She said that it is a way to deal with her nightmares. From our view of trauma as a moral rupture, prayer may function to comfort and console, but it is also an attempt by individuals to reconstruct their belief in a meaningful world.

The transition to positive affect from depression, anxiety, and fear is important to document, and this will be the focus of the next chapter. However, it is relevant to note references to happiness in the context of our discussion of trauma, qualified by the fact that happiness is often a long time coming. For example, a survivor said, "It took me ten years after the genocide until I felt joy and a reason to live." During this period, survivors potentially go through several stages. Initially, they are simply coping with the fundamental needs of health, shelter, and food. They may feel emotionally numb, inhuman, going through the routine of physically sustaining their body, sometimes in the most minimal ways.

In our interviews, happiness and joy—to the extent that they are referenced—are inevitably mixed with tears and sadness. Happiness, for example, was cited by a widow who says she is happy when her children have something to eat and when they can go to school. Another widow said that she is happy when friends from her prayer group come and spend the night with her when she is distressed. Other survivors said they are happy when they are with individuals who have experienced the same thing as they have, and together they are praising and worshipping God. In general, happiness was referenced when someone is in an environment where they felt loved, accepted, and comforted.

What is missing in the references to happiness and joy are any of the individualistic formulas proposed by self-help guides from Western countries. Rather, as the next chapter explores further, survivors potentially become "whole" again when they are reintegrated into a community that cares and listens, and in which social meaning and purpose can be restored. Put differently, joy has a social quality for survivors, restored in the slow but steady reconstruction of loving relationships. Grief and sadness are not denied; rather, they are accepted as part of the experience of being human and as part of the survivor's life narrative.

For those survivors who testify to being happy and joyful, they do not deny the terrible events that occurred during the genocide, but they are also able to celebrate the gift of life and the joy of communal experiences. Tears and laughter, mourning and dancing, may be experienced in near simultaneity. The usual formulation of progression from melancholy to happiness may not be appropriate to genocide survivors. They may live with high levels of PTSD for many years and yet be relatively functional human beings, capable of joy and responsible caregiving.

In the following chapter, we transition from a focus on trauma to the healing process, looking in particular detail at the practices of Solace Ministries in Kigali. This case demonstrates that when trust in the moral order is broken through extreme social ruptures, trust can potentially be rebuilt through human interactions wherein survivors experience love, empathy, and compassionate concern and care. Because the breakdown of trust was experienced as a rift in the social contract, the work of restoration is effectively mediated through a community of loving people who accept the survivor as she is, bearing witness to her pain, and journeying with her through the long road to recovery.

CHAPTER 7

A Holistic Model of Healing

There is a voluminous literature on different strategies for dealing with trauma, ranging from individual and group therapy to various medical interventions. It is not our place to evaluate the relative effectiveness of these particular approaches. In this chapter, we instead focus on one case study of a grassroots healing community that has met with substantial success. In what follows, we describe what we experienced at Solace Ministries during more than a decade of careful observation of group meetings; visits to the homes of survivors; over one hundred interviews with survivors; and in-depth, repeat interviews with the leadership of the organization.

By devoting this chapter to a description of a community-based program to deal with survivor trauma, we are not disparaging individual-oriented therapeutic interventions. These can be extremely helpful to individuals who have had traumatic experiences, and, in fact, individual counseling is an element within Solace Ministries. But in the case of Rwanda and other instances of mass violence, individual therapy is often not a realistic goal when tens of thousands of people suffer from long-term trauma. Hence, we hold up Solace Ministries as an example of a large-scale intervention that may have applications in other contexts where there is mass trauma.

In contrast to models of individual and group therapy, Solace can best be seen as a holistic healing community whose approach to postgenocide recovery has been developed organically by an inspired process of trial, error, development, and faith—and with the deep insights of a leadership made up of survivors themselves. Solace's approach is not limited to one-on-one client-therapist interactions; nor is it a therapy group that runs for a dozen sessions. Rather, for survivors of the genocide, Solace literally becomes a surrogate family, one that replaces the family and community lost through genocide. And while Solace is rooted in the Christian faith, it is not a church, it is not identified with a particular denomination, and it does not exclude Muslims or people of no faith. In the context of Rwanda, in which the majority of the population is Christian, a faith-based approach to therapeutic intervention has resonance for many people.[1]

FINDING SOLACE

We will never forget one of our first experiences of Solace Ministries. Sixty women were packed in a partially constructed building. The glass had not been installed in the windows and it was raining ferociously. Women who had been perched on the window ledges in the crowded room had to huddle even closer with the survivors who were sitting on wooden benches. Led by Mama Lambert, the routine was the same this Wednesday during their four-hour meeting as, we later learned, was true every Wednesday. Alternating between songs, scripture reading, and words of comfort, survivors stood and testified about their experience of the genocide. Sometimes they could choke out only a paragraph or two and then collapse into tears. The meeting would stop, and fellow survivors would gather around them, holding and comforting the individual. On occasion the survivor giving testimony needed to leave the room in order to collect herself emotionally; other times she would sit down, to continue her story another week.

One Wednesday, a teenage boy stood to testify. He told the most awful story of his mother being beheaded. There was no expression of emotion on his face, not a tear. Jean Gakwandi, the director of Solace Ministries who was translating for us, said, "Just give him time. He will learn to cry and then his healing can start." Another Wednesday, a widow stood and rambled for a long time while the audience patiently listened. She jumped from incident to incident, but there was no coherence to what she was saying. Later Jean indicated that as she deals with her trauma, she will develop a narrative of what happened, and this will signal that she is on the road to healing.

Group dancing during the Wednesday meetings was one of the more surprising things we witnessed on a weekly basis at Solace. Survivors who had been weeping during a meeting or interview a few hours or days prior were ecstatically dancing to the pounding of a drum, often by an orphan. There were smiles on their faces. Those who were crippled from machete blows were moving, aided by a cane, in rhythm with everyone else. They were quite literally dancing their sorrows away. Later in the meeting, Jean Gakwandi would read from scripture passages of comfort and hope, gently telling those in attendance that they had a future. They were loved by God as people made in his image. They had been stomped on, but their intrinsic value was unchanged.

The Wednesday meetings in Kigali are repeated in other locations throughout Rwanda, including in small groups that meet in the homes of survivors—some of which Solace has helped build. Thus, while Solace has an established headquarters in the capital, their group meetings and the communities and programs that grow out of them operate on a cell model throughout the country.

Over the years that we interviewed survivors at Solace Ministries, we witnessed their strategy at work. Survivor after survivor told us that they first came to Solace out of utter desperation and sometimes in a crazed state. One woman said she had been running around her neighborhood half naked, ripping off her clothes. Another woman said she had been prostituting herself in order to feed her children. She had been raped repeatedly during the genocide and said she had lost her dignity and all sense of self-respect. An orphaned young man said that he escaped into drugs and alcohol after the genocide, trying to wash away the memory of his parents being killed. Somehow, through Solace, this desperation found a sounding board, and, as one widow put it, one by one, over time, survivors transitioned from being "ghosts" to becoming "human" again.

Solace does no advertising; survivors come to Solace because they hear from others that this is a place where they can be comforted. Survivors may attend meetings for months, even years, before they have the courage to stand and testify. And when they finally share their story, it often comes out in bits and pieces. Many of the survivors will first share their story individually with the founder of Solace, Jean Gakwandi, or Mama Lambert, who leads the meetings in Kigali. But it is important that they also testify publicly. It is important to have the community validate and help carry the burden of their trauma.

As noted in the previous chapter, trauma does not exist in isolation but rather interacts with the present-day material context of the survivor. So Solace takes a holistic approach to their ministry. They listen to the pain of survivors with a loving and empathetic heart. Solace provides basic forms of relief to survivors—housing, food, medical care, and medication. It creates a surrogate family where people can heal from their trauma and find new roles that give them meaning and purpose. Then, over time, Solace assists survivors in becoming economically self-sufficient. This is done through things like tuition assistance for university students, community gardens to grow vegetables, the gift of milk cows or goats, and microcredit loans.

Solace's ministry is tied directly to the Christian gospel of hope, which was shattered for many survivors when they witnessed their loved ones being killed in churches, sometimes with the complicity of the local priest or pastor. However cynical one may be about the role of the priestly class during the genocide, where many clergy abandoned the principles of their faith to align themselves politically with the Hutu Power movement, it is difficult to be cynical about Solace, which is helping to give new life to survivors. On several occasions, we took visitors who are completely secular to these meetings. We remember a retired investment banker saying afterward that this was religion in its most authentic form, even though he was not a churchgoing person.

THE SEEDS OF SOLACE MINISTRIES

Jean Gakwandi, the founder and director of Solace Ministries, recalls that in 1959 his father was put in prison for several months after the Tutsi king of Rwanda was killed and Hutus assumed political power. Jean was only six years old, but he vividly remembers the homes of Tutsis being burned. His family fled to a mission compound where they stayed until things calmed down. Afterward he recalls that Tutsi children were denied educational rights even if they were the highest-performing students in their class.

In 1963, Jean said that many more people were killed, especially in his home area. He saw Tutsi cattle being stolen and slaughtered. Many Tutsi children were orphaned. And while his family survived, their house was looted, and they lost everything.

A decade later, in 1973, he was working as an administrator in a hospital and many Tutsis fled to neighboring countries, fearing for their lives. He decided to stay, but for several weeks he did not report to work. Eventually he was called back to his job, but as a Tutsi he was very afraid and didn't talk publicly about any of the political issues that were unfolding for fear of being arrested or killed.

In 1989, he heard that there was a plan to kill Tutsis. It is for that reason that Jean does not believe the 1990 attacks by the rebel army nor the fact that the president's plane was shot down on April 6, 1994, were the cause of the genocide. He said the propaganda machine was in full effect prior to the onset of the genocide. The Hutu population was led to believe that they were bad citizens if they did not exterminate the Tutsis, including babies and small children—since these were the family members of the rebel forces that had fled with their families during earlier persecutions of Tutsis and were now seeking to redress their place in Rwanda.

In April 1994, Jean was living in Kigali with his wife, son, and three daughters. Because they had heard shots during the evening of April 6, when they heard someone ring the bell at their gate early in the morning on the seventh they immediately went into the storeroom in the kitchen where food was kept. The killers shot the lock on the gate, then the doors, windows, wardrobes, and mattresses, but finally they assumed that no one was there—that the residents had already fled.

The family remained in the storeroom that day, and the next day Jean pulled the telephone cord into this small room and started calling friends that he thought might help them. One of these individuals was the teacher with whom he had been studying German. She immediately went to work and contacted the Swiss embassy, and after thirty-seven hours of hiding, a representative of the embassy came to their home and took Jean and his family to the house of this German teacher, where they stayed for the next eighty-nine days, even though the owners were evacuated along with other foreign nationals after a few days.

Jean remembers hiding in a wardrobe in this house with his family, including his four-year-old daughter. She was very hungry; in fact, Jean could feel her ribs in the darkness and realized that she was losing weight from not eating. As he crouched in this dark location he accidentally hit the shelf above him and something fell down. Picking it up, he felt it and realized that it was a piece of chocolate. So, he reached his hand up on the shelf and discovered it was filled with boxes of chocolate and other sweets. For a while, they lived on this and water that they would get from the bathroom where they crawled when it got dark.

After five days, however, they were discovered by the killers and forced out of their hiding places, only to discover that there were other Tutsis also hiding in the house—a total of fifteen of them altogether. One of the soldiers who had entered the house recognized Jean—he was one of his patients at the hospital where Jean had worked—and said, "What are you doing here?" Jean answered simply, "We are hiding." And then he lied and said that all of the individuals in the house were members of his family. The soldiers then left and seemingly forgot about them for the next three months, which is how they survived. However, almost every member of Jean's extended family who were living elsewhere in Rwanda were killed while he was there, including his siblings, parents, aunts, and uncles.

THE ROLE OF GOD AND FAITH

Jean said about his past that he entered secondary school feeling very diminished—"I was afraid of myself." Specifically, he was fearful that people would know that he was a Tutsi, and this had led to considerable self-doubt. Furthermore, he said that he mistrusted and had anger toward everyone. Not only had he witnessed his father being imprisoned for no reason other than his identity, but also he said that his brothers and sisters were very clever but never passed the national exams, even though they were first in their classes.

In 1970, when he was eighteen years old, he said that he could not sleep; there was a deep unease inside him. He was a self-proclaimed atheist because he could not reconcile the injustice he had observed with a God who was good. On a whim, he went to a religious revival meeting one night to mock the preacher. Instead, he found himself weeping and praying for God to take control of his life. The next day he said the world looked radically different. He had lost his desire to drink—which was how he put himself to sleep at night—he felt physically "light," at peace, and had a feeling of love for humanity that he had not previously experienced. Even the trees seemed greener, he said.

Such transformational experiences are not particularly unusual, at least according to William James, the author of the classic work *Varieties of Religious Experience*.[2] For Jean, however, this experience left him with a desire to understand what was happening to him, and as a result he started reading the Bible from cover to cover, as well as other religious books, in an effort to understand his emerging Christian faith. He said that he was a new person, filled with joy and a transcendent sort of connection that gave him a sense of hope and purpose.

With this as context, we return to the evening of April 6, 1994. Jean heard shots being fired throughout the city, and while praying and reading the Bible that night he encountered this verse from scripture, "God is a strong fortress," and he took this as a promise that God would protect his family. During the three months that they were in the German teacher's house, he continued to pray and meditate on scripture. When the genocide ended in July, his faith was further solidified—he felt God had a purpose for his life or else he would not have been spared.

THE BIRTH AND PHILOSOPHY OF A HEALING COMMUNITY

The situation immediately after the genocide was incomprehensible. People were wandering the streets with amputated limbs. Survivors had no place to sleep because their houses had been destroyed. Food was scarce. Orphans were everywhere. Institutions were not functioning. Jean said that people had lost their identity as human beings. They had internalized the message that they were worthless cockroaches and snakes. Their support system of family and kin was completely broken. As Jean encountered survivors, he said that they were dead inside. Physically, they might be alive, but internally they were empty.

Wrestling with what his response should be, Jean read a verse in the Old Testament book of Isaiah, which he took as a command from God: "Comfort, comfort my people."[3] In response, he invited a few people he knew to attend a meeting. The first week, only eight widows showed up. Jean said that they shared their experiences of loss, prayed, and cried together. The next week there were twenty widows. The third week there were forty. The fourth week it was raining, and they only had eighteen. But by the fifth meeting, there were 150. And this was the beginning of what is now Solace Ministries.

Although later Solace would go on to develop a number of projects and programs that deal with housing, medical care, farming, education, and economic self-sufficiency, Jean said that his most fundamental insight after the genocide was that survivors not only needed material things, they also needed comfort. They needed someone to listen and to acknowledge their experience of horror. People would talk to Jean for hours, pouring out their story, interrupted by tears and bouts of weeping. Jean's response was to listen and to weep with them, and then to offer some words of hope.

Jean said, person after person would come to him and say, "I have problems." This was the totality of their identity, problems. They had lost all sense of themselves as persons with an identity or purpose, a "self" constructed through relationships and social roles. It was only as Jean and other members of Solace listened to them that they could start the journey to once again become human—not just a bundle of problems. Yes, dealing with their financial and medical problems was critical, but equally important was helping them build a new identity that was not solely defined by their multiple losses, trauma, and problems.

To the extent that their previous identity was socially constructed, defined by being a mother, a wife, a homeowner, or a good neighbor—these were gone. And as Jean encountered widows and young women who had been raped, the situation was even worse. They had become alienated even from their own bodies. In fact, Jean believes that 60 percent of the women who were raped during the genocide were infected with the AIDS virus.

When Jean reflects back on his own emotions immediately after the genocide, he said that, like other survivors, for several months he was numb emotionally; he had no feelings. But as he prayed and searched the scriptures for promises of hope, he said that God comforted him and in turn he had the strength to start sharing the burdens of others, comforting them.

SOLACE MINISTRIES: PROGRAMS AND ORGANIZATION

In 2015, we attended the twentieth anniversary of Solace Ministries. What began as a handful of widows gathering together to share their stories had expanded dramatically. When we first visited Solace in 2001, they had been given a prime piece of property not too far from where the US embassy is located. By faith, Jean had started the foundation for a building, lacking funding to build even a single story. A few years later, donors had provided the funds to build a second story and then a third.

Jean's method was to invite donors to meet with survivors, attend meetings where survivors shared their testimonies of tragedy and hope, and never ask for money. People saw the need, the integrity of the program, and they signed on as partners. Sometimes the donors were religious people who shared Jean's Christian convictions; other times they simply saw the fruit of what was being done and wanted to contribute to the program.

By the twentieth anniversary, the Kigali facility had expanded to include another multilevel building with a large hall, offices to house the staff of this expanding ministry, and a number of guestrooms for international visitors that generated income to support the work of Solace. In addition, Solace had opened a medical clinic on the outskirts of Kigali and was in the process of building a maternity hospital—once again by faith, laying the foundation and then waiting for donors to see the need and respond. Solace also had several well-developed demonstration farms and plant nurseries where survivors were learning animal husbandry and cultivation, so they could be economically self-sufficient.

Beyond the facility in Kigali, by 2015, there were sixty Solace cell communities spread through the country. A few of these communities had formal buildings, but many groups of survivors met in homes or rented facilities, including some who met outdoors. Each community had elected its own officers. Some communities were only a dozen members or so; others were several hundred.

Within the central headquarters in Kigali and each of these cell communities, the Wednesday meeting model was adopted. Once Wednesday meetings were established and a community was formed, other aid and sustainability projects were birthed. For example, with the help of an international organization, some of the widows had been given high-quality milk cows. Hundreds of survivors had been given goats and chickens. There was also a fledgling project to develop beehives. Whenever someone was helped with housing, they were asked to plant ten fruit trees on their property. And when survivors had excess produce from these trees or from farms they were cultivating, they shared it with other survivors.

Solace was also paying the school fees for several hundred orphans and children of widows as well as buying their uniforms and school supplies. And although it is expensive, they were helping a number of college students pay their tuition at local universities. On the other end of the age spectrum were elderly women who were unable to support themselves, so Solace also was giving them assistance, even though their philosophy is to help people be self-sufficient.

Solace is committed to long-term solutions, which is the reason for the focus on education and financial autonomy. But Jean says that it is impossible to ignore crisis moments, such as a child who has not eaten for two or three days—a reality that we repeatedly confirmed in our interviews. Likewise, if someone is being evicted because they cannot pay rent, one cannot ignore their predicament. Solace also has a revolving loan fund and teaches survivors basic concepts related to being an entrepreneur, even if it simply means selling vegetables on the street.

Jean also believes that every child has the right to play, so they developed a football team that is coached by a former professional player. One of the benefits of this sports program is that Hutu and Tutsi young people play together, united in athletics rather than political differences.

In short, Solace takes a holistic and community approach to the trauma genocide survivors experience. While it is important to comfort those who have been traumatized, comfort can only take survivors so far without the construction of a new life and set of relationships. Conversely, material assistance or even steps toward self-sustainability can set the context for healing to occur, but they are ineffective if the individual still suffers from extreme symptoms of PTSD and moral rupture. Both sides of the coin are necessary for survivors to begin to build a new postgenocide life and sense of purpose.

A CLOSER LOOK AT THE HEALING PROCESS

Mama Lambert, currently one of the key staff members at Solace, was one of the first survivors to attend a Solace meeting. She was filled with despair over the deaths of five of her children as well as her husband. At night, she couldn't sleep. And at the end of the first meeting she attended, Jean Gakwandi asked if he could pray for anyone. Mama Lambert told him that she had terrible insomnia. In an autobiography that she wrote years later, she recalled: "Jean laid his hands on my head and he prayed so passionately for me that the women began to cry. Jean prayed to God that there would be peace throughout our land; he prayed for all of the widows and orphans; he asked God to help these people by easing and taking away their sorrow and suffering."[4] That night, for the first time, she slept peacefully, Mama Lambert said.

At the second meeting she attended, widows once again testified about their experiences during the genocide, often in very demonstrative ways. She recalled, "Some beat themselves on the head, others on their thighs. The women stamped on the ground, trembled and screamed it out."[5] She said, "All the misery and sorrow came flooding out. The hellish pain of these violent memories came from so deep within their hearts, it was screamed out in an assortment of the same words repeated over and over again. . . . Distraught, the women put their hands on their heads and walked around in a daze."[6] In response to this emotional outpouring, she said that Jean moved among the group, passionately praying. She said that he also attempted to lighten the mood by singing. Reflecting back on the early days of Solace, Mama Lambert said, "The more often we gathered together, the more our strength returned. We felt ourselves becoming stronger. Very slowly and little by little, we started to become human again, physically as well as mentally."[7]

One day in 1995, Mama Lambert made an appointment to see Jean. She brought with her photographs of her two daughters who had been killed, Joyeuse and Claudette. When Mama Lambert burst into tears, Jean joined her, while also comforting her and asking her to have the courage to live her life. "It was such an unforgettable experience, meeting someone who showed himself to be so deeply compassionate and empathetic, who showed me his sorrow by openly shedding his tears over the deaths of my children. This gave me a lot of faith."[8]

In 2000, Mama Lambert started volunteering for Solace Ministries and two years later was offered a contract for employment, where she currently heads the counseling department and also oversees the Wednesday meetings. She also visits widows in their homes and coordinates some of the programs for orphans. In several long interviews with Mama Lambert, we asked her to further explain the process of healing as she has observed it over the last two decades.

Mama Lambert said the first step in dealing with the trauma of the genocide is that survivors need to tell their story within a safe and supportive space. At first, it may be to Mama Lambert or Jean in private, but then it is healing for survivors to tell their story publicly so that the community of survivors can embrace the individual and carry her burdens with them. It is almost like "coming out of the closet" regarding one's traumatic experience. Keeping these secrets bottled up inside kills the human spirit—survivors can think of nothing else but their trauma. But by sharing their experience, the heart is opened to feel, to empathize with others, to rejoin the human community of care, concern, and love.

The role of the community, in turn, is to affirm what the survivor has been through and then to communicate to the survivor that she still has value. Mama Lambert asserts that it is not alone but in community that one is able to experience dignity, self-respect, and worth as a human being. For members of Solace, this message is gently wrapped in the view that everyone has value in God's eyes even if they can no longer see or feel their own worth. This abstract concept must in turn be embodied, and this is the role of the community of fellow survivors—to be God's hands in the world, embracing the individual.

Perhaps an example can illustrate the theological concept embodied at Solace. At one Wednesday meeting, a guest speaker addressed the women and children, taking a 5,000 franc bill out of his pocket. He asked the survivors, what was the value of the money? They responded, "5,000 francs." He then crumpled it, spat on it, threw it to the ground and stomped on it. After jumping up and down on the bill he picked it up—now crumpled and dirty—opened it up and asked again, "What is this bill worth?" Women laughed and cried and embraced each other. The answer was obvious. In spite of survivors being stomped on, they still had worth in the eyes of God.

Because the Wednesday meetings are such a central element of the healing process, and one that is repeated every week, we asked Mama Lambert to further describe the various elements of the meeting, which almost always follow the same progression.

Singing is the first thing that is done as survivors gather. The goal, says Mama Lambert, is to lighten the heart and "sing away one's tears and one's hurts." Depending on the week, there may be as few as fifty or sixty people present, but at the Kigali facility often there is a hundred or more. The majority are women, but there is typically a sprinkling of orphans, both males and females. Some of the younger women have babies on their backs, and these children are passed from lap to lap and are free to wander, if they want. The women are dressed in colorful long dresses, with many also having beautiful head scarfs. Chairs are neatly arranged in rows, and at the front of the room is a desk. On the far side of the front row is someone keeping time to the singing with a drum. Otherwise there is no accompaniment.

After the initial singing, newcomers are welcomed. They introduce themselves and may mention where they are from. Many of the survivors walk to the meeting, oftentimes a number of miles. Others will ride in one of the minivans that circulate through the city or hire a ride on the back of a motorcycle. Inevitably, a friend has invited newcomers. They are there to check out the meeting and see why their friend has found it valuable. There is no pressure to participate and, as previously stated, newcomers may sit in these meetings for months before they decide to stand and share their story.

The third element is the act of testifying for as long or as short a period as a survivor wishes. Each week, participants who want to testify write their name on a scrap of paper and hand it to whoever is leading the meeting. Then sprinkled throughout the meeting, they are invited to stand and tell their story. As they do, fellow survivors empathize emotionally and vocally. Those who are not ready to stand before the group may meet privately with Mama Lambert at another time. This experience of sharing one-on-one with her builds trust and enables the survivor to later share her story with the larger group.

Prayer is the fourth element of the Wednesday meeting. This is a time to give thanks for what God has provided, and often very material things are mentioned. In prayer, survivors also call out to God for strength and invite the Holy Spirit to fill their meeting with joy and hope. There is a public element to these prayers— it is an opportunity for survivors to be encouraged by what they perceive God is doing in their lives. While the leader of the meeting may orchestrate the prayers, there is ample opportunity for members of the audience to participate.

Prayer is followed by dancing. Nearly everyone stands to their feet and moves in rhythm to the drumming that has now intensified. Some of the survivors move to the front, dancing in a growing circle. For the moment, their worries and cares are bracketed. Physically, spiritually, and mentally, they are in a different space. The demons of the past have been chased away. They are experiencing the joy of being part of a loving and accepting community.

Then there is a short homily by Jean, Mama Lambert, a guest, or one of the members of Solace. Various biblical references are noted, which always have to do with hope, God's presence in spite of challenges, and the promise that new life is possible after a tragedy. A frequent statement heard at Solace is that "God is the father to the fatherless and a husband to the widows." Typically, there is also an invitation to newcomers to explore a relationship with God in a new way.

Finally, the meeting ends with more singing. People embrace, hug, and show their affection for one another. Since the meetings often last four hours, sometimes there is something to drink or eat after the meeting. People linger, chat, and catch up with each other's lives. This is a community gathering, not simply a religious service where one comes for an hour and then heads for the exit.

IN THE WORDS OF SURVIVORS

While survivors often mention the physical and financial support they receive at Solace, one of the elements they return to over and over again is the role of Solace as a loving community, and one that is consistent, compassionate, and dependable. For example, a survivor said, "In Solace we hug each other and ask each other news and we feel at home." Another survivor said, "Sometimes we talk about things that made us sad; we cry, and we end up laughing and the anger disappears." Still another survivor said, "I think of it [Solace] as my family, because when I reach there I feel free to say whatever I want about my story or my problems."

Orphans often live alone, especially when they are sole survivors. An orphan said, "If I had not found Solace, I would have died out of loneliness." In addition to finding surrogate parents, aunts and uncles at Solace Ministries, orphans also find surrogate siblings, such as this individual who said, "I was able to get another family here at Solace; I was able to get mothers, sisters, and brothers. Before I wouldn't even talk with elder women because I would compare them to my mother were she alive. But now I am able to talk with them." We heard a similar refrain from widows who had lost children during the genocide. One woman said, "Now I have children who visit me and bring life back to me. . . . I have a family now."

Orphans also find in Solace an important and trustworthy source of authority, which they value, as stated by this individual: "Other organizations just give you aid. But Solace is like a family. We not only come for help, but we listen to advice from elders. They teach us how to behave." Sometimes the advice is very concrete: "They even teach us that we should wash and clean up, so that those who wanted us dead will see that we are well dressed." Another survivor elaborated: "We shouldn't behave like dogs. We should always aim to be proud of ourselves, even when we are not happy." An orphan in his twenties summed up the goals he had developed in his association with Solace: "One of my objectives is to be a respected man so that others can see what God has done for me. To get to a level where my word counts. My healing would be to feel normal, at the same level as those who have parents."

Accountability is another role of Solace, much like one experiences in a family. A survivor said that Solace had helped him find purpose in attending school, explaining: "Since I had lost all my family, I didn't see the reason for being good or studying. I didn't see why I should achieve good things. I didn't have anyone to show my achievements." Echoing this view, a survivor said that Solace may help you with school fees, but like a parent they want to know how you are doing as a person. In short, Solace becomes a nurturing reference group to orphans, acknowledging their achievements, urging them to do better, and offering words of encouragement when they are struggling.

The other component of Solace is that survivors experience it as a place filled with joy and happiness, in spite of the sorrows that unite them. As mentioned in the last chapter on trauma, joy is often described as a social emotion. Repeatedly, survivors mentioned the freedom that they experience at Solace: They are free to laugh, to dance, to sing, and to worship. At traditional churches, the genocide may be mentioned during commemoration periods, but at Solace the genocide is acknowledged every week.

BECOMING HUMAN AGAIN

Many survivors explained their contact with Solace as being a journey of arriving in a ghostlike state, and slowly but surely coming alive again. Perhaps the most succinct statement was from a survivor who said about her experience at Solace, "I was able to become human again." This idea was elaborated in other statements by survivors: "When I first came to Solace I was going crazy. I would come only wearing one cloth and not even cover myself properly." Another survivor said, "I was like a mad person. I would spend the whole day walking, with no hope," before joining Solace.

When asked what Solace does, one survivor explained that Solace deals with "heart" issues, including despair, anger, hatred, purpose, and meaning. There is no denial of the genocide and the horrific things that occurred, and no attempt to minimize the pain that one experienced—both mental and physical. Telling one's own first-person account is difficult, because it may require publicly saying that one was raped, how one's children were killed, and other memories that continually circle in one's mind but seldom are expressed.

One survivor who initially could not bear to testify publicly said, "Mama Lambert took away my fear and whenever I was before her I had the courage to tell her my testimony and now I feel I have no fear to testify to anyone else." Another survivor said, "I listened to people's testimonies and people in Solace kept comforting us until I reached a point where I regained hope and felt valued, and I started to value myself too." And a survivor who finally gained the courage to publicly share her testimony said, "When I saw that those who were testifying had lighter hearts, I told myself I could do it." Similarly, a survivor said, "I saw how those who testified were changed afterward. I decided to also take that step. When I was testifying, it was really hard for me. But once it was done I felt relieved."

It was not unusual for survivors to report that their headaches lessened after testifying or that their insomnia was better. A survivor said, "When I give my testimony, it is like a wound which is getting healed." Another survivor said that after testifying, "I felt something going out of my body." Survivors said that in the act of testifying they feel accepted, once again as a part of the human community. They no longer feel marginalized, disrespected.

A devastating element of the dehumanizing experience of genocide is that individuals lose their ability to love as well as experience love. A survivor said, "Before I came to Solace, I was very sad and I hated myself, but ever since I joined Solace I am relieved; I love myself, and I know that life goes on." Nearly identical statements echoed through the interviews with other survivors, and especially women who had been raped. A survivor said, "There [at Solace] I was able to love myself again, because I hated myself before, feeling lifeless due to the problems I had encountered." Another survivor said, "When I first came here, I was traumatized. I did not love anyone and did not want anyone to get close to me. But when I came to Solace, I got love."

INTERPRETING THE MODEL PSYCHOLOGICALLY

Judith Herman, one of the early pioneers in studying trauma, says that there are three stages of recovery for individuals who have been traumatized.[9] First, the survivor needs to feel safe from further violence. Second, the individual needs to reconstruct their trauma story, integrating it into their larger life narrative. And, third, the connection between the individual and a community must be restored so that the individual can once again experience trust in others.

These three stages parallel the practice of Solace Ministries. As was seen in the preceding pages, Solace is a safe place where one can be with other survivors who are struggling with trauma. They are comforted, often one-on-one, in private counseling sessions where their experiences are affirmed, and they are invited to participate in the Wednesday meetings at whatever level they desire, including sitting silently for weeks and months. If they need food, shelter, and medical help, Solace does what it can to meet these needs within the limitations of the organization's resources, recognizing that the psychological and the physical go hand in hand.

The leadership as well as fellow survivors at Solace recognize the symptoms of trauma. They are met with a loving embrace, not medication or formulaic responses. Jean Gakwandi appreciates the insights of psychotherapy, but he said rather pointedly in one of our interviews, "If you don't have love, you will fail." And he is rather unorthodox in that he believes that comforting survivors means that you come down to the level of the people you are counseling— "When they weep, you weep with them." Solace believes in heart-to-heart communication. Comfort is not a morally neutral activity.

Second, the group meetings provide an opportunity for survivors to testify about their experiences, or—in Herman's words—to "reconstruct their trauma story." Because this is done collectively, they realize that they are not alone in their suffering. In fact, other survivors may have had even worse experiences. Eventually they have the courage to stand and share their experience—not once, but multiple times if they desire, honing it until it holds its rightful place in a life story rather than dominating that story. As they recount various experiences, they begin to develop a narrative that links elements of their past together, and, in time—perhaps months and even years— they find a purpose for living, both presently and in the future. Many survivors even accept the opportunity to write their story and contribute to a growing archive that documents there is "life after the death"—the title of the first conference we attended in Rwanda in 2001.

Herman's observations parallel what we heard from both Mama Lambert and Jean Gakwandi and what we observed in meetings. Herman states, "The survivor's initial account of the event may be repetitious, stereotyped, and emotionless."[10] She says that this initial description of the trauma is a "prenarrative." It has little feeling or interpretation. In fact, she describes it as being like a "silent movie." In her view, "the role of therapy is to provide the music and words."[11] At Solace, the music takes the form of singing and dancing and the words are wrapped in biblical accounts of hope.

Third, Solace survivors discover that they have a community, a new family of people who understand their struggle to once again become whole. These bonds grow strong as they assume responsibility for the welfare of other survivors and build meaning structures that make sense in the midst of tragedy. It is in community that a new self has the opportunity to blossom, one constructed in the context of a newfound "family" and friends. One may even gain surrogate children, or, if an orphan, surrogate parents.

The parallels to Judith Herman's categories are striking. For example, she says that the self has to be rebuilt after trauma—"rebuilt only as it was built initially, in connection with others."[12] She believes that traumatic events shatter the connection between the individual and the community, which creates a "crisis of faith." She says about traumatized people: "They lose their trust in themselves, in other people, and in God," although she does not elaborate or probe the God question except to acknowledge that faith in God is often shattered when one loses hope in an orderly and predictable set of relationships.[13] She also affirms what we heard from Jean Gakwandi, saying: "This work of reconstruction actually transforms the traumatic memory, so that it can be integrated into the survivor's life story."[14] According to Herman, "Recovery can take place only within the context of relationships, it cannot occur in isolation."[15] Finally, it is important to note that healing is not linear. As Herman writes, "Resolution of the trauma is never final; recovery is never complete."[16] Trauma does not disappear; it is integrated into one's life in different ways and to different degrees that may change based on the context in which the survivor finds herself.

In concluding this chapter, we want to address the role of religion more broadly, noting some of religion's problematic elements but also its potential to contribute to human flourishing. To summarize, we see two types of religion: *culturally accommodating religion* that mirrors the cultural and political mores, baptizing them with religious language, and *compassionate liberating religion* that appeals to a transcendent source, prophetically challenging policy makers as it embodies the true essence of religion—compassion, care, love, and equal treatment of all.

THE ROLE OF RELIGION

Religion is always a complex topic to address, but especially for survivors of the genocide, since many felt abandoned by God, and yet later they may have found comfort in religion as they pursued the process of healing from the trauma that they had experienced. As we have seen, many survivors, including those who currently are religiously devout, said that they felt that God was absent during the one hundred days of the genocide. They could not reconcile their condition and what they were experiencing with a God who was good, all-powerful, and was concerned with his creation. In despair, they would call out to God for help, and the killing and suffering simply continued. In a few instances, Hutus chided them, saying that the Tutsi God was on vacation, and that is how they felt, that God had forgotten them.[17]

After the genocide ended, many survivors continued to have difficulty reconciling their Christian heritage with what had occurred. Numerous survivors were ambivalent entering a church, and especially one in their hometown where family members had been killed. Clergy had lost credibility in their eyes. Either they had passively observed the slaughter in their churches or, in some instances, clergy had actually participated actively in the propaganda and the extermination of Tutsis. Therefore, it was not just that survivors' faith in God had been challenged, but his representatives—priests, nuns, and pastors—had also failed or even betrayed them.

It is little wonder that when survivors did join churches after the genocide, it was often not the church of their childhood—Catholic, Anglican, Seventh-Day Adventist. Instead, it was one of the new Pentecostal churches that spread like wildfire around the country. These churches didn't carry the baggage of traditional religion and the imagery of betrayal and killing. Furthermore, these charismatic churches were highly expressive, tapping the emotional dimension of life that had gone dead for survivors.

The problem of theodicy—how a good, all knowing, and all-powerful God could allow evil—is finally not solvable, at least logically. It is one of the great challenges that people of faith confront, and we certainly are not going to tackle this profound philosophical question in these pages. However, an alternative tact is to see how religion functions in people's lives, with prayer being a universal element of all religions and therefore an act that provides a window into the role of religion. We humans do not operate purely by rationality; the "heart" also plays a profound role, and one expression of the heart, understood metaphorically, is the act of prayer, which takes many different forms.

PRAYER AS A RESOURCE

For many survivors, prayer is a profound and important element of their everyday lives. Several individuals told us that they wake up at three in the morning to pray, sometimes calling each other on their cell phones to join them. Other survivors practice monthly the combined acts of fasting and prayer. But more routinely, survivors pray on a daily basis, sometimes throughout the day but often when they wake and when they retire at night.

The focus of prayer is oftentimes for things that are immediate and highly personal. Both mothers and orphans reported asking God for food, shelter, and clothing—which are primal needs when one is unemployed and one's housing was destroyed. Older orphans pray for admittance to the university and for a donor to pay for their tuition and associated school fees. Survivors also pray and plead for release from insomnia, recurring memories, and dreams—especially of rape and other violent acts—and for reduction of pain, healing from AIDS, and that they will survive long enough to care for their children. And survivors pray for their country, their president, and, in one instance, for all countries where violence such as they experienced is occurring.

Sometimes prayers are uttered in the middle of the night when things seem bleakest. For example, a survivor said, "I would have nightmares of the people who raped me coming back to do it again. I would get up and pray." Similarly, a survivor said, "When I have bad dreams, I get up and pray a lot. I plead with God to take away these bad dreams." For widows and orphans who are alone and have no other resource, prayer offers a relationship, someone to turn to. A survivor said, "I am always talking to him [God] asking him to give me strength to go on looking after my children, saying, 'Please Lord, help me to live long.'" Another said, "I have an intimacy with God when I pray." She went on to say, "I finish praying feeling that God has done something for me . . . he understands me. He loves me."

Survivors also address God with their mundane, everyday concerns and future goals. For example, a survivor said, "I pray that God helps me finish school, get a job afterward, get out of this kind of life, change my history, and not go back to the life I had before." Survivors sometimes connect their personal needs with a concern for their country, such as this survivor who said, "I pray that the war will not happen again." Or this survivor who had a more universal view: "I pray for employment and for every country I hear of with impending war, because I compare them with what we passed through and I pray for them."

Finally, survivors use prayer to work through feelings of rage and anger toward the perpetrators of the genocide, as well as for internal healing. One survivor, for example, said that through prayer she felt her "heart cooling" when she thinks about her attackers. Another survivor said, "I used to hate life, even hate myself. But now, praying helps me." In summary, survivors use prayer to work through difficult emotions and the processes of acceptance and forgiveness; in this way, prayer is viewed as a source of strength, mercy, and grace.

Clearly, prayer is not a panacea for personal problems. As one survivor stated succinctly, "Prayer alone is not enough." But it cannot be ignored as a resource for many survivors. As the quotes above attest, prayer is used in a number of different ways: it is a form of catharsis, a type of companionship, a source of strength and courage, and a daily source of comfort and hope. Whether God has ontological reality is not our focus in this book; for many survivors, God is perceived to be real. God is someone they speak to in highly personal and intimate ways.

Cynics would say that God is merely functioning for these survivors as a crutch, especially when they turn in prayer to God for help. For some existentialists, prayer is an expression of "bad faith," it is a form of escapism. However, judgments like this need to be put alongside the experience of survivors and how religion functions in their lives, rather than viewing religion from the philosopher's armchair. Especially after the genocide ended, survivors report that prayer gave them strength to live again, that it sustained them day in and day out against the most difficult of odds. For them, God functioned as someone with whom they could experience trust and intimacy, an entity with whom they could build a relationship after so many of their relationships were decimated. Even if they felt their life was of no value, they felt that God still valued them and was concerned about their welfare.

RECONCILING THE TWO FACES OF RELIGION

During the course of our research we made a point of visiting several churches where the Hutu pastor chose to die with his parishioners, protesting the ideologically driven racism of the Hutu Power movement. These clergy clearly made a distinction between the ethical values of the Christian tradition, which honor the value and dignity of all people, regardless of tribe or nationality, and the genocidal desire to purify the nation of "outsiders." In our view, if the clergy had stood as a group against the genocide, rather than mirroring the racist ideology of the government, the genocide would likely never have occurred on the scale that it did, with neighbors killing neighbors. But the clergy did not fulfill their role as moral prophets. Instead, many clergy aligned themselves with government ideology—putting their quest for personal power above their role as moral shepherds of their people.

Authentic religion is always independent from government and tribe, drawing on transcendent values to inspire people to work for justice, equality, and compassionate care of others. It is important to note that the civil rights movement, women's suffrage, LGBT rights, antiwar movements, and many other attempts to honor the dignity and equality of people have been inspired and led by religious leaders. At the same time, there are always elements within the religious community that align themselves with the dominant ideology and justify oppression by cherry-picking passages from sacred texts, as was classically demonstrated during slavery in the United States and apartheid in South Africa.

In debates about religion, there is a tendency to polarize the discussion, arguing either for the efficacy of religion and its positive benefits or proclaiming that it is an illusion, an opiate of the people and a force for human oppression. In fact, both cases can be made. The error is in generalizing that all religion is the same, which it is not. There is compassionate liberating religion that appeals to transcendent values and there is culturally accommodating religion that stems from humanity's baser instincts. To deny the destructive role of religion is to ignore human history, especially when we look at a case like Rwanda. On the other hand, religion has also been a source of hope, social vision, and compassionate care.

CONCLUSION

In the next chapter we address another complex topic, the issue of forgiveness. It too can be superficial, inauthentic, and escapist. On the other hand, forgiveness can be profoundly liberating, releasing one from revolving thoughts, rage, and revenge—but only if it is first preceded by a degree of healing. As we will argue, forgiveness is a process, and there are multiple contexts and types of forgiveness. Following that chapter, we then examine the issue of reconciliation—which is different from forgiveness—both at the individual and social-political levels. Overshadowing all of the chapters in the second half of this book is our profound sense that genocide constitutes a moral and social rupture that needs to be addressed and healed. Only then can individuals flourish, becoming fully human again.

CHAPTER 8

Forgiveness

In 1996, Mama Lambert embarked on the task of trying to discover the remains of the five children she had lost during the genocide, with the goal of giving them a proper burial. In her memoir, she recalls the agonizing process of unearthing the body of one of her daughters: "One day I came across a body and dug it out very carefully. To my great dismay, the body turned out to be my daughter, Joyeuse. Her murderers had cut off her head and stuffed it into her vest. I found Claudette too, with her hands missing. They had been cut off."[1] Later, she discovered the bodies of her other three children: Germain, Olivier and Rutayisire. As she and other survivors continued to search, eventually they dug up 347 bodies and seventeen heads whose bodies they could not find.

As referenced in the first chapter, two years later she was sitting in her office at work and someone entered, holding an envelope in her hand. It was Mukansanga, the mother of Manasse, who had killed Mama Lambert's children along with many other Tutsis in her neighborhood. On seeing this woman, Mama Lambert said, "My heart stopped. For a moment I stared at her, stunned. Then I jumped up, flinched backward and went crazy. I started to scream."[2] Mukansanga had brought a letter to Mama Lambert from her son who was in prison. In it, he acknowledged his criminal acts, detailing the people he had killed, and begged for forgiveness. He was explicit in stating the methods used, saying that he and others had used clubs and small pickaxes to break the skulls of their victims. In one day alone, he said that he had killed thirty-eight people.

Her work colleagues gathered around Mama Lambert, and one of them read the letter out loud to the group. When he was finished reading, Mama Lambert shouted for Mukansanga to leave the premises. That night she was in deep agony and put the letter and its plea for forgiveness aside. All she could think of was the ways in which Manasse had gone about his killing, not only with a nail-spiked club and pickax but also throwing stones at the heads and bodies of his victims.

Two years later she received another letter from Manasse who was still in prison. Again, he acknowledged his crimes and asked for forgiveness. This time Mama Lambert said that she read the letter line by line, letting its message and request sink in. She realized that she was totally preoccupied with the deaths of her children as well as her husband. Ideas of revenge as well as hatred kept revolving in her mind. In the midst of her sorrow, she said, "I became ever more conscious of the fact that there was only one way to get Manasse out of my head, to give my damaged existence a reason, and to make my life livable again. I would have to forgive him."[3]

In our interviews with Mama Lambert years later, she stressed that forgiveness is a process. You don't decide that today you will forgive, nor do you forgive because you have been taught to forgive. "It is something that comes from the heart." In her view, forgiveness is something that gradually may unfold through prayer, reading the Bible, and thinking about your own condition. Fundamental to forgiveness, for her, is "breaking the bond" that connects you to the people who killed your family or assaulted you. However, based on her own experience, the forgiveness process is uneven.

After receiving the first letter, she said, "I felt like killing myself or killing him at that moment. He went on narrating how he killed my children and how some were stoned in the chest and others had their heads cut off. When I read this, I was so confused and I actually got so angry with the leaders of the prison for having allowed him to send me this kind of letter. Well, I knew that my children were killed, but I did not know all those horrible details. To tell you the truth, I did not forgive him at that moment. I did not even value this letter."

Reflecting on the second letter from Manasse, she said that he had obviously been reading the Bible while in prison. "He wrote to me some biblical verses. He quoted Proverbs 28. So, when I read this passage, I found that it was about forgiveness. After reading these words is when I took time to pray for this person." In the midst of offering this account, Mama Lambert paused and said in disbelief about this young man, "We had supported the perpetrator's family before the genocide because they were very poor. Actually, my husband was paying the school fees of his elder brother to go to secondary school. So, what hurt me most is that we had done a lot of good things for this family."

In our interviews, Mama Lambert acknowledged her struggle with forgiveness and the fact that she was plagued with questions about how God could allow the genocide to occur. She is still bothered by the fact that her husband's bones lie at the bottom of a lake and she has not been able to give him proper burial as she did with her children who died. She also says that she sometimes still gets angry, especially in the month of April when the rains come, and she is reminded of the onset of the genocide. In fact, she described a conversation from the previous day that made her very angry as an orphan girl described being raped and then giving birth to the child born of this rape. She also described the agonizing process of encouraging women who have been raped to be tested for HIV/AIDS, and the difficulty of informing them of test results if they are positive.

At the same time, there are also things that give her strength and comfort. She spends hours each week in prayer, sometimes alone and other times with friends. She also mentioned in one of our interviews that she found strength in returning with us to the site where her children were killed. There was something symbolic to her and a witness to her former Hutu neighbors that she could bring "white" people to her home, without fear. In her words, "See, you tried to kill us, but you didn't succeed." She also finds healing in the fact that on a daily basis she is helping survivors restore their sense of humanity. As painful and anger-producing as it is to hear their stories, she also gains strength in being able to comfort others and see them deal with their trauma.

For her there is also comfort in the belief that she will see her loved ones some day in heaven, although this doesn't compromise her desire to commemorate and honor her slain relatives in this life. She still feels outraged that her father was cut into two pieces and thrown into a river. As stated earlier, she still wants to exhume her husband's bones from the lake near their house. In fact, she said that she would also like to rebuild her house as a way of saying to neighbors that the genocide did not destroy the legal rights to the family's property. In her view, survivors who have been able to bury their people are much more likely to experience healing and the ability to forgive than those who still do not know what happened and the whereabouts of their deceased family members.

In her words, "A person cannot forgive until he or she is healed." Forgiveness cannot occur when there is still an open wound. Furthermore, there are circumstances that keep the wound from healing. In her experience, it is women who are HIV positive who struggle the hardest with forgiveness, and especially those who also lost all their children during the genocide. She also worries about orphans who lost their parents and siblings but says that if they can go to school—including university—they have a much better chance of conquering their trauma.

In the following pages, we will comment more broadly on what survivors said about forgiveness, moving beyond the context of Solace Ministries.[4] It is very clear to us that forgiveness is a process, and for many individuals a lifetime process, even though there may be turning points in their healing when forgiveness is experienced, sometimes in poignant and even dramatic ways. For example, survivors described how they wrestled in prayer with the desire to forgive the perpetrators of violence against them and against their family members. There was nothing superficial about this struggle. And yet over a period of time, which inevitably also corresponded with their own internal healing process, they were able to forgive the killers, the rapists, and sadists—those with seemingly no conscience about what they were doing.

Sometimes these acts of forgiveness were in response to heartfelt apologies; other times there was no formal apology, and, in fact, sometimes the victim did not even know the identity of the perpetrator. One of our major insights in wrestling with the idea of forgiveness is that forgiveness, fundamentally, is not for the perpetrator; the benefit is for the victim. It is a way for the victim to free herself from obsessing about the past—especially feelings of hatred, revenge, and violation—and instead focus on the possibility of building a new life, one that is forward-looking.

To summarize, there are two elements to forgiveness. The first is *freedom from* the images and experiences that are enslaving one; the other is *freedom to* pursue a life that is rooted in love, community, and positive engagement with the world. As will become evident in the following pages, this is not an easy process. Indeed, it may be the highest expression of our humanity—what truly marks us as a unique species.

A SIX-FOLD TYPOLOGY OF FORGIVENESS

In examining hundreds of interviews, a six-fold typology emerges that is useful in understanding the complexity of the forgiveness process. It is important to note that these "types" should be viewed as constructions—ideal types in the way social scientists use the term. As with most of the categories in this book, we have arrived at these six expressions inductively, through data analysis, not through the literature.[5] In actual lived experience, the categories overlap, and the messy processes our interviewees describe means that survivors may pass through a combination of these forms of forgiveness or even span several categories simultaneously.

Like trauma, survivors had an implicit understanding of what forgiveness meant—it referred to the idea of coming to grips with the individuals who perpetrated the genocide and, more specifically, the reference typically was to individuals who killed their loved ones or raped them. In terms of our view of genocide, forgiveness deals with the attempt by survivors to heal the wound in the collective conscience—the moral rupture in what it means to be human—at the personal but also the societal level. The typology we have developed ranges from nonforgiveness to heartfelt forgiveness, with four intervening categories. At the outset, it is important to state that this is not a normative typology, meaning that one should progress from the inability to forgive to heartfelt forgiveness. There may be benefits to having experienced heartfelt forgiveness, but it is completely understandable why a survivor might not have achieved the freedom that accompanies full forgiveness. While human agency may be involved in all the various expressions of forgiveness, heartfelt forgiveness is a gift as much as a choice. Indeed, it may involve a transcendent experience—an experience of grace that defies rational cognition.

Here is our six-fold typology of forgiveness:

Nonforgiveness. An inability to forgive the perpetrators of the genocide was very common among survivors, and there were many reasons for this. The primary factor was that perpetrators had not apologized; they had not asked for forgiveness. Or if they had apologized, the survivor doubted the sincerity of the person. And then there were a host of other factors: The horror, degradation, and inhumanity of what they had experienced as well as the ongoing legacy of the genocide (poverty, being infected with AIDS, amputations, inability to envision a positive future, etc.), as well as the fact that they often did not know who had raped them or killed their loved ones. Furthermore, some survivors may be living relatively functional lives but they choose not to forgive. Sometimes they believe that forgiving a perpetrator may encourage a repetition of behavior by this individual or a cohort of individuals who share his same political convictions. And other times, the wound of the genocide has not sufficiently healed for the survivor to even consider forgiveness—their emotions are still too raw; the experience is too undigested.

Resigned Forgiveness. On occasion we encountered individuals who said they had forgiven the perpetrators, but they said this with no emotion, no reflection on the process, and with a spirit of resignation as if there were no other alternatives. These survivors often exhibited a degree of emotional blunting—unable to cry, unable to express positive emotions. There was little expression of human agency on their part; they were victims, they were simply trying to exist one day at a time. When asked about forgiveness, they offered the following responses: "There is nothing else to do but forgive." "We have no alternative." In desperation, or because they had simply grown tired of their revolving thoughts and anger, they resigned themselves to forgiving the killers—typically not even certain what this means.

Transactional Forgiveness. During the *gacaca* courts—described in chapter 9—if a prisoner confessed to a crime and apologized, there was an expectation that the survivor will forgive the perpetrator. This transaction is fraught with difficulties, because the apology by the prisoner may be inauthentic—simply a way to reduce his sentence. Likewise, the survivor may feel that the perpetrator did not tell the whole truth. Nevertheless, within the public space of the *gacaca* court the victim feels obligated to forgive the perpetrator because it is politically mandated. While apology by the perpetrator may be personally healing for them, the victim—typically a relative who survived the genocide—is often left with unresolved feelings. Therefore, the principle benefit of transactional forgiveness is political, symbolically countering divisionism between ethnic groups.

Pragmatic Forgiveness. Some survivors forgive because they need a fresh start; they feel that they simply can't continue to dwell on the past; they want to get on with life. Through daily interactions with Hutus in their neighborhood, markets, and work, survivors begin to see them as fellow humans, just like themselves. Also, they may have gone through a process of politically reframing the past, rationalizing that the genocide was the product of the "old government" (i.e., the killers were pawns of political extremists, following orders). This may not excuse their behavior—justice should still be accomplished through the courts—but they seek release from revolving thoughts of revenge and rage and pursue forgiveness as one avenue to accomplish a resolution of their feelings. Consequently, they exert their personal agency to forgive so that they can move on personally and, pragmatically, they may believe that forgiveness is necessary at a political level so that the nation can heal.

Religiously Inspired Forgiveness. Because Rwanda is a very Christian culture, many survivors referenced religion in their discussion of forgiveness. Christians have the example of Jesus on the cross saying, "Father, forgive them; for they know not what they do," referring to the Roman soldiers who crucified him—which has obvious parallels to Hutu neighbors who were following the orders of their government in killing Tutsis. There is also the statement in the Hebrew scriptures (Deuteronomy 32:35) cited by survivors, "Vengeance is mine, I will repay, says the Lord," implying that retribution comes from a higher power. And there were numerous individuals who credited God with their survival, believing that in gratitude they should forgive the perpetrators of violence against them. The liability of theologically inspired affirmations of forgiveness is that they occur at a cognitive and rational level and do not connect emotionally with the survivor's feelings of injury.

Heartfelt Forgiveness. On occasion, we encountered survivors who seemed to have truly forgiven the killers and those who abused them sexually. They spoke of the liberation and freedom they experienced in the act of forgiveness, although it was typically through an internal struggle involving personal healing, and often prayer, meditation, and an experience of self-transcendence that acknowledged the humanity of the perpetrator. They had made the transition from victim to moral agent, freeing themselves from the revolving memories that previously enslaved them. They were no longer dependent, controlled by the past. Sometimes there had been expressions of apology by the aggressors; often there had been other healing experiences such as proper burial of the deceased, return to the site of the killing, or a transformative religious experience. We do not see heartfelt forgiveness primarily as a cognitive process so much as an emotional experience, a matter of the heart. And for many survivors, it is a gift that is somewhat transcendent in nature.

SEVERAL IMPORTANT QUALIFICATIONS

Survivors repeatedly stated that forgiving perpetrators was a process they embrace for themselves, but it does not mean they forget what the aggressors did. Mama Lambert explicitly says in her memoir, "Forgiveness doesn't erase the crime, doesn't nullify the administration of justice and doesn't revoke the sentence."[6] Rather, forgiveness frees the victim from preoccupation with revenge and constant reliving of the trauma. It is a form of release.

Second, it is also important to note that healing does not require forgiveness. For some people, forgiving the perpetrator—or multiple perpetrators— may simply be out of the question. As previously noted, the ongoing suffering due to AIDS, amputation, extreme poverty, failure to identify the perpetrator, and the lack of apology may compromise the likelihood of forgiveness. While there are many benefits to forgiveness, it should not be viewed as a normative requirement for healing from traumatic life events.

Third, any form of coercion related to forgiveness, including religious expectations, tends to falsify the authenticity of the experience. Jean Gakwandi, for example, says that talk about forgiveness, especially by Hutu religious leaders, can be "cheap." He dismisses seminars on forgiveness that are calculated to end with victim and perpetrator embracing. Forgiveness in his view is something that must come from the heart and is a response to the love that one experiences from God and the community.

Fourth, forgiveness can be detrimental if it comes too early in the healing process. It is important for one to mourn the loss, acknowledge the pain, and contextualize what one experienced. As noted, those survivors who seemed to have least engaged the path of healing, and who expressed minimal affect in telling their story, were also often the individuals who said with little fanfare that they had forgiven. After analyzing the data, our finding is that genuine forgiveness—if it occurs—never happens at the beginning of the process of healing. Rather, it is a by-product near the end of a healing process.

Fifth, forgiveness is typically not a one-time event. As with trauma, survivors may cycle back through emotions of rage and revenge, depending on their personal context or a social or political trigger. Our interviews, time and again, show that forgiveness is a process fraught with conflict, introspection, and is often a step forward followed by a step or two backward. In short, forgiveness is something with which one struggles. And when one experiences true heartfelt forgiveness, it is often viewed as a gift, not an act of the will or a personal achievement.

Finally, forgiveness does not preclude justice. Criminal acts require retribution and appropriate punishment. In this regard, forgiveness is for the victim, not the perpetrator, although the perpetrator may also feel some release from his or her suffering when forgiven. As previously stated, apology is inauthentic when it is done in a calculated manner, hoping, for example, for a reduced prison sentence. Likewise, forgiveness is not a ticket to cathartic release for the perpetrator, although a new freedom is often a correlate of forgiveness.

CONDITIONS AND BARRIERS OF FORGIVENESS

Many survivors said that they could forgive the perpetrators if certain conditions were met, and oftentimes the list of conditions was very similar. First, it was important for survivors that the perpetrator ask for forgiveness and apologize for what they did. For example, an orphan described the manner in which a perpetrator sought him out so that he could make an apology: "He was honest because he searched for me for a long time. He came and asked me to forgive him . . . they had undressed me before they hit me and threw me in the hole. He had kept the jacket I was wearing and right after the war he sent it to me upon hearing that I was alive, although I couldn't wear it again. Then he came to ask me for forgiveness, saying that it was the bad government and so forth. He pleaded for forgiveness and I . . . I forgave him because he was sincere. I totally forgave him."

On the other hand, if the apology is not sincere, then the likelihood of forgiveness is diminished, as for this survivor: "I haven't forgiven them because they haven't apologized or shown their remorse. The fact that they deny having done wrong prohibits me from forgiving them." Another survivor made a similar statement, "I think it is possible to forgive, but I still think it is far off for me. When I see those who did it, I find it good, but I have never seen anyone who came to apologize or even confess. I think that if they confessed, and also explained their reasons, maybe I would. But it's still hard for me since no one has come."

Another survivor said that not all apologies were sincere. "You still hear those who admit their crimes so their [prison] sentences are reduced, but that doesn't mean that they have really asked for forgiveness. For me, for example, the people who came to look for me in Nyanza, who made me lose my arm, have never admitted their crime and come to the point of asking me personally to forgive them. They must admit their crime and say, 'We cut off the arm of Francois' wife and we sincerely ask for pardon.' If I see that it comes from the bottom of their hearts, I will forgive them without problem. I don't speak only for myself. I speak for all the survivors. No one has asked me for pardon, but I am ready to forgive those who ask for forgiveness—in order to rebuild our country."

Apology is not the only factor affecting forgiveness. Survivors also wanted details related to the death of their loved ones. A survivor said, "I can forgive them if they ask for forgiveness and show us where they buried those whom they killed, so that we can bury them again with respect and honor." Another survivor made a very similar statement: "There is something positive if they admit their crimes and say how they carried out the act of killing and, if possible, they show you where they put the dead so that you can give the dead a decent burial."

A widow elaborated on the appropriate elements of apology in this way: "If someone comes and asks me for pardon, before anything else, he must explain how it happened. I believe that I will not hesitate to forgive him. To this day, the problem I have is that I don't even know where my family was killed. But if they come and tell me how and where it happened, because even my neighbors to this day do not admit, 'I took your saucepan, your sheet metal, or your household tools.' If they do that, I will not hesitate to pardon them because this is our country. It belongs to all of us. We must get along. Moreover, a heart that forgives is a pure heart."

The biggest barrier to forgiveness often was the horrific nature of the killing. A survivor cited the following reason why he can't forgive, referencing a friend's experience during the genocide: "We escaped, but his wife was pregnant and she was carrying another child. I noticed her death: they split her belly wanting to see her unborn baby; shot her, but she didn't die. That picture does not leave my mind." The previous chapters of this book give multiple examples of such horrors, but it is important to cite them as examples of why survivors have difficulty forgiving.

Another barrier is that the victim does not see the utility of forgiving. For example, an orphan said regarding the perpetrator: "He can surely do nothing at all, except if he raised my parents from the dead or else if I would go home and find our house there and also my family. Even if he built me a house without my parents, I would not forgive him 100 percent." Another orphan said that he is troubled by forgiveness when he sees that he is getting older, is disabled, and sees no prospect for a decent future.

Furthermore, some survivors reject the idea of forgiving because they feel that it only encourages the behavior that they would be pardoning, such as this individual: "I feel reluctant to forgive because the killers repeat their crimes even after being forgiven—they again kill people." Another survivor echoed the same idea: "I would be making a mistake if I went to court and said that he should go free as I have forgiven him; he would go home and kill others, saying, 'They are stupid.'"

And finally, survivors asked, how could they forgive the person(s) who raped them when they didn't even know who they were. Forgiving someone abstractly, or individuals generically, didn't make any sense to them. Clearly, these individuals had not apologized, nor was it likely that they ever would.

REVENGE

Occasionally, survivors were very forthright in rejecting the possibility of forgiveness. A survivor said, "I don't have the strength to kill them or correct them. . . . I don't have the strength to forgive. On the contrary, if I had a gun I would kill them. If I could find fuel, I would burn them alive. To forgive is a gift from God. For me, it is impossible." Another survivor who had been raped said, "I don't know how I can forgive him because it was not even one man, but they were three. Each of them had his dedicated day—one today, another tomorrow, and another after tomorrow. I think you can understand I do not forgive because of the life I have lived." She followed this statement saying, "Having the authority, I would kill them too."

In spite of the previous quotations, we found a surprising absence of revenge among survivors, even though there were repeated statements of anger regarding what occurred during the genocide. Instead, there was a sense of respect for the government's attempt to minimize ethnic distinctions under the policy, "We are all Rwandans." Other times, survivors relegated justice to God, as in this statement: "Revenge is of the Lord . . . you cannot get a *panga* and cut them like they did to our people or get them and let their children rape them. None of this can be done. So, when you cannot do anything, you leave it to the Lord." Another survivor was theological in his response, rather than pragmatic: "It is not up to us to punish. It is for God to do it." A survivor rationalized, "What I can do is live with them and show them that I am alive and that I need nothing from them. When they see I am alive maybe they will have remorse in their hearts and repent." But most survivors struggle internally with revenge, as stated by this survivor: "Without God helping you, you feel like revenge . . . an eye for an eye, an arm for an arm. . . . God helped me that I can feel forgiveness, but it is not easy."

It is also important to note that attitudes related to revenge sometimes evolved for survivors, such as this individual: "God says that we should love our enemies and pray for them. The more time I spent with God, the more he comforted me. I reconciled with everything related to me and forgave. I didn't have any other choice." While this statement has a degree of theological nobility—"love our enemies and pray for them"—it also reflects the fact that she felt that she didn't have any other alternative than to forgive. This same attitude is mirrored in this statement of a survivor: "I think that God played a role in my survival. . . . I think that I should forgive because God loved me enough to save me. I remember the love of God and think that I have no other choice than forgiving."

THE BENEFITS OF FORGIVING

A common perception of forgiveness is that it is a moral duty, freighted with religious obligation. To some degree this is true. But for survivors who have truly experienced heartfelt forgiveness, it has an altogether different tone; forgiveness that is noncoerced is viewed as an act of liberation. It frees survivors from being bound to hatred and resentment; it frees them from revolving thoughts of revenge; it enables them to look to the future rather than the past.

Perhaps the most succinct statement in our interviews was this: "I forgave to set myself free." Similarly, another survivor defined forgiveness this way: "When you forgive, you have set free your heart from this person that wronged you." The same idea was echoed in this statement: "You forgive so that you will have peace in your heart, so that you will not keep on thinking about this person that wronged you."

Drawing on her own experience, a survivor said, "When you don't forgive you always have a burden in your heart and you feel sad . . . when you forgive, you feel relieved." Another survivor said, "Forgiveness is liberating yourself because before you forgive you are binding yourself." In these cases, it is critical to note again that the primary benefit was not for their aggressors but rather for survivors, as in this statement: "It's mainly me that forgiveness benefits."

Many survivors also noted that forgiveness is for the benefit of the country of Rwanda, such as this individual: "The reason I would forgive is to build my country. We can't live together if we don't forgive each other." Another survivor was more pragmatic, noting that the government can't support one hundred thousand people in prison from the genocide. Hence, for the benefit of the nation it is important that survivors forgive and reconcile. On the other hand, a survivor offered the following qualification: "I would forgive them although I won't forget what happened."

There were also a handful of survivors who looked beyond themselves to focus on the benefit of forgiveness for the perpetrators, recognizing that many of them are filled with guilt and shame and in their own way may be traumatized and imprisoned in revolving thoughts of the atrocities they committed. Regarding the mutual benefit of forgiveness, a survivor said, "You both gain from forgiving—they have a deep feeling in their hearts that they hurt you. . . . When they ask you for forgiveness, they also leave these feelings behind." Another survivor was more explicit, saying that forgiveness is for the perpetrators, but not just to make them free. Rather, perpetrators that apologize and receive forgiveness from survivors will be less likely to repeat their crimes, and this benefits both the victims and the larger society, as reflected in this person's statement: "I personally feel there is something to gain because I feel that the person who wronged me has regrets and he would not repeat it. On his side, he feels relieved because if he feels that if he repeats it, it will be difficult for him to ask to be forgiven. On my side, I would be relieved. I would walk feeling relieved and think that person will not repeat it. That will give me hope to live because he regrets what he did."

THE PROCESS OF FORGIVENESS

Forgiveness is not something that happens instantaneously. It is a process as illustrated by the survivor who said, "Forgiveness doesn't mean you instantly have good relations with them or drink from the same well." Another survivor said, "I have forgiven him but at times the hurt comes back." And many survivors are in the process of considering forgiveness, but they are not yet at this point. Crying, a survivor said, "Even though when I am praying I sometimes say, 'Let me forgive the people that wronged me. It is not easy.'" Nevertheless, for many survivors there is a desire for things to return to normal, to a state where Hutus and Tutsis can live together as one people. A survivor defined forgiveness in this way: "Forgiving is living again with everyone like the way we used to before—loving everyone like before, and everyone feeling at ease."

A survivor said that it took a year to process the idea of forgiveness after discovering the fate of her relatives: "It took a long time in order for me to know where my father had been buried. I had failed to know the place; he had been buried in a latrine behind the house . . . one of those killers who came and asked for forgiveness is the one who told me the place. . . . I managed to get the other dead bodies out. So, when he came to ask for forgiveness is the time he told me the area where my father was buried. I had the courage to forgive him because he came and asked for it." This survivor said that after this experience she was encouraged by her charismatic prayer group to forgive, telling her that her heart would be relieved if she could do this. And so she decided to forgive him.

For some survivors, the healing process occurred after they had the courage to return to the site where loved ones were killed. We recall journeying with a survivor to his hometown. He took us to the church where hundreds of people had been slaughtered, which was the first time since the genocide that he had been to the church. We assumed that he was going to take us into the church, but as we approached the steps, he said that he could not enter—that we should go in alone. He could only venture as far as a memorial outside the church sanctuary. However, on a subsequent trip, he did go into the church. Symbolically, this was a way of facing the horror directly. But it could not be done on the first attempt.

THE ROLE OF RELIGION IN FORGIVENESS

Religion potentially functions at many different levels in the forgiveness process, some of which are cognitive and others that are experiential. At the cognitive level, the vast majority of survivors grew up with a Christian worldview. Hence, it is not surprising that when survivors reflect on forgiveness they sometimes refer to Jesus's death on the cross when he called out to God, saying, "Forgive them for they know not what they do." Likewise, survivors sometimes quote scriptures, such as, "Vengeance is mine says the Lord." Also, survivors occasionally cite a more punitive idea: "He who does not forgive will also not be forgiven"; or the positive interpretation, "Forgive your neighbor and you will also be forgiven." And sometimes survivors viewed forgiveness as a Christian obligation: "The Word of God tells us to forgive everyone."

While these theological concepts are not unimportant, they do not seem to be the "driver" behind heartfelt forgiveness, which many survivors characterize as a gift. Survivors frequently said that they could not forgive without being empowered by God, such as this survivor: "I can do it if I am led by the Spirit, but as a human being I can't forgive." To forgive has a transcendent element in this view.

When survivors reflect on their experience of forgiving, it sometimes is framed in the belief that their life was spared for a purpose. For example, "What made me forgive them is when I thought about how powerful God is and how he protected me during that time . . . and yet I am not as good as those who died. It's a miracle God did for me. So, I thought about the love of God and I also decided to forgive." Similarly, another survivor said, "I think that God played a role in my survival. . . . I think that I should forgive because God loved me enough to save me. I remember the love of God and think that I have no other choice than forgiving." And this statement: "I would forgive them because God has shown me mercy and I am still alive," which was a comment made in response to the question of whether she could forgive those who raped her.

Prayer was the mediating factor as some survivors struggled with the issue of forgiveness, as for this survivor: "God played a big role in enabling me to forgive. I would be praying and I could hear God's voice telling me, 'Forgive those people, they didn't know what they were doing.'" Another survivor said, "I pray for my enemies, even those that killed my relatives." And still another survivor said, "I feel sad but through prayer I know that I should love others as I do myself and forgive him."

Some of the more striking comments were made by survivors who said that they had come to realize that perpetrators are also human and have the potential to change. Perhaps the most philosophical statement was made by a survivor who said, "I can forgive him because I see him as a human being. The person who killed him [her husband] has a soul like him. He will also die in the end. Only God can punish him and forgive him if he confesses."

On the other hand, there were survivors who questioned the humanity of the perpetrators: "When I think of those who assassinated my loved ones, it overwhelms me. It's too much for me. Sometimes I wonder if they were human or if they only resembled humans, because I find that no human could do what they did. Someone who had children could not cut a pregnant woman with a knife to cause an abortion. Nor could a normal man kill his own wife. No, they had lost their minds." But this survivor then went on to say, "If someone who killed my loved ones came to ask me sincerely for forgiveness, I would forgive him. But admitting their crimes in churches or in front of the authorities so that their penalties will be reduced without asking for pardon of the survivors has no value. Anyone who asked to meet me and admitted his crime and sincerely begged for pardon, I would pardon him without hesitation."

As survivors gained strength and dealt with their trauma, some survivors were able to apply specific Christian virtues, not in a negative obligatory way, but as a moral ideal. "God says that we should love our enemies and pray for them. The more time I spent with God, the more he comforted me. I reconciled with everything related to me and forgave. I didn't have any other choice." However, one survivor summarized his feelings in a somewhat ironic way, saying: "Let God himself forgive them and may he forgive me too, because it is impossible for me to forgive such people."

CONCLUSION

In our application for funding from the John Templeton Foundation, we focused on forgiveness as the rationale for the project. As stated in the preface to this book, it was only when we became deeply enmeshed in the interviewing process that we realized that forgiveness cannot be decontextualized, isolated as a stand-alone variable. Survivors do not think of forgiveness in this way. Forgiveness is not a quick fix to trauma. It is not a one-time event in the life of a survivor. Rather, it is a complicated, evolving struggle that involves the emotions more than the will. Theological theorizing can feel very empty unless it is situated within the human struggle for meaning and purpose. Likewise, philosophical theorizing that does not acknowledge the pain associated with moral and social rupture is equally superficial.

In the next chapter we tackle three interrelated issues: the *gacaca* courts, commemorations, and reconciliation. In this regard, we move from the personal issue of forgiveness to the more political and public issue of state-orchestrated efforts at reconciliation, although we continue to draw on survivor perceptions and experiences. While forgiveness and reconciliation are related concepts, we view forgiveness as an internal struggle to deal with perpetrator violence, whereas reconciliation functions at a social and civic level, describing the means by which people of different tribes, races, social status, and political persuasions seek to live together in relative harmony, acknowledging one another's common humanity.

CHAPTER 9

Justice and Reconciliation

While there is a substantial literature on reconciliation and social redress following large-scale violence, in this chapter we focus once again on the words and experiences of the survivors that we interviewed. We address three inter-related processes—*gacaca* trials, interpersonal reconciliation, and official commemorations, asking throughout how these larger processes affect the individual and the country. We do not include discussion of the International Criminal Tribunal for Rwanda (ICTR)[1] in this chapter since none of our interviewees commented on the tribunal, except for one survivor who was very dismissive of a judge who laughed at a witness's description of rape. The ICTR focused on high-ranking military officials, politicians, businessmen, and religious, militia, and media leaders. In total, ninety-three individuals were indicted and sixty-two were sentenced at a cost of more than $1.5 billion. In contrast, the cost of the entire *gacaca* operation was about $43.5 million.[2] The ICTR is the first international tribunal to deliver verdicts in relation to geno-cide and the first to recognize rape as a means of genocide.[3]

In the chapter on trauma, we viewed genocide as a moral rupture in the relationships between two populations of people, Hutu and Tutsi. We argued that this rupture occurs on two levels, the interpersonal and the social-political. In the case study of Solace Ministries, we saw how traumatized survivors are reintegrated back into a caring community that helps them carry the burden of their past memories. In the chapter on forgiveness, we described how heartfelt forgiveness of the perpetrator has the potential to liberate sur-vivors from revolving thoughts of revenge as well as intrusive flashbacks of the horror of the genocide. In this chapter, we move from the individual to the social-political level, asking whether the *gacaca* courts and commemorations have been able to heal the moral breach in the body politic.

GACACA COURTS

When we first became involved with studying the Rwanda genocide, we attended a conference in 2001 that included Rwandan scholars and intellectuals who were grappling with how to administer justice in a context where there were one hundred thousand individuals in prison who had been charged with participating in the genocide. One idea being discussed was to revive the *gacaca* court—a traditional village justice system that had been largely abandoned.[4]

Shortly after this conference, in an attempt to deal efficiently with the prison population as well as promote reconciliation between the Hutu and Tutsi populations, the Rwanda government adopted the *gacaca* process at a statewide level, selecting local people of good character who would hear the testimony of survivors as well as the confessions and defense of individuals who had been imprisoned after the genocide. The *gacaca* courts typically occurred outdoors or in a local hall. The judges had basic training in legal proceedings but were not professional jurists. Several prisoners at a time were brought to the court in their pink prison uniforms. The judges sat at tables in the front. Survivors sat to the side to hear the testimony of the accused. And local residents, sometimes several hundred, formed the audience.

In one of the court sessions that we attended, three prisoners were present and one survivor. The first prisoner got down on his knees before the judges and apologized repeatedly as he described how he and his companions had killed several children and buried them. He was very emotional in his statement as he pleaded for forgiveness. The next two prisoners were more matter of fact; they admitted what had occurred but showed little remorse or emotion. Various witnesses were called and, ironically, onlookers implicated one witness in the killing who subsequently was taken away as a prisoner at the end of the day. At various points the onlookers shouted out opinions based on what they had seen and had to be quieted.

Throughout the trial, a surviving relative of the children who had been killed sat emotionless. And then after testimony had been heard and confessions had been given, the head of the court turned to the survivor and asked if she forgave the killers. Quietly, she said that she did. Sentencing of the prisoners did not occur that day, but the general pattern was for prisoners to be rehabilitated to the community after they had served an appropriate number of years. For lesser crimes, they were ordered to do community service. Those accused of sexual violence were often held in prison. Also, various forms of compensation were to be paid to surviving family members for loss of property, cattle, and land.

According to our interviewees, attending *gacaca* proceedings was often very traumatizing for survivors, since it involved listening in excruciating detail to how their loved ones had been killed. Also, many survivors felt that prisoners were not authentically repentant for what they had done but were merely confessing to lighten their sentence or to get out of prison altogether. For example, a survivor recalled that a prisoner said, "He killed a baby and put him on a spear and put it on his shoulder and acted as if he was a person coming from hunting. When I heard that I stood up and started abusing him." She said that she was forced to leave the court proceedings since abusive language from onlookers was not permitted.

Another survivor said that she decided not to return to *gacaca* because it was setting her back emotionally. "It hurt me . . . they would say how they raped a child, how they killed someone's child, the details. I felt a strong, bad emotion and I decided not to go back there." Women survivors also found it extremely difficult to face their rapists. One woman said that she wrote down her testimony and submitted it to the court. "I could not face him face to face." Another survivor said that she decided not to testify against her rapist because she thought it would bring dishonor to her children. "But when I learned that I was infected with AIDS, I thought that I should go to the courts." Other survivors said that they sat like a mute person throughout the court proceedings, unable to speak. Another survivor said that she could only whisper her testimony to someone who then wrote it down for her.

Other survivors said they felt physically sick listening to testimony. In fact, one survivor said that she fainted during a trial as the names were being read of those who had been killed by the prisoner being tried. And another survivor said, "When I started to talk, my head started becoming dizzy and I did not feel right. So, I told them not to call me again to *gacaca* because I can't manage talking." In another instance, it appears that a survivor was so traumatized that he had lost interest in any expression of justice. "My father-in-law is still alive, but he didn't follow up on anything. Because he lost many children, he didn't care anymore." Another survivor said, "I thought it was a way to make me worse [referring to testifying at *gacaca*], and since, anyway, all my loved ones were killed, there was no point of going there to see those who killed them being happy."

It was also physically and financially demanding to attend the *gacaca* trials, especially if one had moved to another area away from where the killing occurred. Sometimes the trials would last weeks, and survivors would have to walk or pay for transportation back to their hometown. When they were attending *gacaca*, it also meant that they were unable to work, which put a financial strain on survivors. But perhaps even more important is that many survivors did not feel that prisoners were telling the truth. And one survivor said that she feared being laughed at by the prisoners whom she assumed would contradict her account of what occurred.

The view of many survivors was that prisoners confessed to crimes for very instrumental reasons: it was a way to be released from prison and/or to reduce their sentence. Repeatedly, survivors said that confessions were not "heartfelt," they were not sincere, they were not genuine. Furthermore, survivors said that perpetrators would tell some elements of what occurred, but not the whole truth. They would also rationalize the killings, saying that they were simply doing what the government ordered them to do. Another excuse prisoners offered was that they were part of a group that did the killing, but they, themselves, did not do the crime of which they were accused. This was a convenient excuse since oftentimes some of the individuals in the group had escaped to Zaire or other countries and therefore could not be held accountable for the killing.

One of the judges we interviewed said that the apologies she witnessed often did not seem authentic. The request for forgiveness from survivors was part of the protocol, and the survivors had little option but to grant forgiveness if a prisoner confessed and apologized, regardless of the apparent authenticity of the apology. A survivor bluntly said that prisoners apologize simply because the government demands they do so as a condition of their release, and in an attempt to promote reconciliation in the country. Another survivor said that prisoners apologize thinking that this will reduce the compensation that they must pay to survivors.

Several survivors also believed that the families of prisoners bribed witnesses. There were also a few reports of witnesses being killed, but perhaps more important was a perception by survivors that if they testified against a prisoner they might be killed, with poisoning being cited as the most frequent fear. One survivor said that she had been directly threatened in a letter that she would be killed if she testified, so she reported this to authorities with the hope that if she died at least the finger would be pointed at this person. Another survivor gave this example of retribution: "The father had testified; they wanted to kill him, but couldn't find him, so they killed the son."

As we saw in the last chapter, survivors also complained that they seldom received any compensation, even if it was mandated by the *gacaca* court. Occasionally survivors reported that they received a cow or bed or some small partial payment, but no one among our interviewees expressed satisfaction with the settlement. Furthermore, because survivors had often moved away from their home area because their house had been destroyed, it was difficult to lay claim to their land. Instead, perpetrators of the genocide were oftentimes farming the land. And when survivors filed appeals, there were delays or their claim was minimized, as in this case: "It resulted in nothing. . . . I went thinking that they would give me something. But all they did was devalue everything. They said that a house that had almost sixty iron roof sheets had only one. So, in the end I had nothing for they devalued and destroyed everything." Another survivor said, "We went to court about our wealth and won. But nothing was given to us. So, it's worthless."

THE EXPECTATION OF FORGIVENESS IN GACACA TRIALS

As foreshadowed in the previous chapter, forgiveness that is granted at the *gacaca* courts and forgiveness that happens in a more heartfelt way are quite different. When a prisoner confessed at *gacaca*, there was a political expectation that a surviving relative would forgive the prisoner if he apologized. A survivor summarized the expectation as follows: "I could not refuse to forgive because when the government uses the law it is the law that is followed."

Some survivors had a cynical view of the way forgiveness was handled in the *gacaca* courts. For example, one survivor said, "Forgiving is mere talk," and then said that people who have been forgiven may still turn around and poison you. Another survivor was more definitive in this linkage: "We forgave those who confessed and apologized, although they are the ones now poisoning people." A typical exchange in our interviews followed this pattern when we asked about the apology and forgiveness exchanges during *gacaca*:

QUESTION: *Was he sincere?*
ANSWER: He wasn't sincere.

QUESTION: *But you forgave him?*
ANSWER: I forgave him.

There was only one instance in our interviews where a survivor refused to grant forgiveness at *gacaca*: "That is why I never forgave him. He asked me to forgive him and I told him I couldn't forgive him if he can't speak the truth."

Several survivors said that the test of a true apology is not that it is offered at *gacaca*, where it is expected, but when a perpetrator comes to one personally and expresses regret and asks for forgiveness. In only a few instances did our interviewees report heartfelt regret by the perpetrator. In one instance, a killer came personally to a survivor, begging for her forgiveness, but it appeared to her that this was motivated by the desire to get his brother released from prison. Repeatedly, survivors said that genuine forgiveness is only possible when a survivor senses that the perpetrator is no longer expressing hatred and disdain.

THE BENEFITS OF GACACA

In interviews that were done by AOCM prior to the beginning of *gacaca*, when it was still an idea in the making, survivors were quite hopeful about its outcome. An orphan said, "The truth will come from down on the ground, and the government will be able to know who should be punished and not." Another orphan was equally optimistic: "I am hopeful, especially for the *gacaca* courts, which will again resolve justice in the country, reconciling people." And without qualification, an orphan said, "The killers will ask for forgiveness and we will forgive them."

Even after the *gacaca* process began, some survivors were optimistic that the truth about the genocide would be revealed. One survivor said, "If one attempts to deceive, others come up with the whole truth." Another survivor commented on the therapeutic value of being able to testify: "We would go to *gacaca* courts and speak out. This made me change because being able to say what I saw made me feel light at heart."

A real benefit of *gacaca*, however, was that survivors discovered things about their family members that they didn't know. For example, many survivors, prior to *gacaca*, didn't know how their children or spouse had died and, ironically, knowing the details of their death was desired even if it was traumatizing. And as has been mentioned in a previous chapter, because prisoners told survivors where their loved ones had been buried or their bodies disposed, it was possible in some instances for survivors to dig up latrines or other graves, exhume the bones of their loved ones, and give them proper burial.

For those who have not been able to properly bury relatives, it has been difficult for them to heal, as in the case of this widow: "I have not been able to find even a bone of members of my family to bury them. This is a serious problem. It really preoccupies me. If I could have found even the remains of one person among them, it would at least give me a moment of peace." Another survivor said that it has helped her to know at least how her husband was killed, even if she could not bury him. "You see, what grieved me was that I didn't know how they died, but the man who killed my husband, I was told that he killed him and left him in the sewage, but it was the month of April so the rain came and washed him away. I wasn't able to bury him, but it helped to know how he was killed. Because when someone doesn't know how their loved ones died, they still think that they are alive."

The *gacaca* courts were the closest thing that Rwanda had to the Truth and Reconciliation Commission of South Africa, which was so ably orchestrated by Archbishop Desmond Tutu.[5] In July 1995, Tutu came to Kigali from neighboring Burundi and said, "Ultimately we must concentrate on forgiveness and reconciliation because, if we concentrate on retribution, I am fearful that the spiral of violence, resentment and pay-back will never end."[6] There is great truth to this statement, which is why the postgenocide government put so much effort into uniting Tutsis and Hutus, officially banning ethnic and tribal categorical distinctions, and making the case that citizens are simply Rwandans. Whether the *gacaca* courts were successful is an open question. When the *gacaca* process was ending in February 2011, the minister of justice said that 1,222,093 persons had been judged with 12 percent acquitted. And by early 2012, about 40,000 genocide convicts were still in jail.[7]

INTERPERSONAL RECONCILIATION

In the minds of many survivors, reconciliation is different from forgiveness and exists on a number of different levels. First, there is social or interpersonal reconciliation, which has to do with everyday interactions between Hutus and Tutsis when they meet on the street, see each other in the market, or worship together at church. In everyday discourse, there is the perception of harmony between Hutus and Tutsis. But as noted previously, reconciliation is not easy to achieve, especially when one is living next door to the individual who killed your loved ones.

An orphan explained, "After the genocide the government has done its best to reconcile people, but I think it is not from deep in our hearts. In fact, we do it as an obligation. So according to me, there is a kind of hypocrisy between people." This echoes the sentiment in earlier chapters on the "insincere" relationships that exist between survivors and their aggressors. Realistically, it may take several generations before the wounds can heal. One survivor said that younger survivors seem to reconcile more easily than adults, and this is understandable since widows who lost all their children lack the ability to start over in life.

Nevertheless, just as was the case with both trauma and forgiveness, orphans struggle with reconciliation, especially if they lack adequate shelter, have physical disabilities, and are caring for surviving siblings. The orphans who seem to be doing best and are more reconciled, not only to Hutus but to life itself, are those who have been able to get an education, have good employment, and have started raising their own families. On the other hand, there are orphans and widows alike who seem stuck in their circumstances. A survivor said, "Reconciliation is difficult because there are orphans with no one to care for them, no one to whom they can take their worries, as well as widows who don't have the means to live, who have lost everything." Deprivations of this sort are constant reminders of the genocide, making reconciliation a challenge.

Furthermore, the attitudes of some perpetrators make reconciliation difficult. A survivor reflected on a killer who was released from prison after ten years: "It traumatizes me when we meet and he acts very innocent, like someone who doesn't have any punishment . . . that makes me think of beating him with stones." It is also disturbing to survivors when perpetrators are living better than their victims—with homes, farms, and extended families, whereas orphans and widows are lonely, living hand to mouth and lack hope for the future. One survivor said, "Reconciliation is always talked about, but I think it will never be achieved." Another survivor said that it is impossible to live next door to the person who killed her children, saying, "How can you reconcile?" And for children living without parents, a survivor said, "It is not easy to reconcile an orphan with the one who has killed his whole family."

Survivors make distinctions between those who have apologized and sought forgiveness, having served their prison terms, and those who deny any wrongdoing. A survivor said, "There are some perpetrators that I reconcile with and there are those that set me back." The ability to get along and to reconcile is also context-bound, affected by the time of year or the political climate. For example, one survivor said that she gets along okay with Hutus until the month of April and the commemorations, and then for a period she has difficulty talking with Hutus. Another survivor said that he can relate to Hutus that he didn't know before the genocide, but it is difficult to relate to those from his hometown.

Other survivors said that they have civil relations with Hutus at a superficial level, but they avoid deep conversations. One individual said, "Genocide survivors hold their own conversations," elaborating, "You have nothing in common with Hutu perpetrators or their children." An orphan said, "They [perpetrators] seem to be more angry than we survivors." Another survivor said, "When the government speaks of it [reconciliation], you find only the genocide survivors are ready to reconcile, but the killers don't accept this matter and get angry."

Some survivors are still fearful that perpetrators may harm them, such as this individual who said, "I try not to pass when they are passing because I feel as if they are also going to kill me." But sometimes there is avoidance by both survivors and perpetrators. For example, a survivor said that she is always afraid when she meets the person responsible for killing her family members, adding, "both of us know that he killed." And another survivor described the situation when he returns to his home area: "I only meet them when I go back for the issues of land. They don't even dare greet you with their hand, unless you are the one giving it to them. I get scared that they can even poison me and I die. That's why I don't greet them. We just pass by one another." And when exchanges do occur, a survivor said the exchanges are superficial: "We greet each other but we don't have long conversations."

PROBING THE ISSUE OF RECONCILIATION

In lieu of posing more abstract questions about reconciliation, we found discussion of the mundane and day-to-day interactions to be more grounded and revealing. In addition to the discussion about everyday meetings, as described above, we also asked questions that probed the issue of interaction and reconciliation in hypothetical but practically imaginable terms. To the question, "Could you live in the same house with Hutus?" many survivors answered affirmatively. This was especially true for students who might share living accommodations in school dormitories or similar housing. Interacting with Hutus on a social level is something that students do regularly. After all, 85 percent of the population is Hutu. However, more intimate sorts of relationships raised questions about the degree to which Tutsis are reconciled.

To the question, "Could you share your secrets related to the genocide with Hutus?" we received more ambivalent responses. For example, a survivor said, "I feel there is no problem in my heart and I have forgiven them. But to be my friend and share with them my testimony or secrets, this cannot happen." Another survivor said, "We talk about general things related to life . . . we talk about school . . . but nothing concerning the genocide." And a survivor said, "I would talk to them if they started talking to me," but it is apparent that Hutus avoid conversation related to the genocide as do Tutsis in interacting with Hutu friends.

Third, we asked orphans whether they could marry a Hutu, and we asked widows how they would feel if a surviving child married a Hutu. One survivor said, "It would depend on his heart . . . the way I see his heart." And another survivor, a widow referring to her daughter or son marrying a Hutu, said, "I would accept it, but in my heart it wouldn't be right." And commenting further about the importance of context, she continued, "in April it would be really hard." But most survivors dismissed the question with a laugh. "No," it would be impossible to marry a Hutu, even if this person was not involved in the genocide. Hence, in relations among school friends, friendships might be quite easygoing, but in the matter of marriage it was inconceivable to most orphans that they could marry individuals from the perpetrating group.

On the other hand, there was widespread recognition that, in time, it is very important for the future of the country that Hutus and Tutsis reconcile. In fact, survivors acknowledged the leadership of President Paul Kagame related to reconciliation, even if they expressed personal difficulties reconciling with Hutus. In discussing reconciliation with survivors, the bottom line was that "reconciliation goes hand in hand with justice," said Mama Lambert. At the heart of justice is acknowledging the genocide, not denying it, and making certain that perpetrators have punishment appropriate to their crime and that compensation, as ordered by the court, is paid. One survivor said rather plaintively, "If they tell the truth without hiding what they did and what they knew, we would reconcile. We would forgive because they are the only neighbors we have left." She also added, and "if they showed us where they killed and threw our people, we could bury them. At that time, we will reconcile and build our country."

Other survivors pointed to the importance of recovering personally from the trauma they experienced as a necessary condition to reconciliation. A survivor pointedly said, "Reconciling occurs when a person has realized that he is a person of value." This individual, however, aptly stated the problem with reconciliation: "Now I am an orphan. I take care of myself and my children. We have no food today. I am meeting people who have killed my parents. These people look down on me. How can I not suffer from trauma?"

Hence, from our interviews with survivors, it would appear that addressing the issue of psychological trauma, as well as the living situation of survivors, is an important element if reconciliation between Hutus and Tutsis is to occur. A member of the Solace community stated that widows have a responsibility to nurture orphans: "Women and men who survived must approach orphans and bring them up and not leave orphans alone. That is when there will be unity and reconciliation."

THE COMMEMORATION PERIOD AND MEMORIALS

Many survivors have very ambivalent feelings about the commemoration period, which begins in April and extends for one hundred days. On the one hand, they believe that it is important to remember those who died and the events that led to the deaths of their fellow citizens. On the other hand, unresolved feelings and emotions are triggered during the commemoration period that oftentimes are a setback to the healing process. Nevertheless, we did not encounter any survivors who believed that the genocide should not be commemorated, in spite of the pain associated with it. Indeed, many survivors argued for the erection of memorials to commemorate the dead.

One survivor said about the commemoration period: "It helps me remember my family, the good things they did for me and the way we lived together." He admitted that he feels sad during the commemorations, but he also said that he sometimes doesn't want the commemorations to end. It is a dedicated period of time and way of being with his loved ones who were killed. Another survivor was more blunt in assessing the value of the commemorations: "Mourning and remembering are important, because if we didn't, then we would forget our loved ones." But simultaneously this survivor said that she often feels sick during the commemorative period. Dueling emotions inevitably surfaced for many survivors during the commemorations, as expressed by this survivor: "Mourning is good because we remember and cry."

When assessing the value of the commemorations, perhaps the key distinction has to do with the emotional health of the survivor, as stated by this individual: "For those of us who have come to terms with what happened, we find it a good period for we shouldn't forget." Echoing this view an orphan elaborated what he thought should be done: "I think memorials should be built, books written, churches in which people died should be used as memorials, weapons used to kill people during the genocide should be put in those memorials. All this in order to help people to never forget what they have been through and let our next generations know that." Indeed, there was repeated anxiety that within a generation or two, the genocide could be forgotten unless there are memorials reminding people what occurred. An orphan specifically expressed concern about whether her own children would be aware of the genocide if there were not memorials.

A number of survivors vividly described the experience of visiting memorials and attending commemorations of the genocide. A survivor said, "When the month of April begins, I remember from day one where I passed and everywhere I went." Another survivor said that during the commemoration period it is as if the genocide happened yesterday. Some survivors say that it is specific things, such as viewing skulls that are displayed, which immediately takes one back to the killing. Even the sound of commemorative songs being played on the radio may trigger vivid memories of the genocide.

Consequently, for many of our interviewees, interacting with the past is highly problematic. Some survivors go to considerable lengths to avoid any contact with memorials or commemoration ceremonies; the pain and triggering effect are too great. One survivor said, "During the mourning period I lock myself in the house because I don't want to see people. There are times people come knocking; I don't open." Some survivors refuse to turn on the radio or watch TV. A survivor said regarding these triggering stimuli: "I end up wanting to scream and hide all over again." An orphan summarized the issue succinctly: "For me, memorials create problems, because I remember what I have forgotten." And sometimes these memories stimulate very negative feelings, as expressed by this survivor who said that during the commemorations, "We really hate people."

More typically, however, survivors turn these negative emotions on them-selves. In the context of discussing memorials and the mourning period, survivors referred to headaches; their ulcer getting worse; backaches increasing; fainting spells; physical numbness; losing appetite for food; crying repeatedly; being unable to get out of bed; flashbacks to specific events, such as rape and cutting; and being fearful. Some survivors said that they have been hospitalized during the commemorations. In a spirit of resignation, a survivor said, "Of course we have to remember our people who died . . . but it doesn't help our hearts to heal."

ANTICIPATING THE FUTURE

A collective task for Rwandans as they move forward is to figure out how to incorporate the events of 1994 into their national narrative. Currently, the government account focuses strongly on the role of the RPF as the savior of the people, stopping the slaughter of the civil war. This account has been memorialized in a genocide museum installed in the parliament building. The role of the RPF is further articulated in all of the annual commemorations of the genocide. Counter narratives tend to be squashed by the government, accusing people of divisionism.

In spite of the economic advancement in Rwanda since the genocide, there is still considerable poverty in the rural areas. Many young people feel stuck, unable to put together the resources to build a home and marry.[8] And Rwanda scored very low on recent global "happiness" surveys in spite of economic growth rates that have been averaging 7 percent in recent years.[9] Hence, under the veneer of apparent prosperity, multiple challenges confront the govern-ment. Not everyone is satisfied with the social engineering that dominates the national agenda, although certain emphases such as its anticorruption campaign, seem to be appreciated by most people. Furthermore, Rwanda is rightly applauded for the inclusion of women in leadership positions, with approximately half of elected officials being female.[10]

The question that is always just under the surface, but seldom articulated, is whether a Tutsi-led government can continue to define the national agenda or whether something akin to the revolution of the early 1960s might once again occur. Clearly this fear is felt by the current leadership or it would not be as forceful in silencing dissent, whether within its borders or outside. Given the fact that this book is based on oral history, we resist the impulse to prophesy about the future. Instead, we conclude with some broad generalizations.

Firstly, the reality of survivors and killers having to live side by side in Rwanda following the conflict is somewhat distinct when compared, say, to the Armenians who were deported from their ancestral lands and in the postgenocide period lived outside of Turkey where the genocide occurred. This reality presents a number of complex issues around the experience of reconciliation and peaceable coexistence on a day-to-day basis. Is the necessity of interacting daily in a civil manner something that can heal wounds? Or might pent-up revenge motives, on both sides, find expression in a different political climate?

Secondly, whatever one's opinion might be about the success of the *gacaca* courts, the creation of memorials, and the annual commemorations, they served a function in attempting to unite the country. One can be cynical about the government's emphasis that we are all Rwandans, but what is the alternative? Continued ethnic division? Furthermore, one can debate whether the *gacaca* courts were successful, but would it have been better to put a lid on untold, unconfessed acts of violence? In some manner the violence needed to be processed. Only history will tell whether these strategies were a successful stage in healing the wounds of the nation.

Finally, genocide is generational. It does not cease when the last killing occurs.[11] All the orphans we interviewed have now entered adulthood. There is little question but what their disrupted childhood will mark the postgenocide generation. There are consequences to not having role models regarding how to raise children. There are even deeper consequences of missing out on crucial periods of not being loved, affirmed, and nurtured. We also worry about the status of widows. Are they being forgotten as the society marches to the drum of economic advancement? While organizations such as AVEGA and Solace continue to support these women, they struggle with loneliness and the challenge of engaging a hopeful future.

CONCLUSION

As we have argued, genocide creates a moral rupture at two levels—for the individual whose structures of meaning and interpretation have been assaulted; and at a social-political level that requires that the breach in the moral fabric be healed. The Rwandan government has pursued policies of moral repair in multiple ways.[12] Critics of the government play a valuable role in emphasizing democratic values. But the preceding chapters of this book document the extreme challenge that the government faced in reuniting a fractured social order after the genocide. There are undoubtedly stages in moral reconstruction that take years to unfold. In the case of the Holocaust, Bosnia, and other genocides of the twentieth century, the process of healing and reconciling is ongoing. What we know, specifically from the Armenian genocide, is that denial of what occurred is not helpful. It delays the ability of survivors to reconcile with their past and to move forward. Therefore, the fact that the Rwandan government has faced divisionism, including denial, head on is to be applauded.

CHAPTER 10

Becoming Human Again

One of the first survivors we interviewed was Naphtal Ahishakiye, the president of AOCM, the organization of orphan heads of households. Sitting in the garden of the Mille Collines Hotel, he told us his story—very slowly as he searched for words in English to contextualize the deaths of his parents and three brothers. He was hiding in the forest when the killers found his father, killed him, and put his body in a latrine; Naphtal watched from a distance. Several of his siblings were thrown into the river near their house after they were killed. Naphtal survived by hiding in a swamp, breathing through a reed under water whenever the killers came searching for Tutsis. For two months, he was on the run, and then when the genocide ended he lived in the homes of Hutus who had fled to Zaire and elsewhere, sometimes with ten or twelve orphans to a house—surviving off the gardens that had been abandoned.

In 1995, he went back to school and finished his secondary education. In 1999, at age twenty-four, he enrolled in university. And in 2000, he and some fellow students started AOCM, realizing that they needed to create a support system for one another. By the time we left Rwanda after our first visit, we were bonded to Naphtal. He reminded Lorna of her father, who also had lost his family during a genocide. Like Lorna's father, Naphtal carried himself with great dignity. He was a natural leader, expressing himself in measured and thoughtful ways—always choosing his words carefully.

We were on another visit to Rwanda and staying at the Mille Collines Hotel when Naphtal excitedly rushed to our room. He wanted us to see his new baby, who was only a few hours old. So, we took a taxi to the nearby hospital and were the first ones to congratulate the new parents as his wife cradled their firstborn in her arms. It was a joyous moment! We were witnessing the birth of the second generation of survivors.

Since babies are not named at birth in Rwanda, it was with enormous pride that we were told later that they decided to give their child an Armenian name, Arpi, which is the name of our daughter. This was a very symbolic gesture. In the Armenian language, "Arpi" means the early rays of sunshine in the morning and, indeed, this child was the beginning of new life for Naphtal. Arpi had brought sunshine into Naphtal's life.

In subsequent visits, we kept meeting the newest additions to their family. On one of our last trips to Rwanda, there were four vivacious children. Baby Arpi was now fourteen years old. She looked very scholarly with her glasses, and Naphtal said that she regularly corrects his English. She also is fluent in French and Kinyarwanda.

Currently, Naphtal is the executive secretary of IBUKA, the umbrella organization for survivor groups in Rwanda. He owns a home that he built step-by-step over several years, and works through IBUKA on a variety of issues important to the 390,000 survivors in Rwanda—the majority of whom are young adults.

The orphan association that Naphtal helped start eventually ended as the leadership married and orphans reached adulthood. There were no longer child-headed households; the orphans had grown up; they were adults. But AOCM served a tremendous need at the time and is a model for crisis situations around the world where orphans are put in the unfortunate role of caring for their younger siblings. At the peak of the organization, there were 1,300 orphan families networked with each other through AOCM. They advocated with the government to provide educational assistance for orphan children, and they met regularly in small groups to carry their collective burdens together.

Another of our memorable experiences during the early years of visiting Rwanda was traveling to a village outside of Kigali where AOCM had constructed nearly two dozen homes with the help of an NGO. Each one was tidy and neat, but lacking many furnishings. Flowers had been planted in the yards. A shed had been constructed for pigs that they were raising. As we talked with the "parents" in these homes, there was something rather resigned in their demeanor. Individuals were struggling with the burden of caring for children, employment was difficult, and the legacy of memories from the genocide was clearly weighing on them.

Several years ago, we sat down with Naphtal and asked him how he was doing emotionally. He said that he went through a rather rational process a few years after the genocide. He decided that the best punishment for the perpetrators of the genocide was to become educated and prosper in life. As stated, in 1995, he went back to school and finished his secondary education. He said, "I rebuilt my life in order to punish the perpetrators." And a few moments later he added: "I decided to go back to school for my parents, my country, and to show the Hutu perpetrators that I am able to do it."

Immediately after the genocide, he said that he wrestled with the trauma of what he had experienced. Insomnia was a real problem. At one point, for a week he could barely sleep. He had numerous flashback memories from the genocide, frequently waking up from dreams in which the killers were pursuing him. "Today," he said, "I cannot say that the trauma is over. What we have is the capacity to *manage* the trauma.

For Naphtal and many other survivors, exhuming the bodies of loved ones was important. We were invited to attend a ceremony in which Naphtal, years later, ritually buried his father and other loved ones. Such occasions are a way of laying to rest, quite literally, the remains of those one has loved. With these burials, there is a degree of closure for the survivor.

Compensatory experiences and achievements play an important role in mitigating past traumas. For Naphtal, having a family brought new hope into his life. Survivors also compensate for their loss through achievement in their work, as is the case with Naphtal, who chose to return to school and be the best he could as a way of making his father proud but also as a way of punishing the perpetrators who sought to destroy his entire family. But recovery after genocide also often requires a helping hand.

For example, we met Francine when she was working as a maid in a guesthouse in Kigali. Her parents had survived the genocide but were extremely poor and had told her that she was their only hope. Through the intervention of a good-willed person who paid her tuition, she was able to go to university. Every year we saw her, she would show us her report cards from school, where she was prospering. When she graduated, she got a job working for a bank and was so successful that she was sent to Nairobi for further training. With some of her early paychecks, she built a home for her parents in a rural area of Rwanda. She then married and now has two adorable children. Meanwhile, one of her coworkers at the guesthouse is still working as a maid. Yes, education made all the difference.

We could cite numerous other examples of the role that education played in the lives of survivors. Modeste was the only one in his entire extended family to survive, yet he now has a master's degree in public health from a university in Egypt and has an excellent job working for the Department of Health in Rwanda. One of Jean Gakwandi's daughters went on to get a PhD, and all of his children are prospering in high-level jobs. But there are also individuals who struggled to finish university and were late in applying to higher education, including Agnes, who with the help of a donor was able to eventually complete her studies and now is married with two children. We frequently think back to the circumstances where we first met her when she was living in a hovel of a house with two other orphan girls. And there are survivors who we have tracked over nearly two decades who didn't have the privilege of going to university but showed an entrepreneurial spirit once they got a permanent job. Jean Claude is a good example. He needed money to attend driving school, where he eventually got a good job as a driving instructor. We were recently invited to dinner at his home, which he had substantially improved from our first visit some years ago. His new bride prepared a lovely vegetarian meal following the tradition of her Adventist church. We couldn't help but remember the time we bought him a large sack of beans when we noticed how thin he had become.

These success stories, however, must always be tempered with the reality of survivors who did not have a supportive hand to assist them after the genocide. For example, in the Rwanda Mental Health Survey referenced in the trauma chapter, researchers classified the economic situation of the respondents into four categories. Two-thirds of genocide survivors fit into the first two categories: being without a house or unable to rent and hardly able to get food and other domestic necessities or, second, able to afford shelter but rarely have full-time work and eat one or two meals a day.[1] Hence, success stories must always be tempered by the reality of most survivors. In spite of the tremendous strides made by Rwanda since the genocide, it is still a very poor country.

THE MULTIPLE LEVELS OF RECONSTRUCTION

Throughout most of this book we have been focused at the individual level—accounts of survivor experiences and perceptions. In this concluding chapter, it is important to restate that individuals exist within a larger social system of interlocking and yet separate levels of influence and support. They are born into families with parents, aunts, uncles, grandparents, and godparents. They grow up in communities with traditions, religious organizations, schools, businesses, and a social ecology of relationships. And every community is governed by local, national, and international laws.

For survivors in Rwanda, all of these levels collapsed or were called into question by the end of the genocide. Families were destroyed, including extended family networks. Communities were broken apart by ethnic killing, so that trust between neighbors was nearly nonexistent. Schools and other local institutions ceased to function, and economic activity was replaced by looting and theft. By the end of the one hundred days of killing, all forms of governance, including the judicial system, were destroyed. Rwanda was a failed state.

When various NGOs and aid organizations rushed in at the end of the genocide, it was often to help the Hutu refugees who numbered in the hundreds of thousands. The rebel victors, the Rwandan Patriotic Front, were faced with reconstructing the nation from the bottom up. It was in the ashes of destruction that organizations such as AVEGA, Solace, and AOCM emerged to help survivors with the most basic needs of food, shelter, and medical care. As Jean Gakwandi, the founder of Solace Ministries, told us, his initial response to psychological trauma was simply to cry with survivors, feeling their pain and accepting it. And for many survivors, they were so shell-shocked that they could not even cry. It was only later, in the healing process, that they could begin to feel emotions once again.

At a conference prior to the twentieth commemoration of the genocide, Mukesh Kapila, one of the aid workers to arrive first on the scene after the genocide, said that he created a program called "school in a box," which contained the fundamental elements to get kids back to school so that they could normalize their lives.[2] There was a need for structure—to wake up in the morning and have someplace to go and something to do. Sociologists use the word "anomie" to describe the state of "normlessness" that leads to despair. Hence, it is not surprising that many survivors attempted or contemplated suicide during and after the genocide when their network of family, friends, and institutions—including the church—was no longer present to support them. Meaning is not an individual enterprise; it is a communal achievement. And during the genocide, the basic structures of community were ruptured.

What is remarkable about Rwanda today is that it has been able to reconstitute society at a highly functional level. In no small part, this is due to the leadership of President Paul Kagame, the leader of the RPF rebel group that stopped the genocide. The Rwandan economy is flourishing.[3] There are new high-class hotels throughout the capital city of Kigali. There is a magnificent new conference center that is equipped to handle major events. A network of paved roadways now extends throughout the country. There is a new industrial park that hosts a number of manufacturing facilities, including some from China. Fiber optic cable has been laid throughout Rwanda connecting many secondary schools and universities to the internet. The government has consolidated a burgeoning number of private universities under a single structure to avoid duplication of course offerings and specializations. Downtown Kigali is filled with financial services and banks with connections to other countries. A new airport is under construction, and a number of major airlines now service Rwanda. In addition, there is a national health care system that provides for everyone, even those who are poor, if they pay a small yearly fee. And, finally, security in the country is excellent, which is one reason that so many international and regional conferences are now taking place in Kigali.

It would be incorrect to say that the genocide is being forgotten by Rwanda, and certainly not by survivors. Also, there are criticisms by some outsiders of political governance in Rwanda.[4] In reading the RwandAir magazine on a recent flight from Nairobi to Kigali, it was interesting that only veiled reference was made to the past—all the articles were future oriented, stressing the business opportunities in Rwanda and the country's scenic beauty. Rwanda is sometimes referred to as the "Singapore of Africa," and there are parallels. Neither Singapore nor Rwanda have great natural resources. The key resource is their people and dynamic leadership.

In one of our last conversations with Naphtal, he said that trauma is surfacing for many survivors in new ways, including at happy moments such as weddings and the birth of children. He said that it is difficult to know why this is the case, but it is probably because these were times when extended families celebrated together. Culturally, he said that families often suppressed awareness of trauma for fear that it would affect the marriage prospects of a daughter. But now there are more counseling resources and so people are more open about their trauma. It is also possible that another dimension is at play. Namely, as people's lower-level needs for food, shelter, and medical care are being addressed, survivors are now able to deal with suppressed emotional feelings. Also, perhaps they can feel safe about articulating them in a more stable political environment.

SUMMING UP

There is never a happy ending to a book on genocide, and particularly this one. Therefore, perhaps the best strategy is to conclude with some summary generalizations about this work. In the foregoing chapters, we have been mired in particularities, which is the stuff of oral history. While the details are painful to read, we believe the first half of the book reveals some important subtleties in the study of genocide. The interviews impart an immediate experience of genocide—how it unfolds, what it looks, feels, sounds, and even smells like. The details present compelling bits of knowledge, such as how goodbyes were carried out between parents and children, what family survival strategies were adopted, and the excruciating decisions parents faced in the hopes of increasing their children's survival.

Stepping back from the details of the killing period itself, our work also highlights the importance of studying the aftermath of genocide. This is the case not only because healing, reconciliation, and forgiveness processes are important to understand, but we can also better understand the multiple layers of destruction that define genocide in practice. A population can go from being a class of landowners, fostered over generations, to being landless in a period of months. Survivors' entire social networks were destroyed: family, colleagues, faith communities, neighbors, not to mention institutions like schools and local government. With the loss of those social networks comes the destruction of generations of knowledge, know-how, the wisdom of elders, and advice for society's youth.

Moreover, once all the relations that helped define a person are gone, who is that person? In examining genocide's aftermath, the social construction of identity is made clear. After the killing, many interviewees stated that they felt they were no one, nothing; they had no self-worth. Prior to the killing, survivors constructed their identity around being mothers, sons, spouses, people of faith, good neighbors, successful workers, landowners. In the healing process, as people came out of total isolation and began to experiment tentatively, cautiously, with new relationships, the social qualities of self-identity become clear. In short, it is in seeing what had to be rebuilt, both at the material and social level, that elements of life otherwise taken for granted become visible. And it is in witnessing this excruciating reconstruction, at all levels, that genocide's devastation is truly understood.

In the second half of the book, we transitioned from the immediate aftermath of genocide to the longer processes of healing, forgiveness, and reconciliation. In addition to the classic symptoms of trauma, we identified a root issue associated with the genocide—moral rupture—the total collapse in meaning structures and social trust. While individual counseling was important for survivors when they had access to it, social healing was just as important. Healing entailed coming out of isolation into a community of love, acceptance, and trust—a community that would receive a woman as she is now, with her new postgenocide self, not only as she was. This community, embodied in organizations such as Solace Ministries, is a community willing to listen to and accept the horrors of one's experiences, and thus validate one's understanding of the moral breach that occurred and the terror and loss that one experienced.

This re-creation of self has a very social quality to it—the community embraces the new self, with all its ruptures, and the individual finds a new place and a new role for their personhood in community as surrogate mother, companion, and so on. The healing community works to combat the loneliness, humiliation, self-hatred, loss of dignity that is repeated throughout the interviews. It is easier for a community to accept and acknowledge the new self than for the woman to do it herself; with external affirmation, a new love for that fragile and raw postgenocide self can begin to blossom.

The postgenocide experience potentially reveals something hopeful, remarkable, and even surprising about the capability of the human species, with individuals like Mama Lambert, Jean Gakwandi, and Naphtal being perfect embodiments. Despite the utter destruction and extreme decimation that define genocide at every level, despite a degree of horror and traumatic experience beyond our worst nightmares, survivors go on. They go on to survive and sometimes even thrive. They rebuild societies, they produce new generations, and while always fragile they potentially find measures of emotional health and inspiration. If we walk away from this study with one human insight, it is not merely how evil humans can be; it is how wondrously resilient and indefatigable is the human spirit. As more than one survivor told us, after genocide it is possible to become human again.

CONCLUDING REFLECTIONS

As we pen the final paragraphs of this book, it is having just passed our milestone of fifty years of marriage. In a few days, we are taking the entire family to the Republic of Armenia to celebrate, including grandchildren ranging from five years of age to fourteen. For the first time, these one-quarter Armenian children will visit the genocide memorial in Yerevan. As we stand around the eternal flame, Lorna will tell them about the survival of their great-grandparents, mixing stories of heroism and initiative with the realism of the 1915 genocide of Armenians in Turkey. She will tell how her father lived in six different countries before bringing his family to America, and how everyone of his children got a college education even though he only went through fifth grade.

Ironically, we will arrive in Armenia on the same day that the Rwanda genocide started twenty-five years earlier. Do we bring this grim story of the dark side of humanity into the conversation with our grandchildren? Probably not: we are there to celebrate the union that brought their parents and four grandchildren into the world. Nevertheless, we are aware that Rwandan survivors will be struggling with what stories to tell their children about the events of a quarter century ago. Yesterday we read a poignant story in the *New York Times* about mothers who were raped in 1994 and the awkward conversations they have had with their children born of sexual violence, their fathers being killers. And the last time we were with Naphtal, while riding in his car and talking with him about the genocide, fourteen-year-old Arpi asked, "What are you talking about?"

As we enjoy springtime in Armenia with our grandchildren, we are anticipating their question: "Will genocide keep happening in our lifetime?" Unfortunately, the answer is "yes." The adage, "Never Again" is morally praiseworthy, but a false hope. More accurate is the refrain, "Once Again," as history has demonstrated. If anything, we anticipate an escalation in global violence. With global warming, there will be hundreds of millions of refugees fleeing uninhabitable land and islands. The root cause of genocide will be present: Us versus Them. And, unfortunately, "Them" will be demonized, made to be less than human, searing our conscience as they are rejected, left to die, and treated as "other," not belonging on our privileged plot of land. Right-wing nationalism and anti-immigrant sentiment is sprouting all over the world in response to migration, which will only increase in the future.

In the face of this political realism, it is important to rebuild for every generation a vision of what it means to really be human. We have been inspired rereading a short book by Jean Vanier, *Becoming Human*, that describes his lifetime of living and working with intellectually disabled people—nurturing a movement of hundreds of L'Arche communities around the world where able-bodied and disabled people live together finding meaning in their life together. Vanier states, "The discovery of our common humanity liberates us from self-centred compulsions and inner hurts; it is the discovery that ultimately finds its fulfillment in forgiveness and in loving those who are our enemies. It is the process of becoming human."[5]

We have the option of shielding ourselves from the pain of others, living in a polarized, dichotomized world of Us versus Them. Or we can find our common humanity in trying to build an interconnected world where compassion is at the heart of our being because we dare to open ourselves to the struggles of others. The temptation is to build walls, denying the humanity of those who are not like ourselves. The challenge of being a grandparent in the twenty-first century is to nurture hope and optimism in the next generation while inviting those in the next generation into the struggle to confront the human tendency to demonize the other. As we said in the preface to this book, after every visit to Rwanda, we felt more human because of our conversations and experiences with survivors. They opened our eyes to what is quintessentially at the core of our common humanity.

Methodology

In this appendix, each of the three interview projects will be described separately, since each had a different character. In the concluding section, the coding, analysis, and writing process will be described. But, first, a theoretical point. We did not enter this project with preconceived hypotheses that were to be tested. Instead, we followed a "grounded theory" approach in which ideas and interpretations emerged inductively from the interviews. While we had read some of the literature on the genocide prior to doing the interviews, and in the course of the fifteen years of the project attended several important conferences and, of course, did a great deal of additional reading, we did not try to shoehorn any of our description and analysis into preexisting categories. Every chapter is rooted in the experience of survivors. Our task was to identify themes and representative stories and quotes to illustrate the topics addressed in each chapter. The actual chapter topics emerged inductively from the 238 coding categories that evolved during our line-by-line coding of the interviews.

THE AOCM INTERVIEW PROJECT

AOCM (Association des Orphelins Chefs de Ménages) was created August 20, 2000, by orphans who were caring for their surviving brothers and sisters, and, in some instances, children that they had adopted who had no one to care for them. Objectives of the organization included the following: Addressing the special problems of orphans heading households; promoting a spirit of understanding, unity, and solidarity among their members; fighting for social reintegration into society; assisting with the schooling of members and their children; finding and helping to create jobs for their members; and assisting their members to be self-sufficient.

After proposing the idea of AOCM documenting the genocide experience of their members, the leadership sent us a proposal with a budget. The proposal was well written and indicated their desire to interview one hundred members of their association, using some of the senior members of their organization to do the interviews. In their budget, they proposed giving a gift of $10 to each person who was interviewed and paying their staff $10 for each interview that they did. They also included a budget for transportation to the interview sites, office rental, office supplies, internet connection, funds for transcription and translation of the interviews, hiring a project coordinator, plus a 10 percent management fee that would go to the organization. We would supply the tape recorders, tapes, and two transcribing machines with foot pedals.

The initial goal was to complete the project in three months. However, there were inevitable delays. But after eight months from launching the project on May 29, 2002, we received an email attachment with several thousand pages of perfectly typed transcripts of the translation of one hundred interviews. The mechanics of the transcription process was as follows: Each interviewer hand wrote the transcription of each interview, which was then given to the translator, a journalist who was fluent in English, and had avoided the genocide because she was studying in India. Later, the handwritten transcripts were typed by a secretary in Kinyarwanda, so that AOCM had an official record of the interview. Not only was the transcribing process extremely laborious, but there was also a challenge with irregular electricity that slowed the typing process.

Interviews were conducted among AOCM members in the following regions of the country: Kigali (where the office was located), Rwamagana, Kibungo, and Kibuye. During the course of the project there were challenges: an essential component of their office computer was stolen, they had flat tires, and so on. We supplemented their budget with additional funds for secretarial assistance, transportation fees, and customs fees for the transcribing machines that we had shipped from South Africa to Rwanda. Altogether, the entire project, not counting the cost of the equipment we supplied and our travel to Rwanda, was slightly over ten thousand dollars.

In late May 2002, we worked with the five AOCM project staff, the president of AOCM, plus the project coordinator, to refine the interview questions, acquaint them with the goals of the project, and practice interviewing each other. In the report at the end of the project from the coordinator, the following summary remarks were made about the interviewing process: "To listen intently to what the person is saying and not correct them or give your personal opinion; to be sympathetic, understanding, and patient as the interviewee is telling their story; to stop the tape recorder and comfort the interviewee if they need to cry or express their emotions; to ask interviewees to describe what they saw personally, not what was told to them; to conduct the interview in an appropriate place where there would be privacy and a lack of distraction."

It was gratifying to see these points summarized in the final report since these were key issues that we discussed with the team in our training period. Two other points should be added. First, while there was an interview guide, the interviewers were told to have a conversation with their fellow orphans and not rigidly follow the questions one by one. Second, each interviewee was asked if they agreed to the interview and if their name could be associated with the interview. In one location, Gitarama, the orphans did not agree to these stipulations and so they were not interviewed.

After the one hundred interviews were transcribed, the project coordinator created a database that included the following fields: (1) date of the interview, (2) name of the interviewee, (3) gender, (4) contact information, (5) length in minutes of the interview, (6) number of members in the family, (7) number of family members killed, (8) number that survived, (9) number of children the orphan head of household was caring for, (10) whether the interviewee was raped, (11) whether they had suffered a debilitating injury, including amputation, and (12) whether their house was destroyed. Here are the summary results from this database:

Interviews averaged about an hour in length; the shortest interview was thirty-nine minutes and the longest interview was ninety minutes. Of the one hundred interviewees, forty-one were female and fifty-nine were male. In the one hundred households, prior to the genocide there were 805 family members. As a result of the genocide, 522 (65 percent) were killed and 283 (35 percent) survived. Of the forty-one orphan girls, five were raped, and one male was raped. Of the one hundred interviewees, twenty-five suffered serious physical injuries, including amputation. And seventy-nine homes of the one hundred interviewees were destroyed in the genocide.

AVEGA (WIDOWS ASSOCIATION)

On January 15, 2004, an interview project was launched with AVEGA AGAHOZO (Association des Veuves du Génocide Agahozo), the largest association of widows in Rwanda. It was modeled after the AOCM interviews except that questions were developed that focused on the experience of women rather than orphans. Jean Munyaneza was the coordinator for this project as well as the AOCM project, which enabled continuity in terms of methodology. The target was to do five interviews with members of AVEGA in each of twelve provinces of Rwanda: City of Kigali, Kigali Ngali, Ruhengeri, Gisenyi, Kibuye, Cyangugu, Gikongoro, Butare, Gitarama, Kibungo, Byumba, and Umutara. While the goal was sixty interviews, there was equipment failure on three interviews so that eventually only fifty-seven interviews were transcribed and translated.

In the report written by Jean Munyaneza at the end of the project, it was estimated that there were 25,000 widowed members of AVEGA and the number of orphan heads of households was over 65,000. In this report, the main objectives of AVEGA were summarized as follows: To protect and promote widows of the genocide severely tested by atrocities committed in their areas; to conduct activities with the view of improving the living conditions of the widows and their children; to promote solidarity between members of the association; to promote the education of the orphans of the genocide; to defend the rights of the widows, be it social, economic, political and others; to perpetuate the memory of the victims of the genocide and to fight for justice; to actively participate in the process of national reconciliation and reconstruction of the country; to collaborate with national and international associations that have the same objective. At the time this report was written in 2004, AVEGA had identified 1,032 victims of sexual assault. The number of members tested and ill from HIV/AIDS was 753, with 190 benefiting from antiviral medication.

Five members of AVEGA conducted the interviews after a three-day training period, which was modeled after the training for AOCM. The interviews were done very expeditiously over six days, visiting two provinces each day. The transcription lasted almost three months and was done by the interviewers in their homes, and the translation into French took another two months and was done by three members of AVEGA who were fluent in French, each doing approximately twenty interviews. The transcripts that we coded were translated into English from French. An important generalization is that the AVEGA interviews were more detailed and the conceptualization of what happened was more sophisticated than in the AOCM orphan interviews. There are probably two reasons for this: First, the widows were older and more mature at the time of the genocide, and, second, the AVEGA interviewees were handpicked by the leadership because they had an important story to tell.

Within the fifty-seven survivors who were interviewed, there were 389 family members, for an average family size of approximately seven people including parents and children. Almost equal numbers were killed (191) and survived (198). Twenty-two of the fifty-five women interviewed were raped (two widowers were also interviewed). Nine of these women had been tested and were HIV positive. Over half of the women (thirty-three) had sustained some type of injury, including amputation.

The budget for this project was similar to the AOCM budget. Interviewers received $10 for each person they interviewed. Interviewees received a gift of $15. Transportation, telephone, internet, computer purchase, and salaries for the coordinator, secretaries, translators, and so on were all included in the budget as well as a 10 percent administrative fee that went to AVEGA as an organization. The total budget for the project was $13,300.

SOLACE MINISTRIES

At Solace Ministries, we collaborated in an ongoing basis with our project coordinator, Agnes Mukamkusi. Working with Jean Gakwandi, the founder of Solace Ministries, and Mama Lambert, who leads their Wednesday meeting and counsels hundreds of survivors each year, Agnes identified one hundred widows and orphans who were willing to be interviewed. Prior to our interview, Agnes met personally with each survivor, explained the project, and gathered some demographic information about the individual. What was intended to be a short conversation turned into a mini-interview in which survivors wanted to tell their story even though it was not being recorded. Agnes took careful notes during these conversations and filled out a long form, which we consulted before beginning the interview with the survivor.

Interviews were done in three different settings: A recording studio at Solace Ministries that was soundproof but became extremely hot when the air conditioner was not on, a guesthouse room on the premises of Solace, and an apartment that we rented that was across the street from Solace Ministries. Because we were videotaping the interviews, the recording studio was ideal, but the air conditioner in the room created a loud hum on the recording and so we tended to turn it off while actually recording. Our apartment was very comfortable for us, but probably a little foreign feeling to our interviewees, at least compared with their homes. And the guestroom was very adequate, although it seemed like there was always construction going on while we were interviewing, so one frequently heard pounding of one sort or another on the tape.

Our interviews began with us introducing ourselves and briefly explaining the project, indicating that we were writing a book and, also, that the interviews would become part of an archive library at Solace Ministries. After survivors agreed to the interview, we asked them if they were willing to sign a consent form. All but one survivor agreed that we could use their name in our research, although we have been very careful to change names in the book if there is any reference to rape or other difficult details. Typically, Lorna would begin the interview while Don focused the video camera on the subject. Our translator and project manager sat next to us and translated every few sentences or sometimes paragraphs if a survivor was in the middle of a thought or reflection. Later, the project manager transcribed each interview from the audio portion of the videotape and translated the interview from Kinyarwanda to English.

All of the interviewees were members of Solace Ministries. Since we had spent considerable time at Solace Ministries over a number of years, we were familiar to many of our interviewees. Furthermore, as described in the chapter on healing, many of the survivors we interviewed had told their story publicly before other survivors, so this was not a unique experience. Even though survivors sometimes became quite emotional during the interview—and we always had tissues available so they could wipe away the tears—survivors often spontaneously thanked us for the interview when it finished. They wanted their story to be told. And in the caring atmosphere of Solace, we believe giving their "testimony," as they called it, was a healing experience. If we were interviewing on a Wednesday, we usually joined survivors during our break to enjoy their dancing and singing. We became very used to being hugged and embraced, with kisses on alternating cheeks, three times.

On occasion, we provided refreshments for everyone attending the Wednesday meetings, and a few days after the interview, Agnes would give the survivor we interviewed a gift of about $50 in local money. Every one of these survivors had extreme need; we did not view this as payment for the interview but an expression of our concern for their welfare. Over the years, we also were able to channel considerable funds to Solace for the university tuition of orphans, for the needs of teenage girls, and occasionally for capital improvement projects. Sometimes this was money from our own pocket, but other times it was from people we knew who had heard us speak or from people whose trip to visit Rwanda we had facilitated.

As mentioned in chapter 1, we made a practice of trying to visit the homes of survivors who we had interviewed, often doing this in the afternoon after a long morning of interviewing. These were often incredible experiences and provided some of the ethnographic elements that helped us contextualize the humanity of our interview subjects. We were fortunate to have had a similar experience with AOCM and AVEGA, although not to the same degree as with Solace Ministries. The bottom line is that this is not simply an interview-based study but involves years of informal ethnographic observation. For example, we attended the wedding of the project manager for the AOCM and AVEGA interviews and ended up providing two cows for the bride price as well as attending several days of festivities related to the wedding, including drinking banana beer out of a common straw. We also spent a considerable amount of time "hanging out" with the leadership of AOCM. And the former president, Naphtal, has become a lifelong friend, along with his adorable family, as well as Jean Gakwandi and Mama Lambert. It is an amazing collection of friends.

Not included in the count of 260 interviews are at least twenty additional interviews that we did at various points during the fifteen years of traveling to Rwanda. Not all of these interviews were recorded, and none of them were coded even though they helped inform our understanding of the genocide.

CODING AND WRITING

The most laborious element of this project—besides the actual writing and rewriting—was coding 260 interviews. We used the coding program, Atlas.ti, which enabled us to code line-by-line and attach key words to a sentence or paragraph. As previously stated, inductively we created 238 codes. Sometimes a sentence or paragraph would have multiple codes attached if it illustrated more than one theme. Atlas.ti allows one to gather all of the coded material related to a topic into one file. It is also possible to look at a single coded sentence or paragraph, click on it, and then go back to the section of the interview where the code is located to examine the context of the statement. In the process of coding our interviews, we developed multiple subcodes around particular topics. For example, we had fourteen subcodes around the theme of forgiveness, ten subcodes related to "current problems," and nearly a dozen codes related to *gacaca*. And so forth.

In examining the codes, we began to see clusters of codes with similar themes, and these, in turn, suggested potential chapters and subsections within chapters. The task, then, was to identify the appropriate quotation or story that illustrated what we were attempting to say in a chapter. In a project as extensive as ours, inevitably there are too many good quotes and accounts, and so it was a wrenching task to eliminate whole sections from earlier drafts of the manuscript.

In the case of Solace Ministries, we took photos of every person we interviewed. In addition, we went back and watched the videotape of interviews, which reminded us of emotions that were expressed as survivors described their experiences. At this point, we have not decided what to do with several hundred hours of high-quality video from the Solace interviews, but perhaps another project beckons.

In conclusion, we want to say something about vicarious trauma. We especially felt this during the Solace Ministries interviews. Someone would pour out a heart-wrenching story; something that was unbelievable. And their needs would be so blatant and obvious. The interview would end, we would look at our watch, have a cup of tea, and then look at our project coordinator and say, "Who's next?" The only comfort was that we knew survivors were in a loving environment that was dedicated to helping them heal and take care of their needs, using whatever resources might be available through Solace Ministries. We felt the same angst while coding and writing. There are some things that no amount of framing or rationalization can explain. No matter how accustomed we became to stories of the genocide, in almost every interview there was something that shocked us and challenged our moral comprehension of what it means to be human.

Survey Results on Distress and Resilience

Beth E. Meyerowitz and Lauren C. Ng

In order to complement the in-depth interviews described in this volume, we invited members of AOCM and Solace Ministries to complete surveys that were designed to assess specific areas of distress and resilience that survivors reported more than a decade after the genocide, including concerns that might not have been mentioned spontaneously during the interviews. The quantitative component of this project augmented the interviews by providing data on the frequency and severity of the wide range of challenges that survivors live with daily, as well as areas of personal strength and resilience. In this appendix we provide a summary of some of the key findings.

The value of any survey depends on the extent to which the questions resonate with the lived experiences of the individuals who are invited to respond. In order to ensure that our measures included the most important issues facing survivors, with attention to the cultural context and in language that was appropriate and easily understood, we went through a multistage, months-long process in close collaboration with our local partners. Our approach included extensive reviews of the available literature, focus groups with survivors throughout the country, translation and back-translation of all materials, evaluation of the psychometric properties of the measures, and review and revision by multiple survivors. At each stage of selection and development of the survey materials, we consulted extensively with the leaders of organizations representing survivors.

Through this process we chose measures to assess five areas of adjustment following genocide, specifically posttraumatic stress reactions, emotional distress and physical symptoms, social support, coping strategies, and overall quality of life. Sixty-one AOCM beneficiaries completed the questionnaires in 2008 as a follow-up to the testimony described in this volume.[1] Their mean age was 29 years (range = 20 to 42 years), and 42% were women. The 100 survivors who participated from Solace Ministries were significantly older on average, with a mean age of 36.7 years (range = 16 to 77 years), and were significantly more likely to be women (82%). Solace Ministries survivors also completed the questionnaires in 2008 at approximately the same time that they were interviewed. The questionnaires were well received by survivors, with no one dropping out of the study after seeing the questions and with few cases of missing data or nonresponse. To the contrary, survivors were dedicated to offering their experiences to help others.

DISTRESS: POSTTRAUMATIC STRESS, PHYSICAL SYMPTOMS, EMOTIONAL DIFFICULTIES, AND BEHAVIORAL PROBLEMS

Not surprisingly, survivors reported numerous areas of distress, consistent with their discussions during the interviews. The results from the surveys documented that the powerful examples of individual experiences described through the interviews represented areas of distress common to many other survivors. We found high levels of distress in every category that we measured.

Survivors completed a survey[2] that assessed symptoms of posttraumatic stress "with regard to the genocide" over the preceding two months on a scale ranging from 0 = not at all to 4 = extremely. Although this measure was not designed to provide a diagnosis of posttraumatic stress disorder (PTSD), research has identified a mean of 1.5 or greater as having the best diagnostic accuracy for assessing the disorder.[3] Survivors in our study scored well above that threshold, with a mean score of 2.2 (83.7% of AOCM survivors and 76.8% of Solace Ministries survivors scored higher than 1.5). The mean scores for each subscale also were very high (mean for intrusion = 2.5, mean for avoidance = 2.2, mean for hyperarousal = 1.9). There were no significant differences between the AOCM and Solace Ministries survivors on any of these scores.[4] It is worth noting that such high rates of posttraumatic stress symptoms are not unique to these survivors. High rates of PTSD also were reported in a study of national prevalence rates in postgenocide Rwanda, which found that 59% of people aged 16 years and older had probable PTSD.[5] The estimated probable PTSD rates found on our survey, while higher, seem in line with this larger representative sample, particularly given the fact that all of the AOCM and Solace participants were survivors of the genocide, which is not the case for the nationally representative sample.

In addition to asking about symptoms of PTSD, we also asked survivors whether they had experienced each of 35 physical, psychological, or behavioral difficulties during the preceding two months. For those items that received an affirmative response, they were asked to indicate the severity of the problem ranging from 0 = not at all severe to 4 = extremely severe. The list of difficulties was developed for this study, based on recommendations from survivors in our conversations and focus groups.

Again, we see high levels of distress. Survivors endorsed 16 different areas of distress on average, with a range from a low of 3 to a high of 32. Three of the four physical symptoms included on the survey had been experienced in the past two months by over half of the survivors. Specifically, 76.3% reported headaches, 68.1% reported difficulty falling or staying asleep, and 58.5% reported stomachaches, with no significant differences between survivors from AOCM and Solace Ministries. Being fatigued/having difficulty staying awake was common among survivors from Solace Ministries (68.0%) but significantly less common in responses from AOCM survivors (16.4%).

Everyone reported having experienced recent emotional distress 14 years after the genocide. The most common difficulties, experienced equally by members of both groups, were feeling sad and depressed (88.1%), feeling anxious and nervous (74.4%), being scared (73.0%), having nightmares (68.6%), feeling like crying (68.1%), and feeling lonely (56.9%). It was less common for individuals to feel hopeless (41.3%), be irritable/angered by little things (37.5%), feel ashamed (36.7%), think about taking revenge (23.8%), lack interest/be unmotivated (28.8%), or be fearful of getting HIV/AIDS testing (11.9%). Significantly more AOCM survivors, as compared to Solace Ministries survivors, reported feeling desperate (86.4% vs. 24.5%), upset (85.3% vs. 69.7%), isolated (63.9% vs. 38.4%), regretful/guilty (49.2% vs. 23.5%), as though life is not worth living (42.6% vs. 15.2%), and restless/having difficulty relaxing (47.5% vs. 23.5%). In contrast, Solace Ministries survivors were significantly more likely than AOCM survivors to report feeling as though they were "losing your mind" (50.5% vs. 18.0%).

The final set of items on this questionnaire asked whether survivors engaged in potentially destructive behaviors or had difficulty in engaging in helpful behaviors. The most frequently reported behavioral problems were having angry outbursts (57.9%) and pushing people away/being detached (31.5%). Potentially destructive or difficult behaviors that were reported less frequently included drinking alcohol, which was significantly more common among AOCM survivors (29.5%) than Solace Ministries survivors (7.1%). There was no significant difference between the two groups in reports of taking drugs (5.6%), getting in fights (6.9%), or bed wetting (3.1%). There were several areas where survivors indicated that they had difficulties with behaviors that might have been helpful. For example, both groups reported having difficulty with remembering things/being forgetful (70.4%), expressing emotions (67.3%), being able to talk about what happened to them (53.2%), and being able to concentrate (40%). There were two additional areas in which survivors from Solace Ministries reported significantly higher levels of difficulty than were reported by survivors from AOCM: being unable to solve problems/feeling useless (93.9% vs. 39.3%) and being unable to help others/being unable to care for the family (63.6% vs. 21.3%).

Although a wide range of symptoms and concerns was identified with most survivors experiencing many of those problems, far fewer problems were rated as severe by most respondents. The average severity rating, which did not differ between the two groups, was 1.1 on the scale that ranged from 0 to 4, with no item receiving an average rating above 3. For AOCM survivors, the problems that were rated as most severe, in descending order from 2.8 to 2.0 in severity, were feeling anxious and nervous, feeling sad and depressed, feeling desperate, having headaches, having nightmares, feeling isolated, and being scared. For Solace Ministries survivors, the problems with the greatest severity were being unable to solve problems/feeling useless, having headaches, feeling sad and depressed, feeling like crying, having difficulty remembering things/being forgetful, being scared, and feeling anxious and nervous (severity ratings ranging from 2.5 to 1.9). While the severity of these problems was moderate overall, it is worth noting that every item received the highest severity rating of 4 by some survivors, with the exception of bed wetting.

RESILIENCE: SOCIAL SUPPORT, AGENCY, AND OPTIMISM

Despite the many difficulties described in the interviews and reported on our surveys, it would be inaccurate to think of these survivors as simply passive victims who were overwhelmed by their circumstances. To the contrary, our findings document that they actively sought to address challenges, with optimism for the future. The chapter on trauma in this volume argues that the healing process following genocide requires regaining a sense of trust and finding a way to move beyond the powerlessness that posttraumatic stress, emotional distress, and physical injury engender. In this section, we describe the results of three questionnaires that assess these signs of resilience, social support, coping, and perceived quality of life.

Levels of social support were strikingly different between the two groups of survivors, with members of AOCM reporting far lower levels of support as compared to members of Solace Ministries. The questionnaire measuring social support included six items on which participants indicated the extent to which they perceived support over the previous two months on a scale ranging from 1 = not at all to 5 = a lot.[6] The mean score for AOCM members (2.0) indicated alarmingly low levels of support, while the mean score of Solace Ministries members (4.7) indicated very high levels of support. Each of the six items received a mean score of greater than 4.1 from the Solace Ministries survivors and a mean score of no higher than 2.2 from the AOCM survivors. It appears that the efforts of Solace Ministries to provide a supportive community for their members may have been successful, especially in light of the low levels of support experienced by another group of survivors. Interestingly, the item that received the lowest mean score for both groups asked whether survivors thought they had someone to help them make decisions. This finding is consistent with the discussion earlier in the volume about survivors' hope to have people to offer advice. This finding may result from the fact that many survivors lost the opportunity to learn from their elders or to discuss issues with their spouses.

Developing strategies for regaining a sense of agency in the face of the many problems that most survivors experience is a key challenge on the path of healing. We designed a questionnaire, based on conversations with survivors and our focus groups, to learn what strategies survivors had attempted or had seen others use in an effort to lessen distress. Respondents indicated whether they had tried each of 24 coping strategies and, if so, whether they had found the strategy helpful on a bi-directional scale where 1 = made matters worse, 2 = resulted in no change, 3 = made matters somewhat better, and 4 = made matters much better. The strategies listed fell into four general categories: religious activity, talking/expressing feelings, seeking improvements in life circumstances for yourself or others, and taking your mind off of difficulties.

Survivors had attempted 17.5 strategies, on average, indicating a flexible and proactive approach to finding useful ways of coping. The number of strategies endorsed ranged from a low of 9 to a high of 23. For the most part, these coping efforts were somewhat helpful (mean helpfulness rating = 3.0). The most frequent and most helpful category of coping, by far, was religious activity. All survivors in both groups reported praying and more than 90% attended religious services. These strategies obtained ratings of approximately 3.5 on helpfulness for both groups, with 53.9% describing prayer as making things much better and only one person reporting that praying made matters worse. Members of Solace, a Christian ministry, would be expected to find prayer comforting and valuable. However, members of AOCM reported that these strategies were just as helpful for them. These findings suggest that faith and prayer may be beneficial, even for individuals who are members of a non-religiously-affiliated group, despite the challenges to faith during the genocide described earlier in this volume.

Some aspect of talking and expressing emotions was used by everyone, which is not surprising given their membership in organizations that were designed to help survivors share their experiences with other survivors. Moreover, anyone who was averse to talking would have been unlikely to have agreed to be interviewed for this project. Nonetheless, there were some differences between the two groups on these strategies. Members of AOCM, as compared to members of Solace Ministries, were significantly more likely to endorse thinking and talking about what happened during the genocide (85.2% vs. 62.9%) and expressing their feelings about the genocide (77.1% vs. 61.6%). There were no differences in the perceived helpfulness of either of these strategies between the two groups, however, with both groups finding these genocide discussions to be somewhat helpful on average. Talking to a counselor was significantly more common among Solace Ministries survivors (85.9%) as compared to AOCM survivors (67.2%), probably because Solace Ministries offered access to counselors. People who did talk to counselors found those conversations helpful overall. Other strategies in this category (talking about experiences during the genocide, talking to others in similar situations, and talking about your relatives) were rated as significantly less helpful by Solace Ministries survivors than by AOCM survivors. Talking to others in similar situations was one of the most helpful strategies for members of AOCM, receiving a 3.5 helpfulness score, as compared to a 3.0 helpfulness rating for members of Solace Ministries. Talking about relatives was especially notable in that 90% of survivors in both groups engaged in that behavior, but 68.2% of Solace Ministries survivors found it made matters worse (with a mean helpfulness score of 1.7) as compared to 8% of AOCM survivors (with a mean helpfulness score of 3.0). These findings suggest that care should be taken in pushing survivors to be self-disclosing in that not all topics are equally useful for everyone. Widows in Solace Ministries, for example, were more likely to have had their children die, which might be an especially painful topic to discuss.

In general, strategies designed to yield improvements in one's life circumstances, such as studying or working and making plans for the future, were viewed as helpful by people who engaged in those strategies. Although AOCM survivors were significantly more likely to make plans for the future, with almost everyone (98.3%) endorsing that item, the strategy was also common among Solace Ministries survivors (87.9%) and was helpful to both groups (> 3.0). It should be noted, however, that these strategies might not be equally available to all survivors, for example, individuals who are too injured to find work. Approximately 93% of respondents in both group indicated that they had tried to be helpful to other people, as well as themselves, and that providing such help was useful in their own adjustment. Fewer people (66.2%) indicated that they had tried to improve their circumstances by learning/reading about how others have solved similar problems. Those survivors who engaged in this coping strategy reported that it was helpful (mean helpfulness rating = 3.1) and might be valuable to a broader range of survivors if such information can be made available.

Survivors also reported engaging in a number of activities that might have served to take their minds off of difficulties. Doing something to forget what happened was endorsed by 71.7% and doing something to help relax/rest your mind was endorsed by 85.3%. Solace Ministries survivors were significantly more likely to daydream (89.8% vs. 67.2%), and AOCM survivors were significantly more likely to engage in sports/play games (53.3% vs. 36.7%). All of these strategies were found to be somewhat helpful. In contrast, 15.1% of survivors reported drinking alcohol or taking drugs, with one-third reporting that those behaviors made matters worse, one-third reporting no change, and one-third reporting some improvement from taking drugs and/or drinking. Not surprisingly, survivors recognized these behaviors as the least helpful strategies for improving their lives, information that might be useful to others who are considering self-medication.

On the final survey that participants completed, they were asked to rate their overall quality of life[7] on a scale ranging from 1 = worst life possible to 10 = best life possible at each of four times, as listed on the table below. Members of Solace Ministries reported significantly higher quality of life than did members of AOCM at each time point, although the pattern over time was the same for both groups. In both cases, survivors saw their quality of life as having improved over the past two years and were optimistic that it would continue to improve over the next two years. However, even with the expectation for a better quality of life in the future, the anticipated level of quality of life in the future tended to be lower than the quality of life that they remembered having prior to the genocide. In addition, the overall level of quality of life at the time the questionnaire was completed, while better than it had been in the recent past, was not high. The combined mean of 5.2 for the present quality of life was substantially lower, for example, than the means of > 7.0 provided by women who had recently completed treatment for breast cancer in the United States.[8]

TABLE I   MEAN RATINGS OF QUALITY OF LIFE

	AOCM	SOLACE
Before the Genocide	7.88	8.84
Two Years Ago	3.38	4.19
Now	4.61	5.52
Two Years from Now	6.05	7.98

1 = worst possible life, 10 = best possible life

CONCLUSIONS

One of the most frequent requests we get from survivors is for help in understanding whether their difficulties are common or extreme. Despite wanting this information, survivors have told us that they are reluctant to share their concerns with doctors, colleagues, friends, or family members for fear of being labeled weak or "crazy." In this appendix we have provided detailed information about a wide range of issues that survivors identified as important in their lives. We have specified which symptoms and concerns were most common and troublesome and which coping efforts were most frequently described as useful. These findings could be conveyed to survivors in order to provide insight into the extent to which their own experiences are shared by others. In some cases, survivors could be comforted to learn that they are not alone in their experiences. In other cases, survivors might be alerted to the need to seek help for difficulties that are not typical. For example, experiencing high levels of post-traumatic stress, feeling sad and depressed, having frequent headaches, and feeling upset were reported by over three-quarters of survivors in this study. However, experiencing multiple areas of very severe difficulties, or relatively uncommon problems, such as getting into fights or drinking/taking drugs, may be atypical responses that require special attention. Survivors might also profit from suggestions of what others have attempted, either successfully or unsuccessfully, to cope with lingering concerns. A dearth of coping responses or a lack of success in attempted responses also were less common and may indicate a need for attention, as might pessimism about the future. Individuals who were children at the time of the genocide seem to be especially in need of help understanding the meaning of their experiences. In one case, for example, a young survivor explained that she had accepted her many symptoms of PTSD and distress because she had assumed they were just what happened to people as they reached adulthood. While it may be valuable to offer survivors this information, it is important to remember that a hallmark of PTSD is the need to avoid reminders of traumatic events, requiring special care in approaching survivors with this information.

Even in cases where levels of posttraumatic stress, emotional distress, physical symptoms, and behavioral problems can be viewed as "normal" in light of the atrocities survivors faced, these challenges should not be accepted with resignation or complacency. Individuals working with genocide survivors in government agencies, NGOs, and public health programs must work to develop programs to help alleviate these problems and the conditions that help to maintain them. The results reported here can be used to prioritize specific targets for interventions, and helpful coping responses can be taught and shared, especially those that appear to be underused. For example, it might be helpful to identify avenues for increased social support when it is not otherwise available, to provide access to counselors without stigmatizing the value of counseling, to offer opportunities for leisure activities, and to disseminate information about how other survivors are managing and thriving.

The high levels of PTSD symptoms reported by these survivors may indicate that serious problems can be coped with but may not naturally resolve without formal treatment. Efforts to provide culturally sensitive, evidence-based treatment for PTSD may be warranted in coordination with other social programs or public health efforts. These interventions should be designed specifically for the needs and circumstances of the recipients, in ways that are cost-effective and sustainable. There are too many examples of well-meaning foreigners arriving for brief periods to offer treatments that have been tested only in very different environments, without sufficient attention to local capacity building or systematic follow-up. While this approach is understandable given the documented success of these interventions, they cannot be assumed to be valuable in a country where reminders of the genocide cannot be avoided. Treatments for PTSD have been successfully implemented in other low-income countries such as the Democratic Republic of Congo[9] and Zambia.[10] These programs trained community-based paraprofessionals to deliver the interventions, making them attractive for implementation within organizations like Solace Ministries and AOCM. Such programs can provide education and employment as well as treatments that are sustainable and effective in the local environment. As with all interventions, these treatments would require systematic scientific evaluation to ensure that they result in significant improvements, without unanticipated negative consequences.

The survey provides some encouraging news. While many symptoms and concerns were endorsed, far fewer were rated as severe. Survivors who had suffered so much may have learned to live with enormous difficulties and, therefore, may require a much higher threshold for considering something "severe" than would be the case for others. It also is possible that individuals had learned over time and with support or resources from their organizations to cope with and adjust to problems, making them more manageable. Most survivors had tried a variety of coping strategies that proved to be at least somewhat helpful. Their willingness to attempt multiple strategies indicates proactive experimentation and valuable flexibility, which are hallmarks of healthy coping. The very fact that survivors, even in the face of serious challenges, had the resilience to participate in grassroots organizations that were designed to improve their lives and allow them to play a role in improving the lives of others is further evidence of active coping. The finding that ratings of quality of life demonstrated improvement over the past two years may provide more evidence of successful coping.

The ability to be optimistic in predicting future quality of life also is suggestive of resilience and positive coping.

Although we have focused on reporting average responses, it is important to remember that no survivor is "average." Each survivor's experience before, during, and after the genocide is unique. Each faces personal daily challenges, lives with private memories, and holds distinctive goals and dreams for the future. Our findings highlight both the diversity and the commonalities within communities of survivors. For most items, we saw a wide range of responses, documenting the unique constellation of concerns and coping among survivors. The only item that was universally endorsed was prayer.

We also revealed a number of differences between the groups of survivors. In some cases, the differences appear to be the result of the differences in membership and goals of the two organizations. For example, many members of Solace Ministries meet together in Kigali on a regular basis to support one another and to join together in prayer. It is not surprising, then, that participants from that group reported very high levels of social support and relatively low levels of feeling isolated and desperate as compared to participants from AOCM, who lived throughout the country and were not often able to gather together as a group to provide and receive emotional support. AOCM had initiated a program of gathering testimony from its members within a few years of the genocide, thus encouraging members to share their feelings about the genocide. A primary focus of the organization was finding funds and other resources to allow its members to continue their education. Our findings indicate that their members were significantly more likely than Solace Ministries members to endorse expressing feelings, talking about the genocide, and planning for the future. Other differences between the two groups of survivors probably had more to do with the nature of the challenges that they were facing. Members of Solace Ministries had major family responsibilities, perhaps leading them to report a perceived inability to solve problems and to help others as especially difficult. On the other hand, members of AOCM may have found their relative isolation, lack of social support, and lower level of responsibility to a community of others to make them feel less like life was worth living and to report lower quality of life than Solace Ministries members.

It is interesting to note that individuals in Solace Ministries could experience very high levels of support while still experiencing high levels of posttraumatic symptoms. These two measures were not significantly correlated, suggesting that survivors can feel fully supported even when they are very distressed. The mission of Solace Ministries involves providing deep support and caring to even the most disturbed survivors, individuals who might not have had access to this level of support in other circumstances. Our survey only collected data at one point, making it impossible to know whether support might have alleviated distress over time. It also is possible that the overwhelming atrocities faced by survivors, as described through this volume, resulted in such severe posttraumatic stress that psychological interventions, as noted above, might be required. Further research is needed to understand fully this unexpected finding.

As described earlier in this volume, healing is an ongoing process that requires regaining the trust, agency, and hope that were lost during the genocide. The survey findings, consistent with the material from the interviews, suggest that while the road to full healing may never be complete, survivors are making progress in their recovery. As we've seen throughout this volume, regaining a sense of humanity does not require the absence of pain or difficulties. Healing is complicated by the fact that many survivors live with poverty, unemployment, lack of access to clean water and sufficient food, and other daily challenges.[11] Nonetheless, most survivors were active participants in their own recovery and had hope for the future. They are finding comfort in their faith and are committed to helping other survivors, as indicated by their willingness to share their stories for this project with honesty and openness.

NOTES

CHAPTER 1. ENCOUNTERING THE GENOCIDE

1. There is dispute over how many Tutsis were killed during the genocide. The figures range from 500,000 to one million. The debate revolves around the size of the Tutsi population in Rwanda at the time of the genocide. Approximately three-fourths of the Tutsi population was killed. See Straus (2006b, 51).

2. The *gacaca* courts were instituted in 2001 as a way to deal with the 100,000 or more individuals who were in prison as potential perpetrators of the genocide as well as heal the moral breach between Tutsis and Hutus. Loosely translated, *gacaca* means "justice among the grass" and was a traditional communal means of settling disputes and administering justice. See Ingelaere (2016) and Doughty (2016).

3. There are three primary ethnic groups in Rwanda: Hutus (84 percent of the population), Tutsi (15 percent), and Twa (1 percent of the population).

4. The Rwandan Patriotic Army was the military arm of the Rwandan Patriotic Front that formed in Uganda after members of the Front fled Rwanda in the early 1960s.

5. Later renamed the Democratic Republic of the Congo (DRC).

6. Des Forges 1999; Straus 2006b; Burnet 2012; Fujii 2009; Thomson 2018; King 2014; Jessee 2017; Hatzfeld 2005a, 2005b, 2006, 2009; Keane 1996; Khan 2001.

7. Mamdani 2001; Des Forges 1999; Melvern 2004; Prunier 1999.

8. Dallaire 2003; Wallis 2006; Melvern 2000; Power 2002; Kuperman 2001; Barnett 2002; Kroslak 2008.

9. Longman 2010; Rittner, Roth, and Whitworth 2004.

10. Straus and Waldorf 2011; Clark 2010; Doughty 2016; Ingelaere 2016.

11. Longman 2017; Thomson 2018; Reyntjens 2013.

12. Staub 2011; Bloxham and Moses 2010.

13. Bloxham and Moses 2010; Totten and Parsons 2009.

14. See appendix I, which describes in further detail the methodology guiding this project, including the number of family members that were killed, raped, or injured.

15. See appendix II, "Survey Results on Distress and Resilience."

16. The United Nations' Convention on the Prevention and Punishment of the Crime of Genocide defines genocide as follows: "In the present Convention, genocide means any of the following acts committed with the intent to destroy, in whole or in part, a national, ethnical, racial or religious group, as such: (a) Killing members of the group; (b) Causing serious bodily or mental harm to members of the group; (c) Deliberately inflicting on the group conditions of life calculated to bring about its physical destruction in whole or in part; (d) Imposing measures intended to prevent births within the group; (e) Forcibly transferring children of the group to another group."

17. Miller and Miller 1993.

18. The Association of Genocide Widows AVEGA AGAHOZO (Association des Veuves du Génocide Agahozo) is a not for profit association established in January 1995 in the aftermath of the genocide perpetrated against the Tutsis in Rwanda.

19. In Kinyarwanda, IBUKA means "remember."

20. Miller and Miller 2003.

21. Gakwandi 2016.

22. See Miller and Miller 1993, 28–30.

23. The issue in recent books is not whether the genocide occurred, but whether the RPF killed a number of innocent Hutus during the course of the civil war. See Rever (2018) in particular.

24. Because this was a civil war in which the RPF was systematically occupying the entire country, thousands of Hutus died and hundreds of thousands fled the country.

25. Longman 2017; Guichaoua 2015; Thomson 2018; Fujii 2009.

26. See the recent book by journalist Judi Rever (2018) that is based on interviews with RPF defectors and Hutu survivors. Also see Straus (2006b), who interviewed Hutu prisoners.

CHAPTER 2. HOW DID IT HAPPEN?

1. This plane was a gift from the French by President Mitterrand, who was a strong ally of the ruling MRND political party.

2. Prunier (1999, 221) speculates that the missiles were either Russian-made SAM-7s or SAM-16s, and that a mercenary might have been hired to shoot them since they are fairly complicated weapons.

3. Des Forges 1999, 181–85; Melvern 2000, 115–16.

4. Prunier (1999, 221) states the most probable hypothesis is that "President Habyarimana was killed by desperate members of his own *akazu* circle who had decided to gamble on their all-or-nothing 'final solution' scheme." He believes it is unlikely that the RPF shot down the plane since they had obtained a good settlement in the Arusha Accords and, furthermore, they did not counterattack until April 8 in response to the massacres of Tutsis that began on April 6 and 7. In contrast, government forces imme-

diately set up roadblocks and began targeted killing of moderate Hutus and influential Tutsis.

5. Des Forges 1999, 222–41.

6. Prunier 1999, 223.

7. Prunier 1999, 230.

8. Prunier 1999, 265.

9. Prunier 1999, 242.

10. Prunier (1999, 189) states: "It [RTLM] knew how to use street slang, obscene jokes and good music to push its racist message . . . [people listened to it] with a kind of stupefied fascination, incredulous at the relaxed joking way in which it defied the most cherished human values."

11. Coalition for the Defense of the Republic, which was an anti-Tutsi political party that sometimes worked together with the MRND but was more extremist in their views.

12. There is a substantial literature on what caused the genocide against Tutsis and how it occurred, but the following are key resources: Prunier 1999; Des Forges 1999; Melvern 2004; Mamdani 2001; Longman 2010.

13. Prunier 1999, 261.

14. For a discussion of the early history of Rwanda and the Lake Kivu region, see Newbury (1991, 2009); Newbury (1988).

15. See discussion of the three ethnic groups by Des Forges (1999, 31).

16. Mamdani 2001, 19–102.

17. Melvern 2000, 7–8.

18. Melvern 2000, 9–10.

19. Des Forges 1999, 34–38; Totten and Ubaldo 2011, 1–4.

20. Melvern 2000, 10.

21. Prunier 1999, 32.

22. Prunier 1999, 27.

23. Des Forges 1999, 38–40.

24. Prunier 1999, 62.

25. Prunier 1999, 63.

26. Melvern 2000, 16–17.

27. Prunier 1999, 56.

28. For a discussion of the use of propaganda, see Des Forges (1999, 65–95).

29. Melvern 2004, 12.

30. Prunier 1999, 60.

31. For a historical perspective on Burundi, see Lemarchand (1994).

32. Prunier 1999, 65.

33. Rwandese Refugee Welfare Foundation.

34. Prunier 1999, 67–73.

35. Melvern 2004, 14.

36. Wallis 2006.

37. Prunier 1999, 93.

38. Prunier 1999, 109.

39. Prunier 1999, 117.

40. Melvern 2004, 17.

41. Melvern 2000, 70–73.

42. Prunier 1999, 163.

43. Des Forges 1999, 123–29.

44. Prunier 1999, 180.

45. Akazu, made up of the president's wife's family and their close associates, took an increasingly racist and hostile posture toward the MRND and its capitulation to the demands of the RPF in the Arusha Accords.

46. Des Forges 1999, 134–40.

47. Prunier 1999, 200.

48. Prunier 1999, 130–33.

49. By April 21, 1994, the UNAMIR had reduced its mission by 90 percent to 270 men (Prunier 1999, 275).

50. Dallaire 2003.

51. In addition to the UN troops, it is also important to note that as part of the Arusha Accords, the RPF was allowed to situate a battalion of six hundred men in the center of the capital at the parliament building. Meanwhile, the French troops had departed from Rwanda, which was a condition set by the RPF in signing the Accords.

52. Prunier 1999, 75.

53. Prunier (1999, 93) states that the rebels took from the NRA in Uganda recoilless guns, machine guns, mortars, rocket launchers, and light automatic cannons.

54. Prunier 1999, 113.

55. Melvern 2000, 32; Des Forges 1999, 97–99.

56. The translation of Interahamwe—"Those who stand together" or "Those who attack together"—was fitting. They often killed in their local community before venturing to neighboring areas. Many of these young men were poor, uneducated, unemployed, and prime instruments for engaging in sadistic violence, including rape. At night they typically returned to their own community, manning checkpoints and seeking out Tutsis the next day who had escaped the killing. Feasting and celebrations were often held at the end of a day's work (Thomson 2018, 73–76; Straus 2006b, 26–31).

57. Prunier 1999, 231.

58. During the genocide, when people did not follow orders, they were replaced—or the army was sent in to ensure that orders were followed.

59. Prunier 1999, 142.

60. Straus 2006b, 89.

61. Straus 2006b, 227.

62. Straus 2006b, 226.

63. Straus 2006b, 229.

64. Straus 2006b, 122.

65. Straus 2006b, 228.

66. Straus 2006b, 122.

67. In our opinion, Straus's explanation does not explain the sadism that was reported by survivors interviewed for this project.

68. Carney 2014.

69. Des Forges 1999, 180–260.

70. Melvern 2004, 20.

71. Longman 2010, 162.

72. Longman 2010, 10.

73. Prunier 1999, 253.

74. Prunier 1999, 298.

75. Prunier 1999, 298.

76. 150,000 Tutsi homes were destroyed from April to June 1994 (Prunier 1999, 365).

77. Prunier 1999, 327.

78. Des Forges 1999, 728. For the full discussion of the Gersony report, see pages 726–35.

79. Prunier 1999, 321–26.

80. Writing two years later after the first publication of his book, Prunier (1999, 359) states: "It is now obvious, from a variety of sources, that the RPF carried out a large number of killings first during the genocide itself and then later during the end of 1994 and even into early 1995, with a diminishing intensity."

81. Prunier 1999, 361.

CHAPTER 3. ORPHAN MEMORIES

1. In instances of rape, the names of survivors have been changed.

2. Survivors typically refer to perpetrators as "killers," and so we follow their nomenclature.

3. It is estimated that 1.2 million children were left orphaned by the end of the genocide and more than 100,000 children lived in child-headed households (King 2014, 111).

4. Of the one hundred interviewees, forty-one were female and fifty-nine were male. In the one hundred households, prior to the genocide there were 805 family members. As a result of the genocide, 522 (65 percent) were killed and 283 (35 percent) survived. Of the forty-one orphan girls, five were raped, and one male was raped. Of the one hundred interviewees, twenty-five suffered serious physical injuries, including amputation. And seventy-nine homes of the one hundred interviewees were destroyed in the genocide. (See appendix I for more details of the research with AOCM.)

5. See Sommers (2012) for an excellent analysis of the struggle of orphans as they achieve adulthood.

6. King 2014, 83.

7. King 2014, 83.

8. Radio-télévision libre des mille collines.

9. National Republican Movement for Democracy and Development.

10. Coalition for the Defense of the Republic.

11. See Totten and Ubaldo (2011, 195–205) for a glossary of terms and political parties. Tutsis living in Rwanda largely favored the PL (Liberal Party).

12. It is estimated that a quarter of a million women were raped during the genocide and perhaps 70 percent of these women were infected with HIV.

13. We call your attention to appendix II, which describes quantitative survey data on emotional distress and various coping mechanisms experienced by members of AOCM as well as Solace Ministries. For example, 86 percent of the AOCM members surveyed reported feeling desperate and 43 percent reported feeling that life is not worth living. Further details regarding survey methodology, resilience of survivors, and comparisons between the two samples are elaborated in this appendix and are well worth reading.

CHAPTER 4. THE EXPERIENCE OF WOMEN

1. See the discussion of women rape victims by Brouwer and Chu (2009). Also, see the excellent analysis by Burnet (2012, 133–46) and the Human Rights report on sexual violence (HRW 1996).

2. The best source on the role of Christians and clergy in the genocide is Longman (2010). Also, see the account by Gourevitch (1998) of the role of a Seventh-Day Adventist pastor.

CHAPTER 5. COPING AFTER GENOCIDE

1. For a parallel discussion of life after genocide, see our chapters on the experience of Armenian survivors of the 1915 genocide (Miller and Miller 1993, 118–51).

CHAPTER 6. TRAUMA AS MORAL RUPTURE

1. See Alexander (2012) and Alexander et al. (2014) for an elaboration of this theme.

2. Durkheim 1995.

3. See the article featuring AOCM in *The Globe*. World's Children's Prize for the Rights of the Child 2006, 42–65.

4. American Psychiatric Association 2013, 271–90.

5. American Psychiatric Association 2013, 271–72.

6. RMHS 2018.

7. See the articles by Ng et al. (2015a and 2015b).

8. Van der Kolk 2014, 61.

9. Van der Kolk 2014, 36–38.

CHAPTER 7. A HOLISTIC MODEL OF HEALING

1. For examples of Christian approaches to trauma interventions, see Gingrich (2013); Park et al. (2017).

2. James 1961.

3. Isaiah 40:1.

4. Over a several-month period, Mama Lambert told her story to Hans Dekkers, who produced a book using her words (Lambert and Dekkers 2015, 149).

5. Lambert and Dekkers 2015, 150.

6. Lambert and Dekkers 2015, 151.

7. Lambert and Dekkers 2015, 152.

8. Lambert and Dekkers 2015, 153.

9. Herman 1997.

10. Herman 1997, 175.

11. Herman 1997.

12. Herman 1997, 61.

13. Herman 1997, 56.

14. Herman 1997.

15. Herman 1997, 133.

16. Herman 1997, 211.

17. See Katongole (2009) on the role of religion.

CHAPTER 8. FORGIVENESS

1. Lambert and Dekkers 2015, 161.

2. Lambert and Dekkers 2015, 169.

3. Lambert and Dekkers 2015, 174–75.

4. One of the most popular books on forgiveness from a religious perspective is Ilibagiza (2006). Also see Rucyahana (2007).

5. There is a substantial literature on forgiveness, including handbooks, edited volumes, and so on. Here is a sample of relevant materials on forgiveness: Bole, Christiansen, and Hennemeyer 2004; Criswold 2007; Govier 2002; Griswold 2007; Helmick and Peterson 2001; Jones 1995; Jones 2009; Larson 2009; Marshall 2001; McCullough 2008; McCullough, Pargament, and Thoresen 2000; Minow 1998; Murphy and Hampton 1988, 2003; Rieff 2016; Rucyahana 2007; Schreiter, Appleby, and Powers 2010; Shriver 1995; Tutu 1999; Wiesenthal 1998; Worthington 2005, 2006.

6. Lambert and Dekkers 2015, 175.

CHAPTER 9. JUSTICE AND RECONCILIATION

1. See Scheffer 2012.

2. Ingelaere 2016, 29.

3. http://unictr.unmict.org/en/tribunal.

4. For discussions of *gacaca*, its origins, application, and limitations, see Ingelaere 2016; Doughty 2016; Clark 2010; Longman 2017; Shaw and Waldorf 2010; Temple-Raston 2005.

5. James and van de Vijver 2001.

6. Los Angeles Times 1995.

7. Reyntjens 2013, 226–27.

8. Sommers 2012.

9. http://worldhappiness.report/ed/2019/changing-world-happiness/.

10. Hunt 2017.

11. Jacobs 2016.

12. See the interesting discussion of moral repair from a philosophical perspective in Walker (2006).

CHAPTER 10. BECOMING HUMAN AGAIN

1. RMHS 2018.

2. Kapila 2013.

3. Crisafulli and Redmond 2012.

4. For a countervailing view of progress in Rwanda, see Longman (2017); Straus (2006b); Reyntjens (2013); and Rever (2018). These authors see the current government as authoritarian and ruled by a Tutsi leadership born in Uganda.

5. Vanier 1998, 5.

APPENDIX II. SURVEY RESULTS ON DISTRESS AND RESILIENCE

1. For more information about the methods and results of the survey project, see Ng et al. (2015a and 2015b) or contact Beth E. Meyerowitz at meyerow@usc.edu.

2. Three of the symptom clusters of PTSD (intrusive thoughts, avoidance, and hyperarousal) were measured by an adapted version of the twenty-two-item Impact of Event Scales—Revised (Weiss and Marmar, 1997).

3. Creamer, Bell, and Failla, 2003.

4. Responses by the two groups of survivors were compared using chi-squared analyses for dichotomous variables and t-test comparisons for continuous variables. Because there were significant differences between the two groups on age and sex, we also conducted regression analyses controlling for those variables. In no case did the results change. Reports of significant differences indicate $p < 0.05$, without correction for multiple analyses.

5. Eytan et al. 2015; Munyandamutsa et al. 2012.

6. This measure was an adapted version of the Medical Outcomes Study Social Support Scale (Sherbourne and Stewart 1991). The specific items assessed the extent to which survivors believed that they had someone they could talk to about things that bothered them, someone who could get to know their feelings, someone who would

take care of them if they were sick, someone to help them make decisions, someone they could trust, and someone they could feel close to always.

7. Cantril 1965 and McDowell and Newell 1996.

8. Ganz et al. 2004.

9. Bass et al. 2013.

10. Murray et al. 2013.

11. Ng et al. 2015a.

REFERENCES AND BIBLIOGRAPHY

Alexander, Jeffrey C. 2012. *Trauma: A Social Theory.* Cambridge: Polity Press.

Alexander, Jeffrey C., Ron Eyerman, Bernard Giesen, Neil J. Smelser, and Piotr Sztompka. 2014. *Cultural Trauma and Collective Identity.* Berkeley: University of California Press.

American Psychiatric Association. 2013. DSM-5: Diagnostic and Statistical Manual of Mental Disorders. 5th ed. Washington, DC: American Psychiatric Publishing.

Barnett, Michael. 2002. *Eyewitness to a Genocide: The United Nations and Rwanda.* Ithaca, NY: Cornell University Press.

Bass, Judith K., J. Annan, S. McIvor Murray, D. Kaysen, S. Griffiths, T. Cetinoglu, . . . and P. A. Bolton. 2013. "Controlled Trial of Psychotherapy for Congolese Survivors of Sexual Violence." *New England Journal of Medicine* 368, no. 23: 2182–91.

Berry, John, and Carol Pott Berry. 1999. *Genocide in Rwanda: A Collective Memory.* Washington, DC: Howard University Press.

Bloxham, Donald, and Dirk A. Moses, eds. 2010. *The Oxford Handbook of Genocide Studies.* Oxford: Oxford University Press.

Bole, William, Drew Christiansen, and Robert T. Hennemeyer. 2004. *Forgiveness in International Politics: An Alternative Road to Peace.* Washington, DC: United States Conference of Catholic Bishops.

Brouwer, Anne-Marie, and Sandra Ka Hon Chu. 2009. *The Men Who Killed Me: Rwandan Survivors of Sexual Violence.* Vancouver, BC: Douglas and McIntyre.

Burnet, Jennie E. 2012. *Genocide Lives in Us: Women, Memory, and Silence in Rwanda.* Madison: University of Wisconsin Press.

Cantril, Hadley. 1965. *The Pattern of Human Concerns.* New Brunswick, NJ: Rutgers University Press.

Carey, Sabine C., Mark Gibney, and Steven C. Poe. 2010. *The Politics of Human Rights: The Quest for Dignity.* Cambridge: Cambridge University Press.

Carney, J. J. 2014. *Rwanda before the Genocide: Catholic Politics and Ethnic Discourse in the Late Colonial Era*. Oxford: Oxford University Press.

Clark, Phil. 2010. *The Gacaca Courts, Post-Genocide Justice, and Reconciliation in Rwanda: Justice without Lawyers*. Cambridge: Cambridge University Press.

Creamer, Mark, R. Bell, and S. Failla. 2003. "Psychometric Properties of the Impact of Event Scale-R." *Behaviour Research and Therapy* 41: 1489–96.

Crisafulli, Patricia, and Andrea Redmond. 2012. *Rwanda, Inc.: How a Devastated Nation Became an Economic Model for the Developing World*. New York: Palgrave Macmillan.

Criswold, Charles L. 2007. *Forgiveness: A Philosophical Exploration*. Cambridge: Cambridge University Press.

Dallaire, Romeo. 2003. *Shake Hands with the Devil*. New York: Carroll and Graf Publishers.

Des Forges, Alison. 1999. *"Leave None to Tell the Story": Genocide in Rwanda*. New York: Human Rights Watch.

Des Forges, Alison Liebhafsky. 2011. *Defeat Is the Only Bad News*. Madison: University of Wisconsin Press.

Doughty, Kristin Conner. 2016. *Remediation in Rwanda: Grassroots Legal Forums*. Philadelphia: University of Pennsylvania Press.

Durkheim, Émile. 1995. *Elementary Forms of the Religious Life*. New York: Free Press.

Eytan, Ariel, N. Munyandamutsa, P. M. Nkubamugisha, and M. Gex-Fabry. 2015. "Long-Term Mental Health Outcome in Post-Conflict Settings: Similarities and Differences between Kosovo and Rwanda." *International Journal of Social Psychiatry* 61, no. 4: 363–72.

Foa, Edna B., Elizabeth A. Hembree, and Barbara Olasov Rothbaum. 2007. *Prolonged Exposure Therapy for PTSD: Emotional Processing of Traumatic Experiences*. Oxford: Oxford University Press.

Fujii, Lee Ann. 2009. *Killing Neighbors: Webs of Violence in Rwanda*. Ithaca, NY: Cornell University Press.

Gakwandi, Jean. 2016. *Solace: The Story of Solace Ministries*. China.

Ganz, Patricia A., L. Kwan, A. L. Stanton, J. L. Krupnick, J. H. Rowland, B. E. Meyerowitz, J. E. Bower, and T. R. Belin. 2004. "Quality of Life at the End of Primary Treatment of Breast Cancer: First Results from the Moving Beyond Cancer Randomized Trial." *Journal of the National Cancer Institute* 96: 376–87.

Gingrich, Heather Davediuk. 2013. *Restoring the Shattered Self: A Christian Counselor's Guide to Complex Trauma*. Downers Grove, IL: IVP Academic.

Gourevitch, Philip. 1998. *We Wish to Inform You That Tomorrow We Will Be Killed with Our Families: Stories from Rwanda*. New York: Farrar, Straus and Giroux.

Govier, Trudy. 2002. *Forgiveness and Revenge*. London: Routledge.

Griswold, Charles L. 2007. *Forgiveness: A Philosophical Exploration*. Cambridge: Cambridge University Press.

Guichaoua, Andre. 2015. *From War to Genocide: Criminal Politics in Rwanda, 1990–1994*. Madison: University of Wisconsin Press.

Hatzfeld, Jean. 2005a. *Into the Quick of Life: The Rwandan Genocide; The Survivors Speak.* Translated by Gerry Feehily. London: Serpent's Tail.

———. 2005b. *Machete Season: The Killers in Rwanda Speak.* Translated by Linda Coverdale. New York: Farrar, Straus and Giroux.

———. 2006. *Life Laid Bare: The Survivors in Rwanda Speak.* Translated by Linda Coverdale. New York: Other Press.

———. 2009. *The Antelope's Strategy: Living in Rwanda after the Genocide.* Translated by Linda Coverdale. New York: Farrar, Straus and Giroux.

Helmick, Raymond G., and Rodney L. Petersen, eds. 2001. *Forgiveness and Reconciliation: Religion, Public Policy, and Conflict Transformation.* Philadelphia: Templeton Foundation Press.

Herman, Judith. 1997. *Trauma and Recovery.* New York: Basic Books.

Hirsch, Herbert. 1995. *Genocide and the Politics of Memory: Studying Death to Preserve Life.* Chapel Hill: University of North Carolina Press.

Human Rights Watch (HRW). 1996. *Shattered Lives: Sexual Violence during the Rwandan Genocide and Its Aftermath.* New York: Human Rights Watch.

Hunt, Swanee. 2017. *Rwandan Women Rising.* Durham, NC: Duke University Press.

Ilibagiza, Immaculée. 2006. *Left to Tell: Discovering God Amidst the Rwandan Holocaust.* Carlsbad, CA: Hay House.

Ingelaere, Bert. 2016. *Inside Rwanda's Gacaca Courts: Seeking Justice after Genocide.* Madison: University of Wisconsin Press.

Jacobs, Janet. 2016. *The Holocaust across Generations: Trauma and Its Inheritance among Descendants of Survivors.* New York: New York University Press.

James, William. 1961. *Varieties of Religious Experience: A Study in Human Nature.* New York: Collier Books.

James, Wilmot, and Linda van de Vijver. 2001. *After the TRC: Reflections on Truth and Reconciliation in South Africa.* Athens: Ohio University Press.

Jessee, Erin. 2017. *Negotiating Genocide in Rwanda: The Politics of History.* London: Palgrave Macmillan.

Jones, L. Gregory. 1995. *Embodying Forgiveness: A Theological Analysis.* Grand Rapids, MI: William B. Eerdmans.

Jones, Serene. 2009. *Trauma and Grace: Theology in a Ruptured World.* Louisville: Westminster John Knox Press.

Kapila, Mukesh. 2013. *Against a Tide of Evil: How One Man Became the Whistleblower to the First Mass Murder of the Twenty-First Century.* San Jose, CA: Pegasus Books.

Katongole, Emmanuel. 2009. *Mirror to the Church: Resurrecting Faith after Genocide in Rwanda.* Grand Rapids, MI: Zondervan.

Kayishema, Jean-Marie, and François Masabo. 2010. "The Rwandan Righteous (Indakemwa): Pilot Study." IBUKA.

Keane, Fergal. 1996. *Season of Blood: A Rwandan Journey.* New York: Penguin Books.

Khan, Shaharyar M. 2001. *The Shallow Graves of Rwanda.* New York: I. B. Tauris.

King, Elisabeth. 2014. *From Classrooms to Conflict in Rwanda.* Cambridge: Cambridge University Press.

Kroslak, Daniela. 2008. *The French Betrayal of Rwanda*. Bloomington: Indiana University Press.

Kuperman, Alan J. 2001. *The Limits of Humanitarian Intervention*. Washington, DC: Brookings Institution Press.

Lambert, Mama, and Hans Dekkers. 2015. *For Those Who Do Not Believe in Miracles: The Resilience of a Rwandan Woman Who Survived the Genocide*. Oisterwijk, Netherlands: Wolf Legal Publishers.

Larson, Catherine Claire. 2009. *As We Forgive: Stories of Reconciliation from Rwanda*. Grand Rapids, MI: Zondervan.

Lemarchand, Rene. 1994. *Burundi: Ethnic Conflict and Genocide*. New York: Woodrow Wilson Center Press.

Longman, Timothy. 2010. *Christianity and Genocide in Rwanda*. Cambridge: Cambridge University Press.

———. 2017. *Memory and Justice in Post-Genocide Rwanda*. Cambridge: Cambridge University Press.

Los Angeles Times. 1995. July 30. "Archbishop Tutu Arrives after New Violence." Reuters.

Mamdani, Mahmood. 2001. *When Victims Become Killers*. Princeton, NJ: Princeton University Press.

Marshall, Christopher D. 2001. *Beyond Retribution: A New Testament Vision for Justice, Crime, and Punishment*. Grand Rapids, MI: William B. Eerdmans.

McCullough, Michael E. 2008. *Beyond Revenge: The Evolution of the Forgiveness Instinct*. San Francisco: Jossey-Bass.

McCullough, Michael E., Kenneth I. Pargament, and Carl E. Thoresen. 2000. *Forgiveness: Theory, Research, and Practice*. New York: Guilford Press.

McDowell, Ian, and C. Newell. 1996. *Measuring Health: A Guide to Rating Scales and Questionnaires*. 2nd ed. New York: Oxford University Press.

Melvern, Linda. 2000. *A People Betrayed: The Role of the West in Rwanda's Genocide*. London: Zed Books.

———. 2004. *Conspiracy to Murder*. New York: Verso.

Miller, Donald E., and Lorna Touryan Miller. 1993. *Survivors: An Oral History of the Armenian Genocide*. Berkeley: University of California Press.

———. 2003. *Armenia: Portraits of Survival and Hope*. Berkeley: University of California Press.

Minow, Martha. 1998. *Between Vengeance and Forgiveness: Facing History after Genocide and Mass Violence*. Boston: Beacon Press.

Munyandamutsa, Naasson, P. M. Nkubamugisha, M. Gex-Fabry, and A. Eytan. 2012. "Mental and Physical Health in Rwanda 14 Years after the Genocide." *Social Psychiatry and Psychiatric Epidemiology* 47, no. 11: 1753–61.

Murphy, Jeffrie G., and Jean Hampton. 1988. *Forgiveness and Mercy*. Cambridge: Cambridge University Press.

———. 2003. *Getting Even: Forgiveness and Its Limits*. Oxford: Oxford University Press.

Murray, Laura, I. Familiar, S. A. Skavenski Van Wyk, E. Jere, J. Cohen, M. Imasiku, . . . and P. A. Bolton. 2013. "An Evaluation of Trauma Focused Cognitive Behavioral Therapy for Children in Zambia." *Child Abuse and Neglect* 37, no. 12: 1175–85.

Mushikiwabo, Louise, and Jack Kramer. 2006. *Rwanda Means the Universe: A Native's Memoir of Blood and Bloodlines*. New York: St. Martin's Press.

Newbury, Catharine. 1988. *The Cohesion of Oppression: Clientship and Ethnicity in Rwanda, 1860–1960*. New York: Columbia University Press.

Newbury, David. 1991. *Kings and Clans: Ijwi Island and the Lake Kivu Rift, 1780–1840*. Madison: University of Wisconsin Press.

———. 2009. *The Land beyond the Mists: Essays on Identity and Authority in Precolonial Congo and Rwanda*. Athens: Ohio University Press.

Ng, Lauren C., N. Ahishakiye, D. E. Miller, and B. E. Meyerowitz. 2015a. "Life after Genocide: Mental Health, Education, and Social Support of Orphaned Survivors." *International Perspectives in Psychology: Research, Practice, Consultation* 4: 83–97.

———. 2015b. "Narrative Characteristics of Genocide Testimonies Predict Post-traumatic Stress Disorder Symptoms Years Later." *Psychological Trauma: Theory, Research, Practice, and Policy* 7: 303–11.

Park, Crystal L., Joseph M. Currier, J. Irene Harris, and Jeanne M. Slattery. 2017. *Trauma, Meaning, and Spirituality: Translating Research Into Clinical Practice*. Washington, DC: American Psychological Association.

Pearlman, Laurie Anne, Camille B. Wortman, Catherine A. Feuer, Christine H. Farber, and Therese A. Rando. 2014. *Treating Traumatic Bereavement: A Practitioner's Guide*. New York: Guilford Press.

Power, Samantha. 2002. *"A Problem from Hell": America and the Age of Genocide*. New York: Basic Books.

Prunier, Gérard. 1999. *The Rwanda Crisis: History of a Genocide*. Kampala: Fountain Publishers.

———. 2009. *Africa's World War: Congo, the Rwandan Genocide, and the Making of a Continental Catastrophe*. New York: Oxford University Press.

Rever, Judi. 2018. *In Praise of Blood: The Crimes of the Rwandan Patriotic Front*. Toronto: Random House Canada.

Reyntjens, Filip. 2013. *Political Governance in Post-Genocide Rwanda*. Cambridge: Cambridge University Press.

Rieff, David. 2016. *In Praise of Forgetting: Historical Memory and Its Ironies*. New Haven, CT: Yale University Press.

Rittner, Carol, John K. Roth, and Wendy Whitworth, eds. 2004. *Genocide in Rwanda: Complicity of the Churches?* Saint Paul, MN: Paragon House.

RMHS. 2018. Rwanda Mental Health Survey. Yvonne Kayiteshonga, Principal Investigator.

Rothbaum, Barbara Olasov, Edna B. Foa, and Elizabeth A. Hembree. *Reclaiming Your Life from a Traumatic Experience*. Oxford: Oxford University Press.

Rucyahana, John. 2007. *The Bishop of Rwanda: Finding Forgiveness Amidst a Pile of Bones*. Nashville: Thomas Nelson.

Rugema, L., I. Mogren, J. Ntaganira, and G. Krantz. 2015. "Traumatic Episodes and Mental Health Effects in Young Men and Women in Rwanda, 17 Years after the Genocide." *BMJ Open* 5, no. 6: e006778.

Scheffer, David. 2012. *All the Missing Souls: A Personal History of the War Crimes Tribunals*. Princeton, NJ: Princeton University Press.

Schreiter, Robert J., R. Scott Appleby, and Gerard F. Powers, eds. 2010. *Peacebuilding: Catholic Theology, Ethics, and Praxis*. Maryknoll, NY: Orbis Books.

Semujanga, Josias. 2003. *Origins of Rwandan Genocide*. Amherst, NY: Humanity Books.

Shaw, Rosalind, and Lars Waldorf, eds. 2010. *Localizing Transitional Justice: Interventions and Priorities after Mass Violence*. Stanford, CA: Stanford University Press.

Sherbourne, Cathy D., and A. L. Stewart. 1991. "The MOS Social Support Survey." *Social Science and Medicine* 32: 705–14.

Shriver, Donald W., Jr. 1995. *An Ethic for Enemies: Forgiveness in Politics*. New York: Oxford University Press.

Sibomana, Andre. 1999. *Hope for Rwanda: Conversations with Laure Guilbert and Herve Deguine*. London: Pluto Press.

Sommers, Marc. 2012. *Stuck: Rwandan Youth and the Struggle for Adulthood*. Athens: University of Georgia Press.

Staub, Ervin. 1989. *The Roots of Evil: The Origins of Genocide and Other Group Violence*. Cambridge: Cambridge University Press.

———. 2011. *Overcoming Evil: Genocide, Violent Conflict, and Terrorism*. New York: Oxford University Press.

———. 2015. *The Roots of Goodness and Resistance to Evil: Inclusive Caring, Moral Courage, Altruism Born of Suffering, Active Bystandership, and Heroism*. London: Oxford University Press.

Straus, Scott. 2006a. *Intimate Enemy: Images and Voices of the Rwandan Genocide*. New York: Zone Books.

———. 2006b. *The Order of Genocide: Race, Power, and War in Rwanda*. Ithaca, NY: Cornell University Press.

Straus, Scott, and Lars Waldorf. 2011. *Remaking Rwanda: State Building and Human Rights after Mass Violence*. Madison: University of Wisconsin Press.

Survivors Fund (SURF). n.d. *Survival against the Odds: A Book of Testimonies of the Rwandan Genocide*. London: Survivors Fund (SURF).

Temple-Raston, Dina. 2005. *Justice on the Grass: Three Rwandan Journalists, Their Trial for War Crimes, and a Nation's Quest for Redemption*. New York: Free Press.

Thomson, Susan. 2018. *Rwanda: From Genocide to Precarious Peace*. New Haven, CT: Yale University Press.

Tick, Edward. 2005. *War and the Soul: Healing Our Nation's Veterans from Posttraumatic Stress Disorder*. Wheaton, IL: Quest Books.

———. 2014. *Warrior's Return: Restoring the Soul after War*. Boulder, CO: Sounds True.

Totten, Samuel, and William Parsons, eds. 2009. *Century of Genocide: Critical Essays and Eyewitness Accounts*. 3rd ed. New York: Routledge.

Totten, Samuel, and Rafiki Ubaldo. 2011. *We Cannot Forget: Interviews with Survivors of the 1994 Genocide in Rwanda*. New Brunswick, NJ: Rutgers University Press.

Tutu, Desmond Mpilo. 1999. *No Future without Forgiveness*. New York: Doubleday.

Van der Kolk, Bessel. 2014. *The Body Keeps Score: Brain, Mind, and Body in the Healing of Trauma*. New York: Penguin Books.

Vanier, Jean. 1998. *Becoming Human*. New York: Paulist Press.

Walker, Margaret Urban. 2006. *Moral Repair: Reconstructing Moral Relations after Wrongdoing*. Cambridge: Cambridge University Press.

Walker, Donald F., Christine A. Courtois, and Jamie D. Aten, eds. 2015. *Spiritually Oriented Psychotherapy for Trauma*. Washington, DC: American Psychological Association.

Wallis, Andrew. 2006. *Silent Accomplice: The Untold Story of France's Role in the Rwandan Genocide*. London: I. B. Tauris.

Weiss, Daniel S., and C. R. Marmar. 1997. "The Impact of Event Scale—Revised." In *Assessing Psychological Trauma and PTSD*, edited by J. P. Wilson and T. R. Keane, 399–411. New York: Guilford Press.

Wiesenthal, Simon. 1998. *The Sunflower: On the Possibilities and Limits of Forgiveness*. New York: Schocken Books.

World's Children's Prize for the Rights of the Child. *The Globe* 42 (2006): 42–65.

Worthington, Everett L., Jr. 2006. *Forgiveness and Reconciliation: Theory and Application*. New York: Routledge.

Worthington, Everett L., Jr., ed. 2005. *Handbook of Forgiveness*. New York: Routledge.

INDEX

adrenaline, 122–23

aftermath of the genocide: overview of, 94, 95–96, 104–7, 187–88, 190; blaming of the victims by perpetrators, 96; and compassion, loss of, 105; and dignity, 107; disabled people and, 63, 97, 98, 102, 106, 108, 137; economy as shattered, 39, 104, 188; emotional difficulties, 98–99, 106, 107; and employment, lacking or insufficient, 104–5, 106; housing, 68, 101–2, 104, 184; Hutu/Tutsi relations, tensions in, 95–96, 102–3, 105; identification of Hutu perpetrators, 96, 103; material context of survival as taking precedence over healing of trauma, 95, 104–5, 106, 107–8; necessity of examining, 10, 109; orphan heads of households and, 96–100, 104–7; orphan reunions and, 70–72; poverty as common to all survivors, 104–5; prostitution of orphan girls, 106; widow reunions and, 8–9, 93–94; widows and, 100–103, 104–7. *See also* food and water; forgiveness; healing; medical treatment in aftermath; reconciliation; reconstruction of the social order; Rwandan government (postgenocide); trauma of genocide survivors

age: as mitigating factor in interpersonal reconciliation, 176; of orphans, as affecting their perception of the genocide, 47, 70, 72–73

agency: loss of, 117; strategies for regaining a sense of, 205–7

Ahishakiye, Naphtal, 14–15, 184–86, 189, 191, 192, 200

AIDS. *See* HIV/AIDS virus transmitted during rape

air travel, 189

akazu circle, 50, 214–15n4, 216n45

Amin, Idi, 30

anger: as ongoing despite forgiveness, 5, 123, 155; ongoing struggle with, and suppression of, 123–24, 125; prayers used to work through, 124, 150; rage and aggression as trauma symptoms, 122–23

Anglican Church, 149

anomie (normlessness), 114, 188

AOCM (L'Association des Orphelins Chefs de Ménages): education assistance advocacy of, 185; ending of, 185; founding of, 107, 184, 188, 195; housing constructed by, 185; methodology of interview project, 12, 14–15, 21, 47–48, 195–97, 200, 217n4; number of families networked through, 185; as prizewinner of "The World's Children's Prize for the Rights of the Child" (Sweden), 115; and survey of distress and resilience by authors, 118, 202–11, 218n13, 220–21nn2,4,6

apartheid, as justified by religion, 151

ARDA (Adventist Relief and Development), 100

Armenian genocide (1915), 11–12, 20, 182, 183, 191–92

United Nations High Commissioner for
Refugees (UNHCR), 39
United States: failure to intervene in the
genocide, 9, 33; Paul Kagame (RPA)
training in, 31; slavery justified by religion,
151; Somalia killings of Americans (1993),
33; Tutsi diaspora in, 31
universities, consolidation by postgenocide
government, 189. *See also* education

value of each survivor, Solace Ministries and
affirmation of, 141–42
Van der Kolk, Bessel, 122, 123
Vanier, Jean, *Becoming Human*, 192–93

war, prayers against, 150
water. *See* food and water
widows: overview, 100–103; adoption of
orphans by, 9, 14, 96, 105, 108, 179; and
alcohol abuse, 122; children of, worries
about, 105–6; counteracting isolation of,
128; and disabilities, 106, 108; emotional
difficulties of, 107, 108; and food and
water, provision of, 104–5; and HIV/
AIDS, 102, 105; and housing, 101–2, 104;
and Hutu neighbors, challenge of living
side-by-side with, 100, 102–3; identifying
perpetrators to the authorities, 103; loneliness of, 105, 108; long-term effects of
genocide on, 182; and loss of partnership
with spouse, 100–101, 105, 108; prayers of,
149, 150; as rape survivors, 102; and reconciliation, 176, 178, 179; reunions with children and adult relatives, 8–9, 93–94;
Solace Ministries programs to assist,
139, 206–7; support of other widows by,
108–9

women: overview, 73, 76–77; appeals to Hutu
neighbors, 8, 76, 77, 78, 81; appeals to
Hutu relatives, 74, 77; carrying and caring
for small children, 76, 90–92; children,
deciding which to save, 92; and church
killings, 83–85; the civil war and repercussions for local Tutsis, 51; fleeing and hiding alone and with children, 3–4, 6–9,
74–76, 79–80, 90–93; genocide of, as
eventual goal, 25; and historical context of
previous Tutsi massacres, 76, 81; hunger
and thirst of children and, 7, 76, 92; Hutu
assistance to, 7, 8, 79–80, 81, 84; injuries
from attacks on, 79–81; killing of pregnant women, 58, 61; leaving children with
Hutus, 7, 78; older women, 92–93; in
postgenocide government leadership, 181;
rescued by the RPA, 8, 80, 90; and suicide, 76, 89; witnessing the killing of their
children, 76, 78–79, 84, 101. *See also* rape
survivors; widows
women, Hutu: charged with crimes after
genocide, 44; sadistic acts by, 58
wooden weapon "impiri," 64
"World's Children's Prize for the Rights of
the Child, The" (Sweden), 115
World War I, 27

Zaire (Democratic Republic of the Congo):
fear of Hutu killers' return from and
repeat of genocide, 125; Hutu killers fleeing to, 8, 96; Hutu refugee camps in, 39;
PTSD treatment programs in, 209; Tutsi
refugees fleeing to (from 1961), 28, 81;
Tutsi refugees joining RPA, 31; Tutsi
saved by Hutu fleeing to, 8–9
Zambia, 209